DRAWING FOR URBAN DESIGN

Published in 2011
by Laurence King Publishing Ltd
361–373 City Road
London EC1V 1LR
Tel +44 (0)20 7841 6900
Fax +44 (0)20 7841 6910
E enquiries@laurenceking.com
www.laurenceking.com

A catalogue record for this book is available from the British Library

ISBN 978 185669 718 7
Designed by John Round Design
Printed in China

LORRAINE FARRELLY

DRAWING FOR URBAN DESIGN

Laurence King Publishing

Contents

Related study material is available on the Laurence King website at
www.laurenceking.com

Introduction

What is drawing?

Drawing is a frame of the imagination, encouraging the gaze to move beyond the frame of the visible to the invisible, the probable to the improbable. Architects and urban designers use drawings to constitute an important part of the process of the thinking about the fabric of the city, the mental construction of the architecture as it evolves and develops. These images can be engaged with as a physical act of drawing, establishing a sheet of paper as a surface and making marks which have a purpose, a scale, a length and weight. Or they can be a set of images that have been produced using a computer programme as an interface. The art is in the selection, manipulation and presentation of these images. There is considerable skill in preparing a freehand or a CAD set of drawings; it needs forethought, consideration and vision.

Architectural representation is establishing a way to convey an impression of the building and cities as they might be, from a hypothetical perspective, suggesting an exciting new world of people and activities, like a film set, to a set of well-worked-out details envisaging how the buildings or spaces within cities might be built or assembled. These interpretations can be quite fantastical and may include computer models that suggest either surreal environments or a photo-realistic sense of place.

Architectural drawing is largely about the art of suggestion. Drawings will not explore every scale or aspect of the idea, but they will provide enough information to allow a glimpse into the possibilities for a scheme. Drawing ideas for a city requires many different scales to be used. Sometimes a diagram sketched over a section of a map may suggest the connection of a site with the broader context of a city or a landscape. For another scheme, it may be that the materials used in the façade need to be described to connect a building to its context or environment, so a street elevation may be needed to explain how a proposed façade relates to its immediate context in terms of scale, mass and material.

It is important to be clear about the intention of a drawing. There are many scales and media available, and before starting to engage in producing drawings time should be taken to be establish how a presentation will work, who the drawing is for, and what it is meant to communicate.

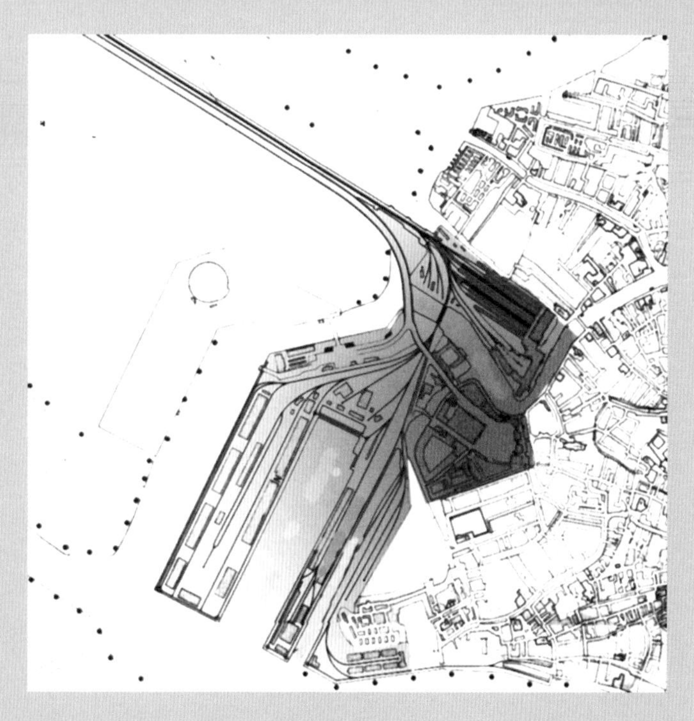

Above
Drawn as part of a student design project (by the European City Studio at Portsmouth School of Architecture) identifying a city site in Venice, this CAD map highlights the site location of the train station.

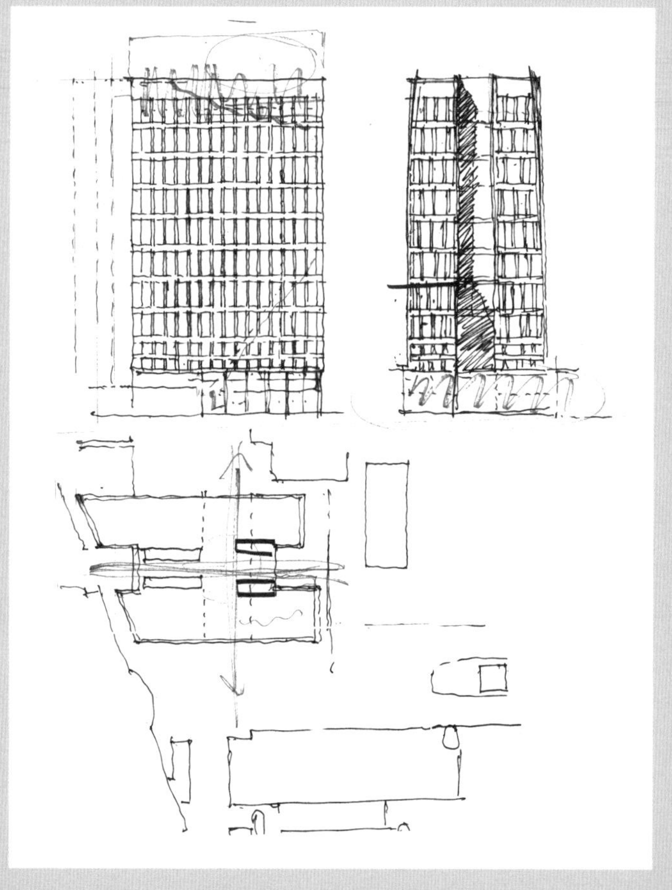

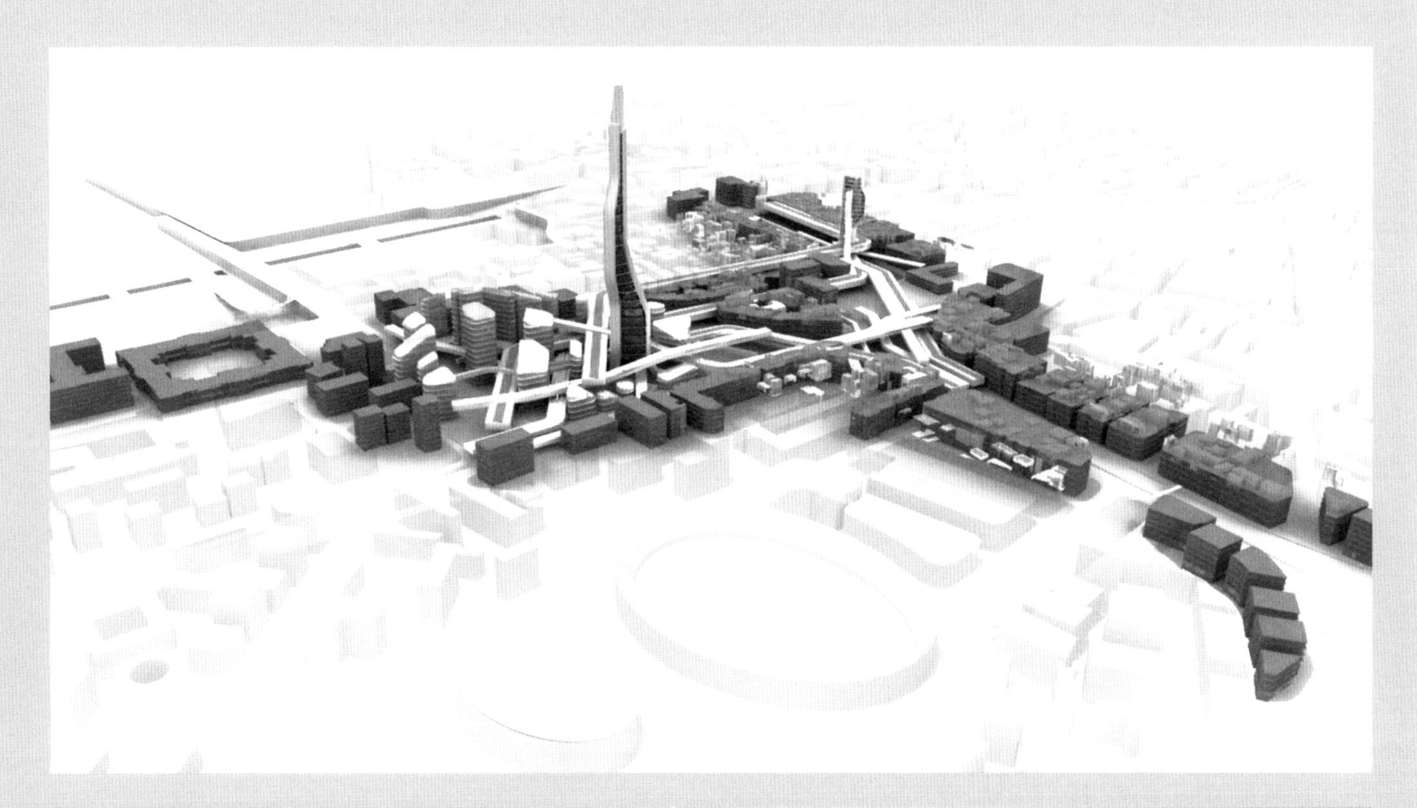

Opposite
A sketch by Eric Parry of a proposed scheme in Aldermanbury Square, London. A plan and two elevations simply explain this proposal for a particular building and its relationship to the streets immediately around it.

Above and top
Architectural visualizations can also be used to convey a much more general overall impression of how a development or indeed an entire city might be.

Drawing the city

Cities are represented by urban designers, planners, architects, politicians and geographers who all have their own language of expression. Drawing the city requires a substantial range of skills to suggest possible situations, environments and experiences.

Architecture is part of the city, so an understanding of architectural systems of plan, section, elevation and measured drawings is necessary to describe the various components. The city is also made up of spaces, places and streets. These are environments where people interact, where the theatre of our existence takes place. So a range of drawings and further subjective representations is needed that can communicate the possibilities that a city offers. A painting, drawing or picture can be used to create an abstract interpretation, or a set of maps can describe relationships of buildings to space. A model, either physical or computer-generated, adds more information and detail.

Sometimes the drawing is intended to be super-accurate, in a way that can never be achieved through building. The drawing has its own expectations, dictated by the scale and framing of the image.

The drawing has to encompass all possibilities from the abstract idea or concept to the engineered construction detail. It needs to communicate to the visionary, the romantic, and to the makers, the builder and the stonemason. Its language needs to be diverse and varied.

The idea that the architect or masterplanner must be the great communicator is of great importance. The drawing is the frame; it needs to allow a child to imagine a place to play, a mason to understand how to build, an engineer to develop his structural idea. For architects to see a building in all these ways and then re-frame the view, they must first imagine, create three-dimensionally and explore, then allow others to reveal the possibilities: through a process of drawing the 'making' is happening. Our language of drawing needs to be mechanical, simple, transparent and stimulating. The city is represented in drawing as a mechanical interpretation through sketches and CAD images, but also through models, both physical and computer-generated, which allow other interpretations of the city and which help us to understand physical context and urban inter-relationships.

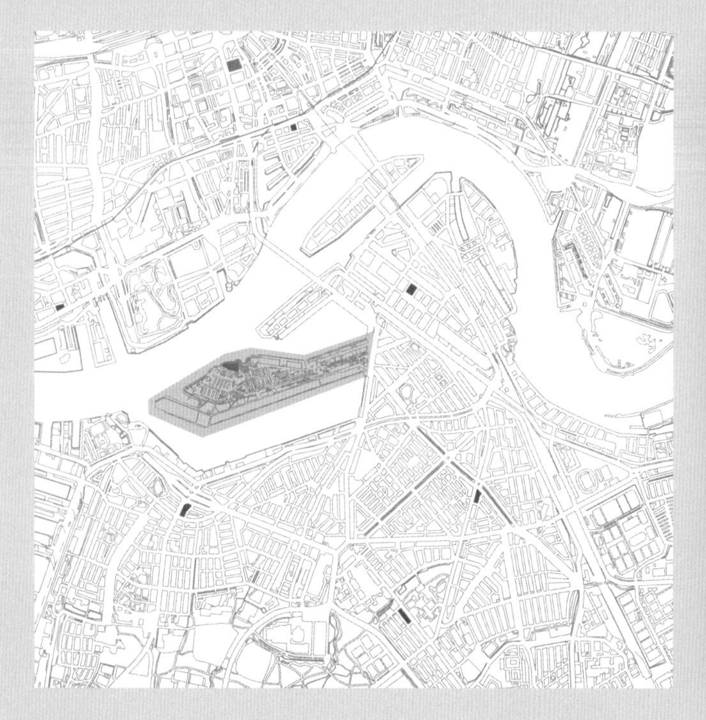

Above
The shaded area of this site plan indicates the location of a proposed scheme in Rotterdam. The map allows the scheme to be studied in relation to local features such as bridges and the waterway.

Above right
This image has been generated using a digital map and explains a concept for a mixed-use urban design scheme that connects different parts of the city of Brighton. The white conceptual lines intersect at a project site.

Above

This image of a proposed campus concept for Oxford Brookes University, Oxford, was created by Design Engine architects using an aerial photo. The new concept was sketched over the site to suggest how the campus could be reinvented.

Left

A masterplan proposal for Venice by the European City Studio at the Portsmouth School of Architecture identifies a possible route across the city that ends at a public piazza which is part of a proposed redevelopment (top right).

About this book

This book has been organized into sections that reflect the broad categories of drawing the city used both professionally and in teaching students how to consider and analyse urban environments.

The first section is entitled The City in Context and describes the key influences in the evolution of representation techniques. There are particular points historically that have affected the expression and style of drawings of our cities. Some are practical, recording what exists, others visionary, predicting a future.

The second section, The City as Object, examines the idea that the city is something that exists and can be treated as a subject of study for observational drawing. There is a subjectivity to this, depending on how we draw and express the existing. The city is drawn by artists and tourists, sometimes to just record what is there and to understand it as a physical place. It influences our experiences, memories and social interactions. This can be expressed as drawing, but also as physical models that show us cities as they exist in three dimensions.

The City as Data is concerned with representing the city as a measured, scientifically defined environment. Some of these measurements analyse it as a series of routes or spaces. Using physical and CAD models to describe the city, and maps which record layers of information, the data informs our understanding of the city as a measured environment. A series of tools is introduced to suggest ways to measure the city. The measurement and interpretation of the data that describe the city are both quantitative and qualitative and such data require both scientific and artistic interpretation.

The City Imagined deals with the range of techniques used to describe future environments, cities that are imagined as either evolving places or completely new cities that have been started from nothing and been portrayed with paintings, drawings and CAD models. These cities are dreams, visions of a future, some of which become a reality or may have informed the development of masterplans that have been implemented.

The last section presents a series of case study masterplanning projects from architects and urban designers around the world who are using the most contemporary techniques and methods of representation to suggest exciting new places and cityscapes.

This book has within it some inspiring representations of the city, from historic precedents to complex computer simulations. There are examples of how to create certain sorts of urban drawings and also tips on how to employ certain techniques of visualization. The key to successful representation for urban design is to use many techniques. The city is complex, and careful thought is needed to decide when to use which type of expression at the concept, development or presentation stage of design.

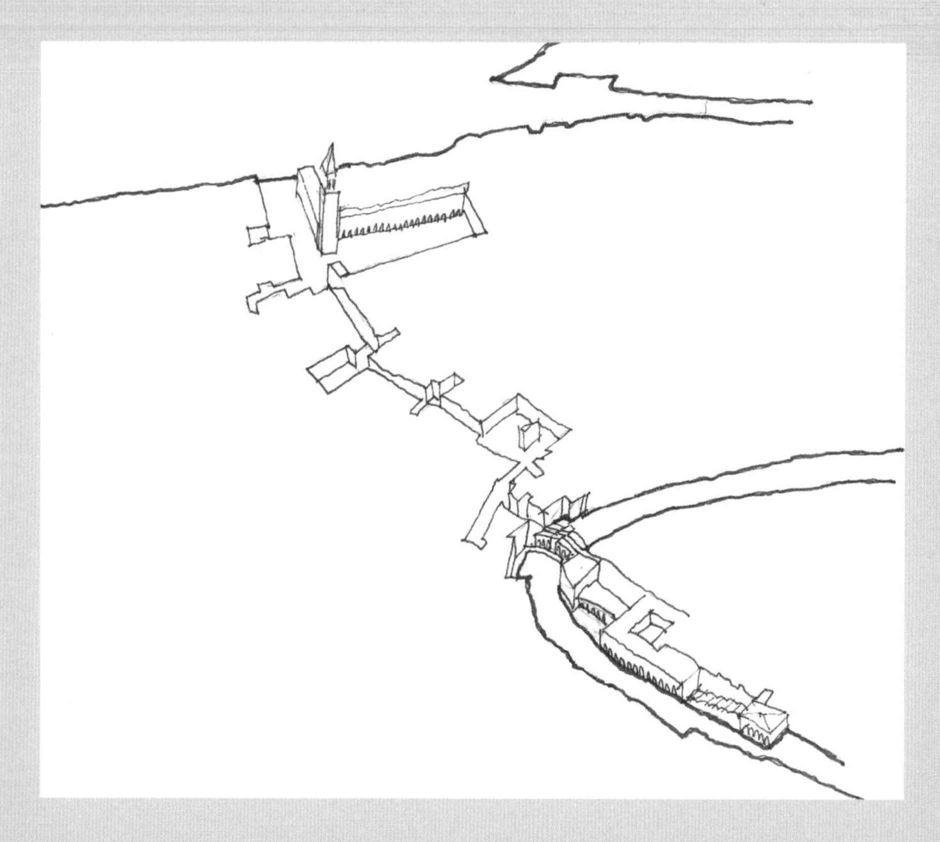

This pencil sketch was based on an aerial photo of Venice and highlights a journey across the city from St Mark's Square to the Rialto Market.

Above
A city can be described with a series of quick sketches to show the shifting scale of buildings and spaces as the location of the viewer changes. This series of sketches describes a route for a student project.

Below
Physical models are an invaluable medium for exploring and describing proposed urban environments.

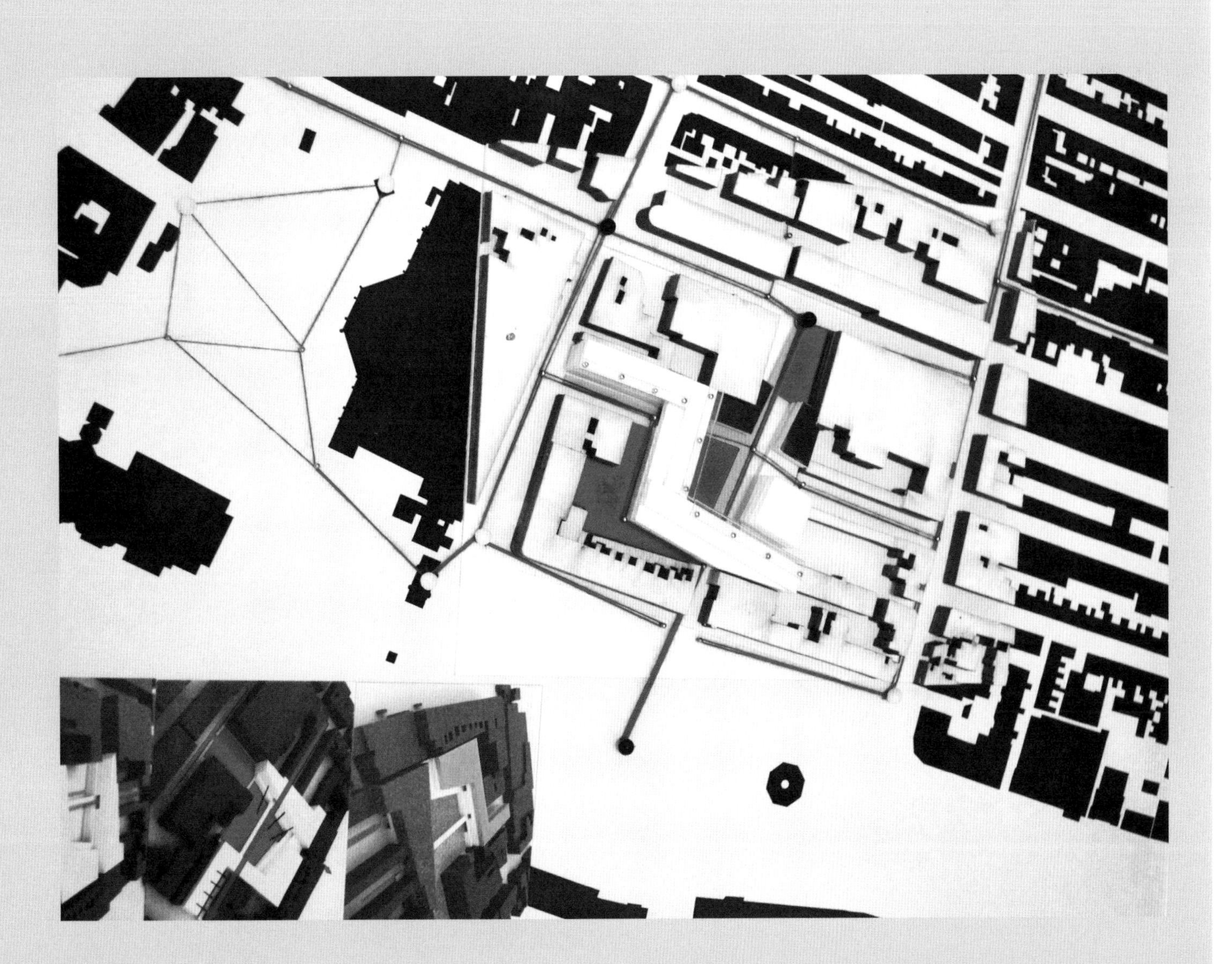

THE CITY IN CONTEXT

Introduction

The city is a discourse and this discourse is truly a language: the city speaks to its inhabitants, we speak to our city, the city where we are, simply by living in it, by wandering through it, by looking at it.

Roland Barthes, 'Semiology and the Urban', in *Rethinking Architecture: A Reader in Cultural Theory*, Neil Leach (ed.), 1997, pp.306–7

Cities have been represented visually since their very beginnings. The methods of their representation have adapted as the worlds around them have evolved. The sense of describing our cities as places where we live, work and exist is an important aspect of cultural and social expression.

These descriptions have been illustrated in our literature and poetry and also our painting and art. The techniques used to express cities began with simple carvings and drawings, which were based on crafts and skills that evolved from building and making. These developed to include photography and modelmaking and, in the twenty-first century, the use of computer software to evoke imagined worlds that can be explored three-dimensionally. The range of expressions has adapted to allow urban environments to be designed in new ways. The technology of representation is challenging the physical possibilities of our knowledge to construct buildings.

Before the Renaissance, architectural drawings weren't used in the way that we understand them today. For example, Gothic architecture was a process that prioritized construction rather than representation. The knowledge was with the master mason who moved from place to place executing his understanding of geometry and tested engineering, informing material assembly. By contrast, the idea of visualization today has developed to the stage that we can construct simulated realities of our cities on computers before we start to build the real environment.

This section of the book will introduce the important references and ideas of representation that have informed the practice of masterplanning and urban design, from painters and engravers to planners and visionaries. Their methods and techniques will be described as important precedents and provide a background for a contemporary interpretation. Each reference explores the importance of the technique of illustration to the idea or design of a city or place.

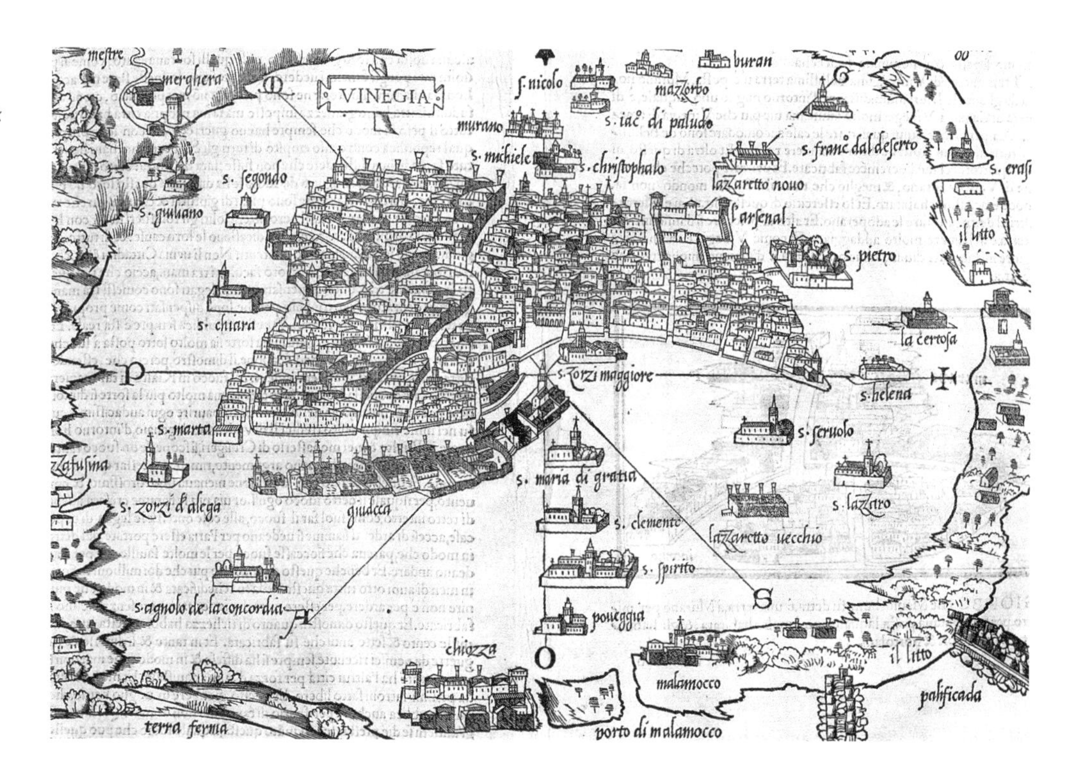

Right
A perspective plan of Venice and the lagoon from the *Isolario* (*Book of Islands*) di Benedetto Bordone, 1528. The map reflects a type that was popular in Italy in the sixteenth century, and which includes new perspective and surveying techniques.

Early views of the city

The earliest views of the city in the medieval period used combinations of views and journeys around the city in a form of abstract mapping and they exaggerated certain features according to their importance. The creation of a map, which wasn't to scale, told a story of important features and buildings that existed within the city or town boundaries. It suggested a set of experiences concentrated around significant locations within the town or village. Such maps are some of the simplest, yet most alluring representations of the town or city.

Early maps recorded the city as text to be read by visitors to describe a realm or the boundaries of a city; they celebrated the culture of a place, its monuments, spaces and buildings. Early medieval maps were akin to diagrams, describing memories within a defined local area, as that was the extent of the map makers' knowledge. Early English city maps were imagined interpretations of buildings describing an emblematic place. Routes were reduced to an imagined straight line; there was no sense of scale or physical space. The concept of the physical world was about a local understanding.

In the sixteenth century, surveying techniques allowed an accuracy of measurement. In the 1540s, scale maps were developed and at the same time perspective techniques were being employed by artists in Europe, which changed the whole sense of spatial representation.

The bird's-eye view of that perspective allowed meant that the landscape and topography of a city could be described. The advent of more accurate measuring and surveying equipment and techniques shifted the idea of representation from the abstract, the imagined, to the more precise and measured.

Maps became tools that allowed for the manipulation and re-imagination of physical space. Many early maps used orthographic perspective or the bird's-eye view as a way of exaggerating aspects of the urban scene and providing a three-dimensional view. Maps are important cultural indicators and represent points in time when particular boundaries and physical relationships existed. If we want to understand the development of a city we compare historical maps to find out how the physical landscape has changed and various pieces of a city have retained their cultural significance through time.

The map is an important device to record a piece of a town or city. In 1748 Giambattista Nolli (1701–56) created a map of Rome which described the city as a figure-ground representation where the buildings are shaded and the spaces are left as gaps in-between. This allows the city to be read as a series of spaces and forms. Nolli clearly records any public spaces that are enclosed, the interiors of churches and colonnades. The figure-ground technique provided a unique map of Rome describing its public spaces.

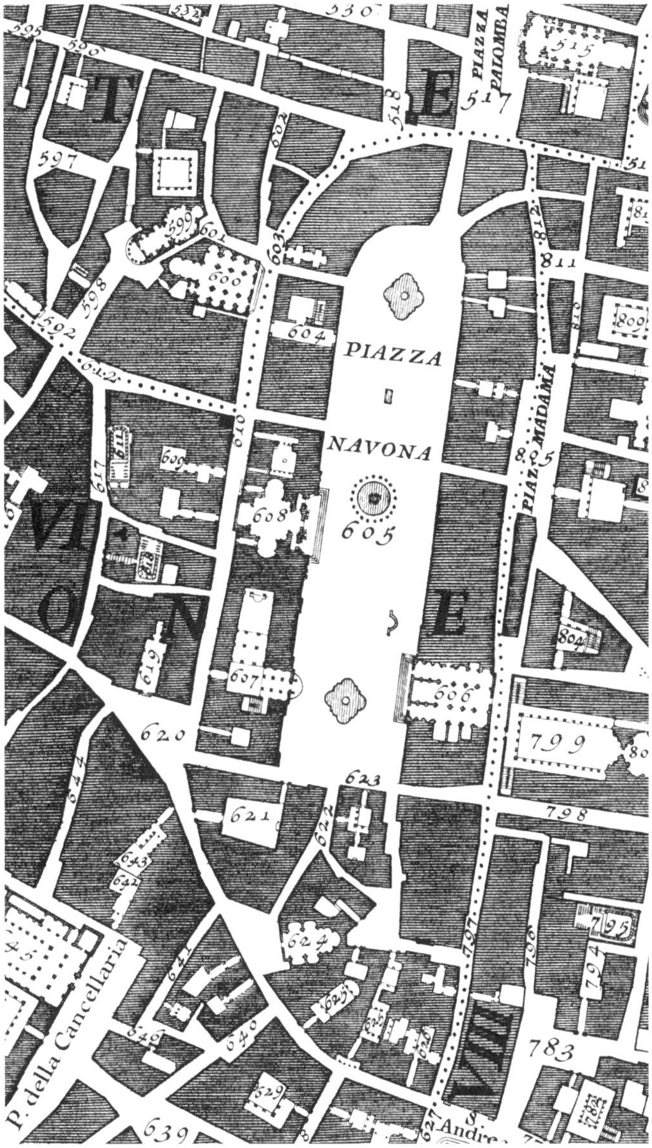

Left
A figure-ground study of Rome by Giambattista Nolli (1748). Built areas are shown as shaded while civic spaces, such as Piazza Navona, and public buildings, such as churches, are left white.

The Renaissance and perspective

In Renaissance Italy, Leon Battista Alberti (1404–72) used painting as a metaphor for a window on the world and saw the painting as an intersection between a viewed point and the viewer of the image. In his treatise on architecture of 1537 (later published as *The Five Books of Architecture*), Sebastiano Serlio (1475–1554) recognizes a series of urban settings for his theatrical productions. He uses the newly developed method of perspective to explore the ideas of the Noble, the Comic and the Satyric. These images describe streets. Each of his street scenes illustrates a different character of the city within the street. The comic scene is chaotic, the noble scene dignified, the satyric scene – as the satyr is half animal, half human – is a hybrid environment, half urban, half rural: the street merging with nature. These drawings were revolutionary in that they created a new system that offered an illusion of depth on a surface but also ordered an image from a single viewpoint. Geometry was introduced to give structure to the representation of space, whether inside buildings or outside in the city. The subjectivity of the viewer remained, as the position of the artist still determined what was drawn, but there was more of a sense of truth and order to perspective.

Perspective can be considered as a series of interconnected spaces, to multiply and disseminate views of the world. When drawing urban environments, the perspective was used to suggest the idea of the street, public space or square, and as it became more developed as a device it was used to create more complicated overviews of the city as axonometric or isometric views. The bird's-eye view, the perspective taken from above, changed the perception of the city.

Perspective extended the idea of a two-dimensional surface, suggesting depth and three dimensions. It was also used in paintings on walls in large family houses to suggest depth within a room or a constructed view of the city beyond. The Renaissance painters and artists were interpreting aspects of the city around them, improvising an accurate impression of the social and cultural experience of the period. The perspective image offers the view of the observer, the participant in the city, and is an invaluable way of explaining the urban environment.

Below
Ambrogio Lorenzetti's *Allegoria del Buon Governo* (1338–40), Sala della Pace, Palazzo Pubblico, Siena. This fresco uses the city as the backdrop to the main scene. The use of perspective in the Renaissance transformed the possibility of the two-dimensional image to suggest a new interpretation of the city.

Artists and their visions of the city

An important artist involved in representing the city is Giovanni Battista Piranesi (1720–78), who was born near Treviso in Italy and studied architecture, etching and engraving. He produced a series of views of the city in 1743, based on his experiences of Rome. Many of Piranesi's engravings are of imaginary environments and spaces within the city, images that are distorted, spaces suggesting incarceration and nightmare that explore the interplay of light and form and appear as extraordinary infinite labyrinthine caves.

The city has been described by a series of visionaries who have suggested different ideas of a future experience of the city. Claude-Nicolas Ledoux (1736–1806) was one of the first exponents of Neoclassical architecture. He had visionary schemes for the ideal city of Chaux and created Utopian ideas of the city and how a new enlightened society might engage with it. The French Revolution prevented many of his ideas from being realized, including his Neoclassical Royal Saltworks at Arc-et-Senans in France.

Many artists have interpreted their view of the city through painting. J M W Turner (1775–1851) was a British painter of the Romantic tradition who depicted the landscape and cities. He used watercolour to represent subtleties of light, surface and colour. His interpretations of cities were realistic, but also suggested a blurred abstraction of the view.

Above
Giovanni Battista Piranesi's engraving 'The Smoking Fire' from *Carceri d'invenzione* (*Imaginary Prisons*), Rome, 1761. Piranesi's work included this series of imaginary environments as well as a famous series of views of Rome.

Left
Plan of the ideal city of Chaux, designed in the 1770s by the French architect Claude-Nicholas Ledoux. The Utopian vision of a city based around a salt works, with schools, a market and social spaces, was never realized.

Giorgio de Chirico (1888–1978), the Greek–Italian painter renowned for his Surrealist impressions of the city, was interested in the metaphysical aspect and exaggerated features of the urban environment. De Chirico captured the mood of the city, focusing on the melancholy and mystery of the street. Some of his most famous impressions use exaggeration of perspective to suggest a shift of scale; objects are juxtaposed in the scene to challenge the idea of scale and the viewer's understanding.

A number of painters have used the city directly as inspiration for their painting and many have inspired urban designers and architects. In particular Piet Mondrian (1872–1944) produced abstract interpretations of his understanding of the city. Reducing complexity to grids and geometry, he painted New York City in 1942 as a series of interlocking lines.

Paul Klee (1879–1940) taught at the Bauhaus and used colour very carefully, with a deep understanding of tone combined with abstract geometry, to interpret landscapes and cities. He used many different media and techniques which have influenced the view of the city.

In contrast, Edward Hopper's (1882–1967) painting *Nighthawks* (1942) is far from abstract, and an important observation of the culture of the US in the 1940s. It suggests that the city is at once full of people and a lonely place, capturing a moment when the inside meets the outside. This painting has influenced architects who are concerned with the social reality of city living and is a commentary on the cultural experience that the city affords. The artistic impression of the streets and squares in which we live provides an important set of cultural references for the explanation of the contemporary city.

Scale

From the map and the global position of a city to the details of the buildings and squares, the understanding and application of scale is important when describing urban places. The architects Charles (1907–78) and Ray (1916–88) Eames created a film in 1968, *Powers of 10*, which contextualized the idea of the body and the city and used the concept of scale to allow the viewer to understand their relationship to the city and beyond. The film starts with a full-size image of a man in a park, then the camera zooms out so the image is ten times smaller, and then zooms out again so it becomes 100 times smaller than the original frame, and so on. *Powers of 10* allows the viewer to understand how scale changes our understanding of people, objects, places and cities.

The notion of scale and the city has been affected in the last decade by the availability of new digital mapping techniques. Online services such as Google Earth create maps by superimposing images from satellite and aerial photography. Google Earth allows the user to see any part of the globe at any scale by zooming in and out and has altered the way we can read cities and understand environments by allowing us to view them at various scales simultaneously. Scale affects our understanding of places, buildings and their context.

Opposite
Italian Square (1912) by Giorgio de Chirico exemplifies the artist's exaggerated urban perspectives.

Below
Google Earth software was developed by Google to allow users to obtain views of the earth incorporating maps generated from satellite imagery. Using the Zoom tool, a chosen location can be pictured at a range of scales, from a view of the entire planet down to streets and buildings. New tools allow a view of the street itself in some locations.

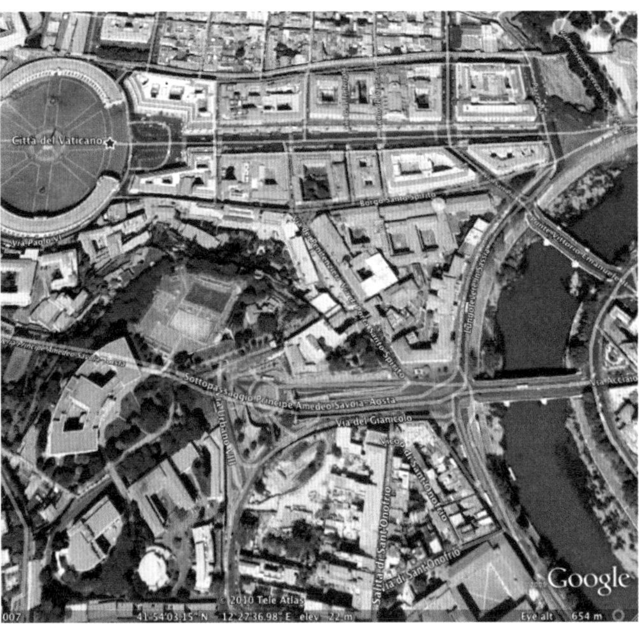

Twentieth-century precedents and realized urban ideas

In 1889, in his book *City Planning According to Artistic Principles*, Camillo Sitte (1843–1903), an Austrian architect and artist, described the city as a series of 'rooms', with urban squares considered as spaces for inhabiting. He was interested in enhancing the experience of the citizens through urban design, approaching the city as a work of art, rather than a technical exercise of geometry and form.

At the start of the twentieth century there were many groups of theorists and artists across the world who were challenging conventions of society, art and thinking. In the early 1900s the French architect and urbanist Eugène Hénard was concerned with aspects of circulation in the city. He suggested proposals for transport systems as well as the idea of public space and parking associated with new road networks. One group that originated in Italy, the Futurists, used Cubist style to describe their vision for the future. They were interested in the new technology, such as cars and aeroplanes. They wanted to challenge historical styles and ideas, arguing that drawing needed to express concepts of dynamism and movement.

Antonio Sant'Elia (1888–1916) famously described his ideas for a Futurist city in a series of drawings called *La Città Nuova* (1912–14), suggesting a world of towers and a mechanized urban environment. The new city was bold and efficient. It was drawn in exaggerated perspective to emphasize the dynamic scale and form of the buildings. While none of his ideas was realized, they became an important reference and impetus for architectural change.

Below right
A figure-ground analysis of a public square taken from Camillo Sitte's 1889 book *City Planning According to Artistic Principles*.

Below
A section drawing from Eugène Hénard's *Les Villes d'avenir* illustrates the relationship between underground Paris and the buildings above.

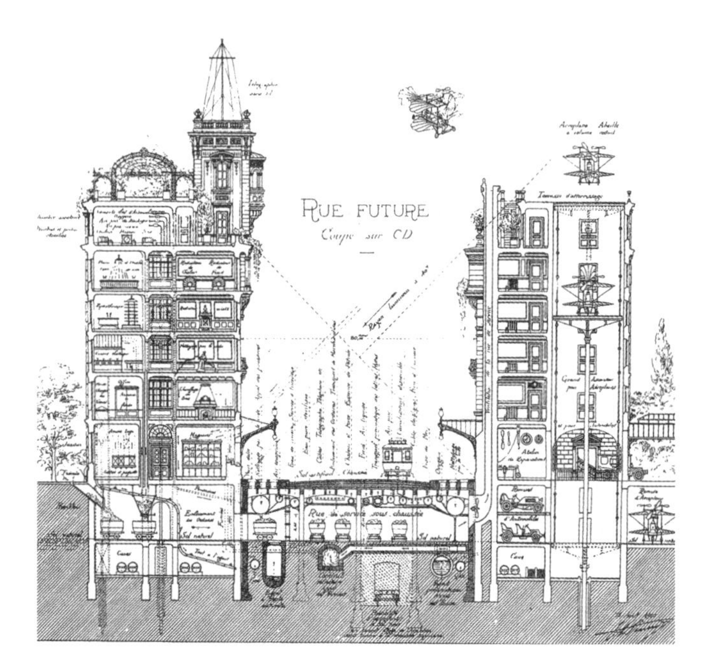

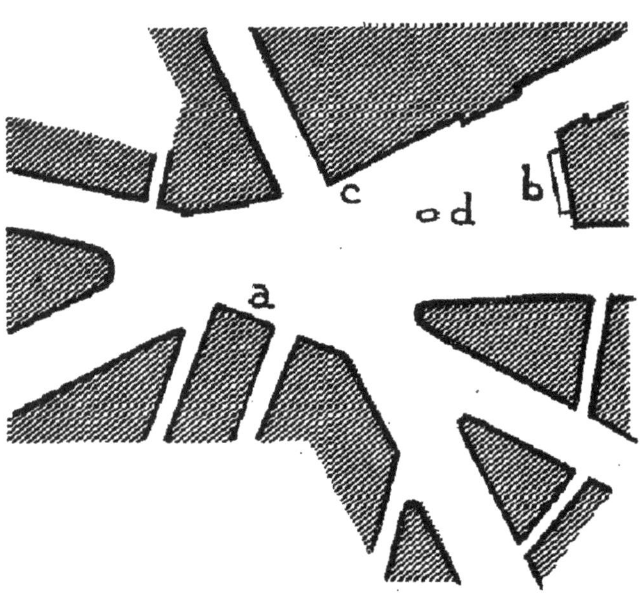

Left
In his series *La Città Nuova* (1912–14) Antonio Sant'Elia used bold tones and a dynamic, exaggerated perspective to promote his vision of the future.

Below
A panoramic aerial impression from French architect Tony Garnier's *Une Cité industrielle* (1917) proposes a design for an imaginary industrial city.

Above
Plate 13 from Bruno Taut's 1919 *Alpine Architektur*. Taut's concept of urban planning could best be described as visionary and dramatic rather than a practical urban design proposal, but it examplifies the imaginative power typical of the time.

Below
In this drawing of 1946 the English modernist architect Joseph Emberton suggested a development of multi-storey buildings surrounding the historic St Paul's Cathedral in London.

Other Futurists, such as Umberto Boccioni (1882–1916), used perspective as a way to connect the viewer with the new emerging world of the city. In his painting *The City Rises* (1910), he represented the struggle between the modern developing industrial world and our response to it, playing on the tension between technology and human endeavour.

Some of Le Corbusier's (1887–1965) most influential work in the twentieth century was concerned with his view of the city. He was a Swiss architect and urban designer whose vision for the city in 1922 was a series of skyscrapers, set within park space. In his proposed Plan Voisin of 1925, Le Corbusier suggested that large areas of Paris should be replaced by parks and skyscrapers. In 1935 he sketched the Ville Radieuse (the Radiant City), based on the idea of increasing the density of the city in housing blocks surrounded by green spaces. He envisaged a future cult of health as an antidote to the congested and polluting environment of the nineteenth-century industrial city.

In the 1930s, Frank Lloyd Wright (1867–1959) developed ideas about the new urban environment outside the city: the suburbs. His Broadacre City proposal was a suburban development where all residents were given one acre of land, using the car to connect to the rest of the city. His ideas were described using plan drawings and perspective imagery.

The Situationists, formed in 1957, were a group of artists and thinkers who questioned capitalist society, proposing alternative ways to read or describe a city. Guy Debord (1931–94) suggested the concept of the *dérive* (or drift) to explore a city without preconceptions. The idea was to drift randomly on foot through the city and observe it in an unpredictable way, as a series of events dependent on experience and circumstance, challenging the notion of using a drawn map to determine a journey or route.

Above
Le Corbusier's 1925 Plan Voisin offers an alternative vision of the relationship between the urban block and surrounding landscape.

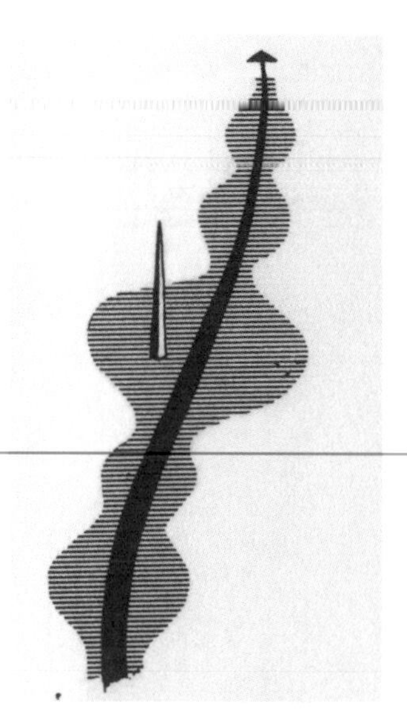

Above
In his book *The Image of the City* Kevin Lynch describes the city using diagrams, maps and abstracted images, such as the examples above.

Below
A series of sketches of a journey through a city taken from the book *The Concise Townscape* by Gordon Cullen.

Kevin Lynch (1918–84) introduced the idea of describing the city conceptually as a series of diagrams. In *A Theory of Good City Form* he uses metaphors to represent the city: the City of Faith, the City as a Machine and the City as an Organism. Reducing the complexity of a city to a diagram can be helpful to communicate and clarify its essential meaning. In his seminal book *The Image of the City* (1960), Lynch used 'mental maps' to describe paths, edges, districts, nodes and landmarks. He took the idea of the city and translated ways to organize the information within it into simple diagrams and drawings.

The Concise Townscape by Gordon Cullen (1914–94) suggests a number of useful ways to interpret a city. One important technique is that of serial views, through which a city can be described as a journey combining a map of the route and a series of images that, as a sequence, illustrate that journey. The journey is both personal to whoever takes and a simple way to explore the city from the point of view of the pedestrian observer. This exercise was described using drawn sections through the city as well as sketches.

Edmund Bacon (1910–2005) was an urban planner in the US and his book *Design of Cities* (1967) is an important text illustrating the development of urban form. It offers new ways to understand and analyse the city, including images that flatten an urban square into a series of elevations, and others showing sections through squares in cities. The drawings represent the city in a distinctive way using geometry, proportion and scale abstracted into conceptual fields.

Cedric Price (1934–2003) was a visionary architect in the late twentieth century. He worked with ideas and theories and influenced many contemporary architects. Price wanted to encourage the reinvention of the city, to challenge conventions and to suggest new paradigms for city experience. He didn't construct many buildings, but wanted to encourage people 'to think the unthinkable'. One of his most important ideas was the Fun Palace: a laboratory of fun where you could go for dancing, music, drama and fireworks. He believed that the flexible and the temporary were key in the city as a non-permanent experience, and that new technology would allow people to have control over their environment, using perspective and axonometric drawings to suggest his ideas.

Left
The city square of Wijk bij Duurstede in the Netherlands, drawn with the elevations flattened against the plan. The drawing is based on an example from Edmund Bacon's *Design of Cities*.

Representing the city in the twentieth century

Twentieth-century urban designers and architects used a variety of representational techniques heavily influenced by contemporary artists. In the 1960s, Archigram used collage and the superimposition of images to suggest a city of the future. It was portrayed as a Computer City, a 'Walking City', a futuristic environment where buildings could move around. Archigram were interested in space-age technology and how this could be used to suggest new paradigms for architecture and cities. They employed the analogy of the machine and the brightly coloured modular unit that could be repeated along with futuristic and space-age imagery.

In 1966, Superstudio, a group of Italian architects, challenged conventional thinking about the city. They used collage, photomontage and sketch techniques to suggest new urban concepts such as a plug-in city under a giant dome. As well as developing ideas about the city, they also designed furniture and were involved in filmmaking.

Aldo Rossi (1931–97) wrote about the city in his book *L'Architettura della città* in 1966. He was interested in the idea of the new city environment that used existing historic forms or types and focused on the city as a repository of human memory. One of the most famous images in this book shows the city as a composition of experiences and ideas, representing it in a completely new way using collage and superimposed images – a layered palimpsest analogous to the layered history of the city.

Rem Koolhaas (1944–) established OMA (Office for Metropolitan Architecture) in 1975 with Madelon Vriesendorp and Elia and Zoe Zenghelis and has written extensively about architecture and urban design. In his text *Delirious New York* he compared the city to an addictive machine. The conceptual City of the Captive Globe was seen as a series of skyscrapers on a grid, referring back to the visions of the early modernists for the city of tomorrow. The imagery suggested a metaphor for the city, an abstract concept of a future environment. It is both painting and three-dimensional representation.

Left
Designs for Sleek Tower (left) and Verandah Tower (right) for Brisbane, Australia (1984), by Peter Cook, the founder of the architectural group Archigram.

Above
In his book *L'Architettura della città* (1966) Aldo Rossi represents the modern city through a collage of emotive and powerful images.

Opposite
This exploded axonometric representation of the 1982 competition-winning design for Parc de la Villette, Paris, by Bernard Tschumi shows his deconstructivist approach to urban design, which uses layers to separate and identify the different concepts behind the park.

Bernard Tschumi (1944–) in his text *Manhattan Transcripts* (1981–82) used techniques and ideas taken from film-making, of the narrative and the storyboard, to suggest new ways to think about the city and to represent it as a series of frames of experience and view. His proposal for the redevelopment of the Parc de la Villette on an industrial site in Paris was produced using a set of exploded three-dimensional axonometric drawings. This type of visualization allows a complex image to be represented as a series of layers so that the concept can be more easily understood. The bottom layer of the drawing represents the map of the site. The next layer represents the 'surface', with a landscape proposal suggesting various surfaces, grass, water and a path. In the next layer, 'points' overlie the ground plane forming a grid that regulates the whole proposal. At each of these gridpoints Tschumi located a red folly structure referencing the Constructivist painter Kasimir Malevich. In the final layer, planes indicate walls, edges that define different areas, walkways and the bridges that intersect the two layers below.

Spiro Kostof (1936–91) in *The City Shaped* (1999) also uses diagrams as abstractions to explore ideas of the city as it developed and evolved, investigating it through diagram, grid and geometry and interpreting new patterns of organization within the city.

More recently, David Grahame Shane in *Recombinant Urbanism* (2005) explores new ways to describe the city, citing the seven ages of Post-Modernism, which include collage, bricolage, superimposition, photomontage, assemblage and decoupage. All these terms refer to concepts of the city as well as methods of representing it.

Urban design and consideration of the city is part of contemporary life and thinking. The many ways to express the city are connected to the philosophies and concepts that relate to the design of the urban environment – the two cannot be separated. The techniques of collage and montage in terms of artistic process have had an effect on the understanding of the contemporary city as a layered, complex and constructed experience.

At the beginning of the twenty-first century, the representation of the city has become exceptionally varied. Sketches or paintings are still valuable forms of personal expression to record the city. In addition, advances in computer software have made CAD models increasingly important. But the physical model remains one of the most significant tools to describe a city. It is real, three-dimensional and allows for quick interpretation of a context. All these methods of communicating the city have evolved: learning from the pioneering thinking and prodigious skill of those who engaged with drawing our cities in the past is the basis from which to express new ideas for the future.

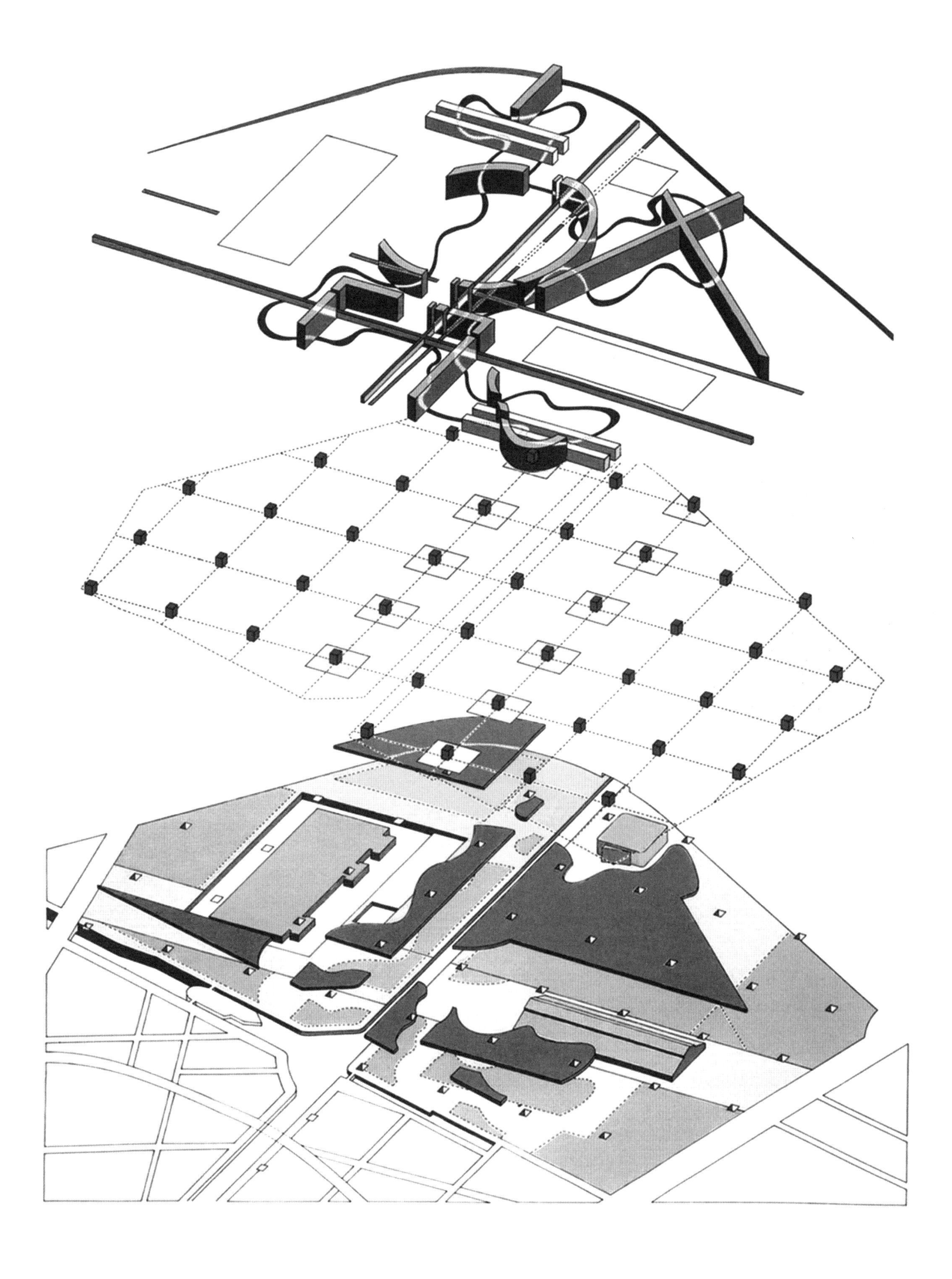

THE CITY AS OBJECT

Introduction

The power of drawing in architecture is to bridge between the imagined and real worlds.

Robin Evans, *The Projective Cast: Architecture and its Three Geometries*, 1997

Below
When used neatly, pencil is excellent for creating a drawing that has depth while maintaining a warm look. Pencil can blur the edges of an image, or suggest a horizon or a detail.

We can record the city as a place that exists through our understanding of it. It can be represented as something seen, experienced and interpreted by the viewer. Or as something to be recorded as one would draw or paint a still-life painting; even this allows for personal interpretation as the record can be made in either a photo-realistic or an abstract way. Many techniques can be brought into play, but freehand drawing and sketching are important methods of communicating – they are as personal interpretation that allows the drawer a sense of engagement with and transition through the surrounding city.

The city as object is the idea that the city exists as something we can engage with, draw and represent as seen and experienced. This section will concentrate primarily on freehand drawing and interpretation of the city, but all freehand methods can be mixed with digital media to represent the urban environment in ever more interpretative and personalized ways. The city needs to be understood as it exists before it can be designed or adapted by urban designers, architects or masterplanners.

Historically, interpreting the city has been about cultural observation, describing activities and experience in the city. Traditionally, freehand drawing and sketching would be the main techniques to depict the city. Now we can use digital techniques such as photography and film to portray our surroundings.

The city is the background for our architectural ideas. To be able to design effectively and develop the urban environment, time needs to be taken to read what exists already, to look, observe and understand. Through this interpretation, the emerging urban landscapes will evolve

sensitively. Through careful drawing and reading of the city, it can be understood as a place for interaction and any design responses – whether they are at the scale of the masterplan of the city remodelled or extended, or a new intervention such as a building or an urban square – will be sensitive to the conditions that exist.

The cityscape inspires artists in different ways to record activity about everyday life through drawing and photography. Careful thought should be given to the scope of the image, whether it is designed to suggest the scale of a street or square, or the idea of material and form, using techniques such as collage or photomontage, which combines photography with drawing and painting techniques. Artists use the idea of mapping city environments to inspire their art and describe 'place', combining techniques from traditional painting, drawing and map-making.

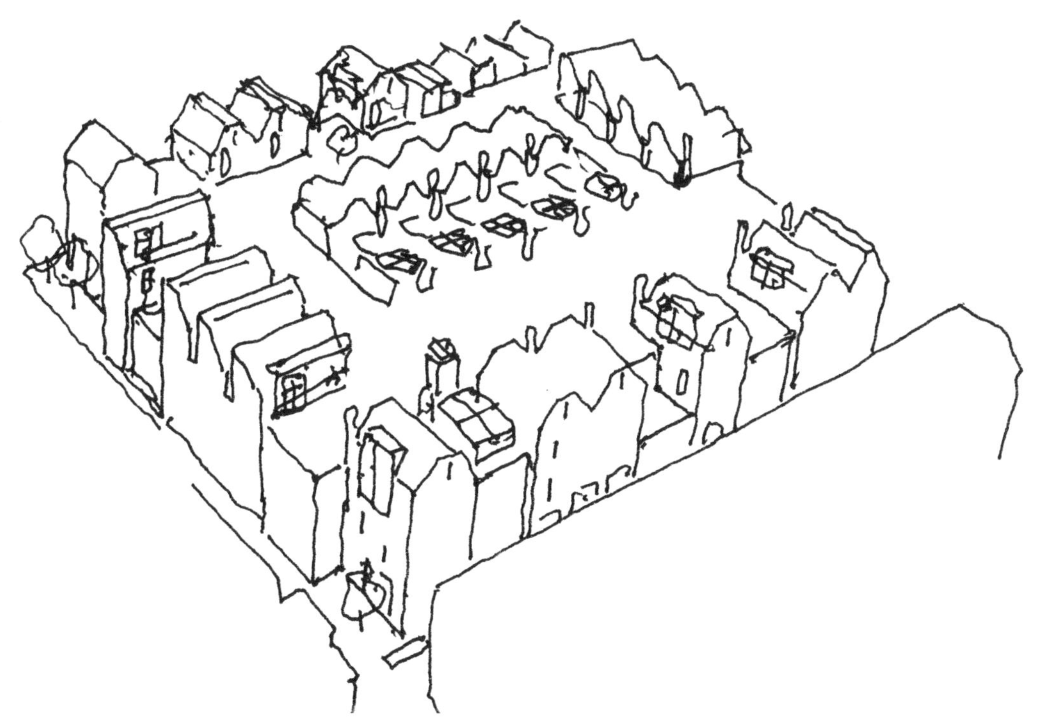

Left
This sketch of a square in Winchester by Allies and Morrison demonstrates how a simple pen drawing can powerfully communicate a three-dimensional understanding of space, mass and form.

Subject

The subject of a drawing could be a description of the context or activities that define that city. Cities are described with various sets of drawings, maps and plans depicting the view from above. In addition there are drawings similar to those used in architecture to represent the physical city as it exists. Elevation drawings express the outer face of the buildings that frame streets and squares, and section drawings convey the notion of cutting through the street, building and square to reveal connections across the city, relative heights and massing. Proportion, proximity and geometry need to be taken into consideration to help to order and understand how the city works, but also to act as helpful references or limitations in a drawing.

It can be useful to limit the subject of the drawing to something focused, for example an experience of opposites. One example might be the difference between shadow and light when moving along a street. Another might be the boundary or threshold between inside and outside, where there may be aspects of private and public space in the city which can be recorded. Or even simple observations to do with the contrasting scale of buildings: large next to small. All of these observations serve to identify each city separately and to define its individual character. When drawing what is seen, it is important to be clear about the intention of the sketch, whether it is to communicate relationships of massing, buildings, form or scale. This intention needs to be identified; it is clarifying a thought about the city. As well as drawing the view in a city, drawing the detail of a building or a part of a square or street is a good way to understand the materiality of a place, to grasp its texture and what it is made from. It may be that the drawing is about a distant view to indicate relative heights of building, or a scene appreciated from beyond the city, exploring the cityscape or landscape with distinguishing features and forms identified from afar.

A city can be described with a close-up sketch to suggest its substance and materiality, and/or with a distant perspective to explain its space, massing and form.

Below
This series of sketches by Khalid Saleh makes up a study that compares the spires of Christopher Wren's London churches. The spires are a distinctive part of the London skyline.

Opposite
This drawing shows an urban site and also gives annotated information regarding the environment, thus providing the viewer with a better understanding of the space.

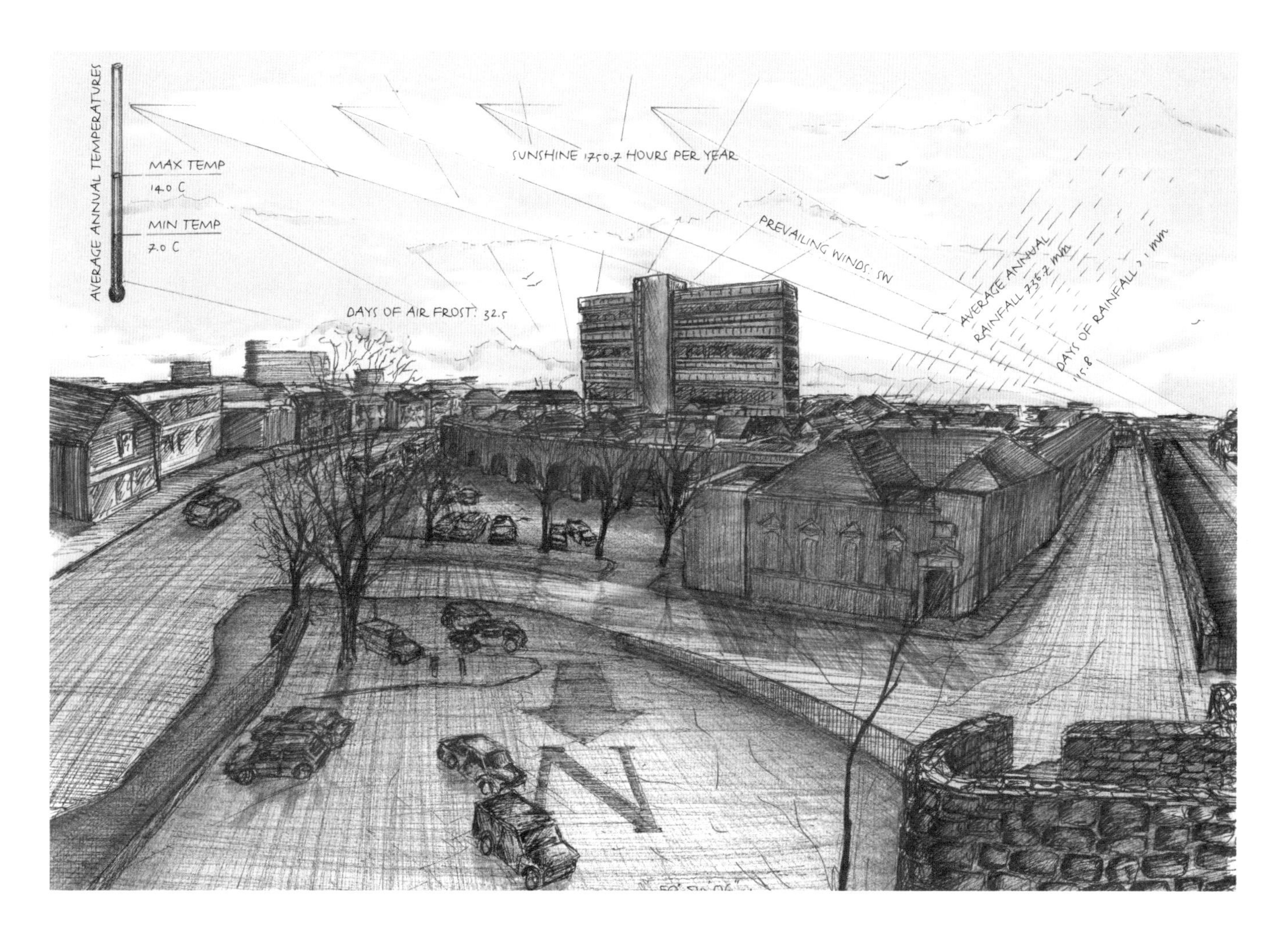
AVERAGE ANNUAL TEMPERATURES
MAX TEMP
14.0 C
MIN TEMP
7.0 C
SUNSHINE 1750.7 HOURS PER YEAR
PREVAILING WINDS: SW
DAYS OF AIR FROST: 32.5
AVERAGE ANNUAL
RAINFALL 736.7 mm
DAYS OF RAINFALL > 1 mm
115.8

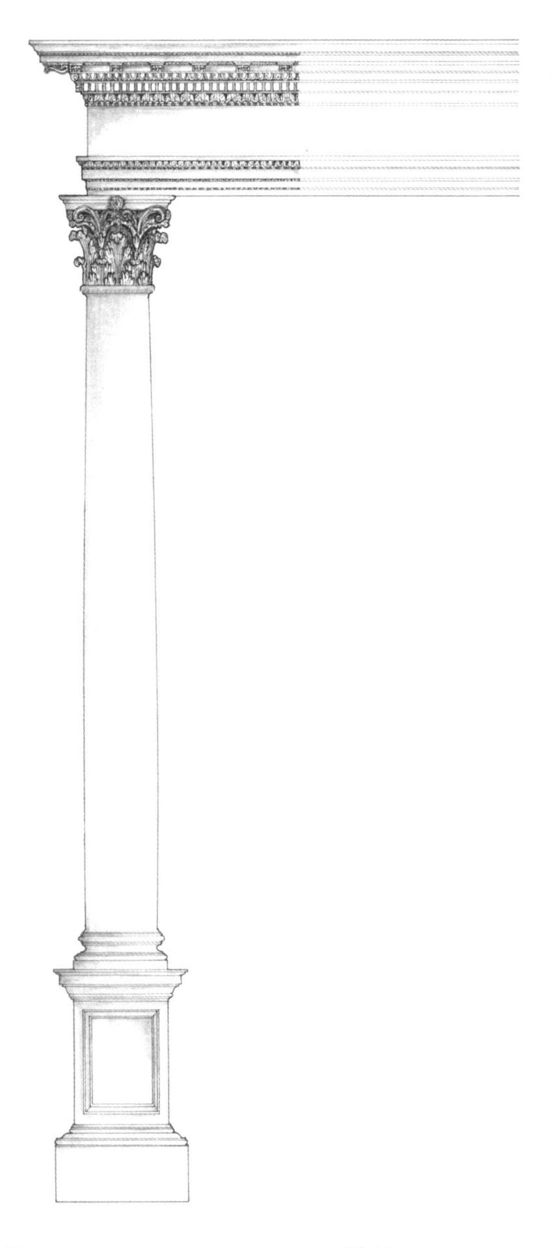

Drawing

There are many drawing types. In architecture and urban design, to draw is to connect with an idea; drawing is an action that transfers thinking into a two-dimensional image. It is planned, considered and exploratory. A city is a complex place, and drawing a city needs careful planning. When we draw, we need to think hard about what we want to communicate. Drawing what you see can explain many things. It can describe an idea of space, an experience, a mood or material. Drawing starts with a blank sheet of paper, it may be in a sketchbook or on a canvas. Before you start to draw, look carefully and think hard.

Drawing the city can be a simple exercise of starting with small square frames on a page and sketching lines to suggest buildings and the relationships between them. It can be a wonderfully precise perspective of a view along a street. Or it can be a multitude of different scales and types of drawing in-between. To draw the city, you need time to explore and experiment. Then the drawings become a record of an experience – first impressions of the scale of a street or urban square, the light as one moves through the city on a bright summer's morning. No words are necessary to describe the experience of the city: a quick sketch, carefully considered, can explain a complex idea.

Above
This technical drawing of a Corinthian column uses ink as a main medium but depth is achieved with clever pencil shading.

Right
Ink can be a fantastic medium for a drawing when you are seeking to create a dramatic contrast.

Above
An abstract drawing of a city can be a more efficient way to give an impression of the urban quality. In this case, the urban site can't be seen but the drawing helps the viewer to understand that there are dynamic forces at play within the space.

Left
This study of a doorway in Rome by Dean Pike brings together an elevation (the main part of the image), section (to the right) and plan drawing (bottom) on one sheet. This type of detailed observation can help to convey the material composition of the city.

Observational sketching

One of the most important considerations when drawing a city is how we interpret the information around us and communicate that to record a general sense of place and particularity of detail.

For each of us the experience of the city is different; even if we take the same journey through the same city as someone else, each of us sees different things along the way. This is something that Gordon Cullen described in *The Concise Townscape* (see page 24), exploring the way that we engage with journeys across a city and how we experience it. This can be expressed as a series of views, related to a journey, with each view building a

A series of sketches showing how one subject can be represented in several ways through the use of different styles, ranging from loose watercolours to ink to ink and coloured pencil.

STEP BY STEP SKETCHING THE DUOMO, FLORENCE

Sketching is the easiest way to start understanding a place, allowing the observer to connect the spaces between the buildings, to understand the scale of spaces and streets, the relative heights of buildings and the massing of the city. This series of sketches was made while standing in a narrow side street in Florence, looking towards a part of the Duomo.

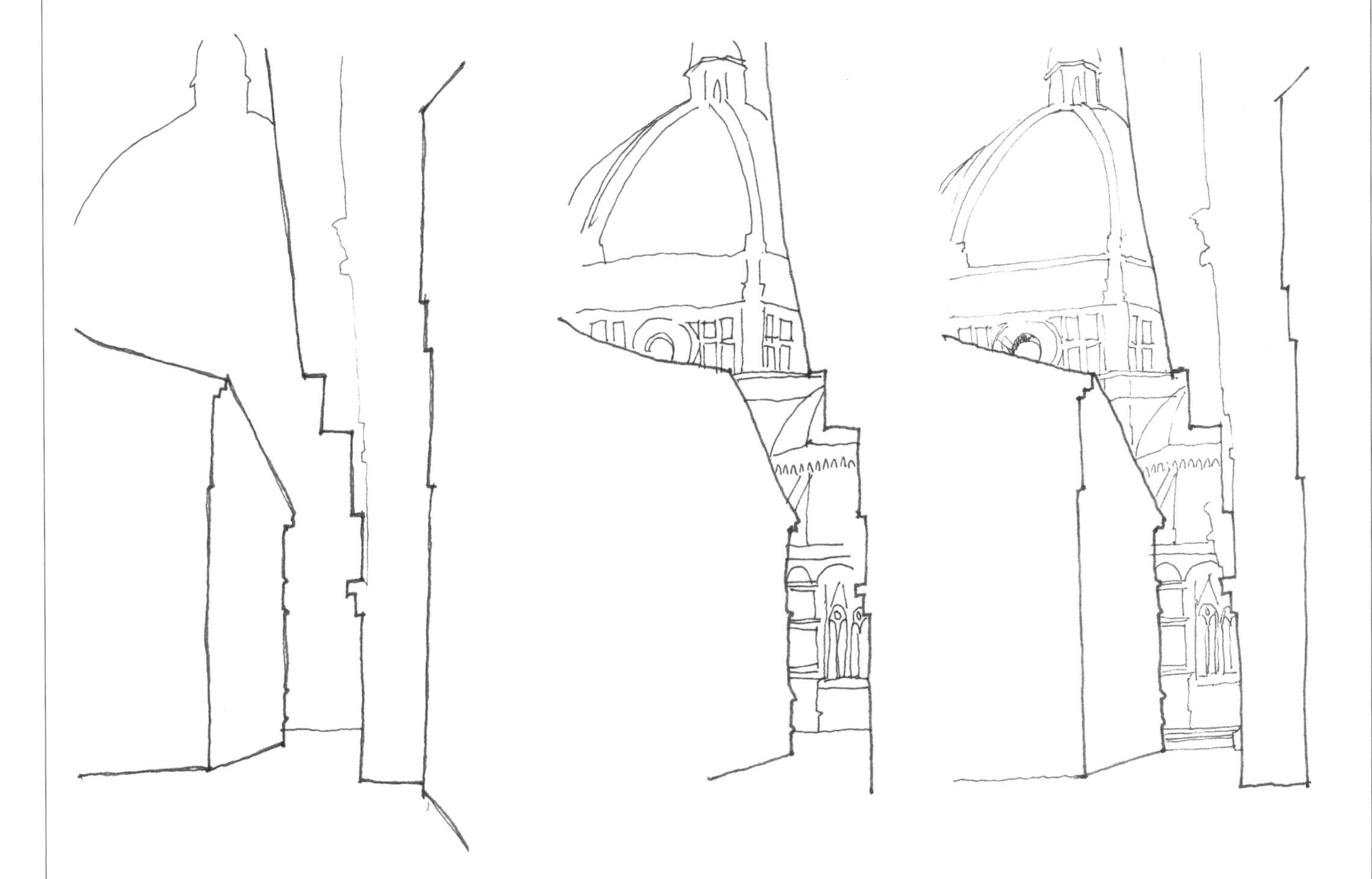

1 An initial sketch. Only the basic outlines of the street, surrounding buildings and the Duomo itself are shown.

2 The main features of the Duomo are sketched in, leaving the surroundings blank.

3 The edges of the neighbouring buildings are then sketched in.

picture of a place. As we turn a corner we encounter a new view with more information and detail. Serial views are a very simple way to interpret a city or even a large building and to describe a personal understanding of that place. This technique uses a series of sketches, with an accompanying sketch map, to describe a journey and the location of the viewpoints.

Observational sketching is important when one first encounters a place in a city. Observing the city can be about perceiving and recording activity, building form or detail, light, colour or spatial characteristics.

To draw a view in perspective could characterize the place in terms of height, mass, scale or form. Again, this type of drawing requires some observation first, to determine what information the drawing is communicating. It may be that the observational drawing serves initially to record relative size or mass of buildings in a street, which can become more detailed with additional information about the view.

When starting a drawing of a place, it is important to take time to understand the nature of the street, square or

Left
A finely detailed ink sketch made while observing a cathedral city.

Above
A page from a sketchbook. Note how details have been drawn at different scales and how these, together with simple annotations, can give the reader a deeper understanding of the subject.

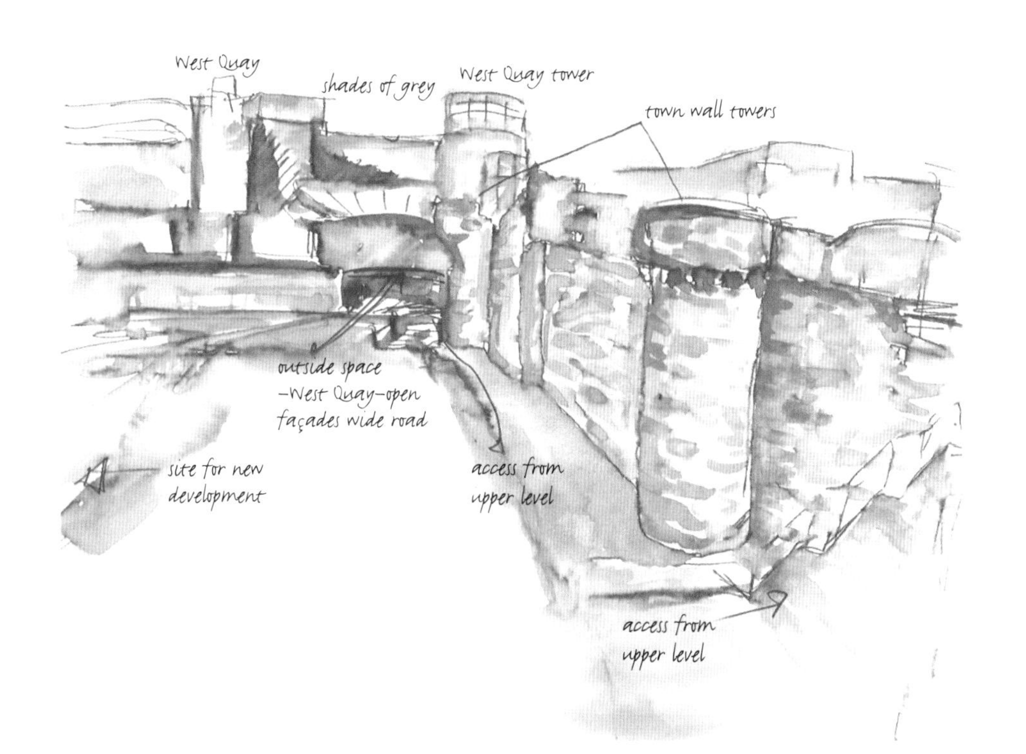

Left and below
Two sketches that use watercolour in different ways. The first sketch replicates the colours of the subject, while the second is a monochromatic study of light and shadow. Annotating a sketch can be a useful way of adding information and thoughts about the space one is sketching.

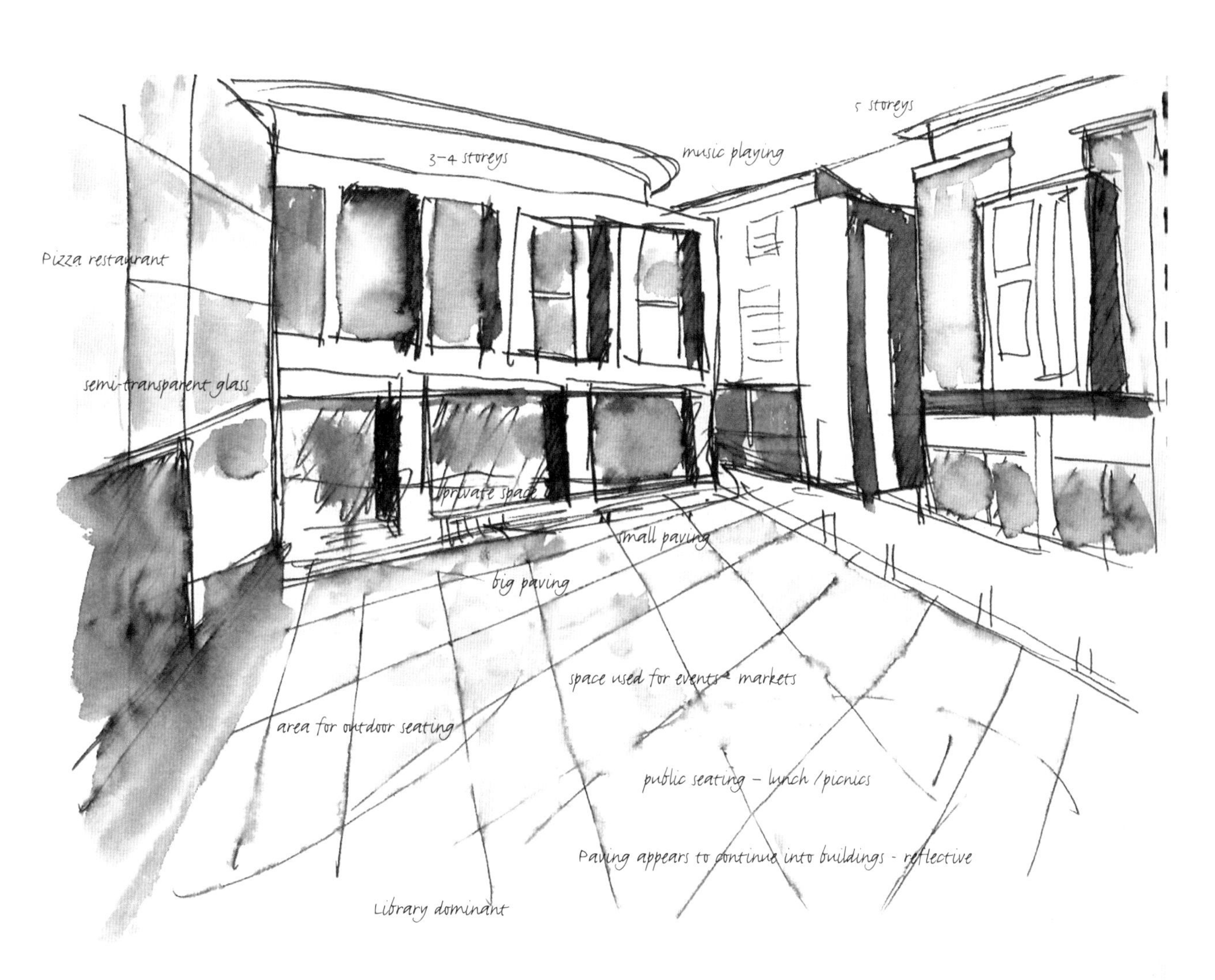

TIP OUTLINE

Adding a thicker line weight can lift an image to give it greater impact. Note that a thicker outline can also add emphasis to CAD drawings.

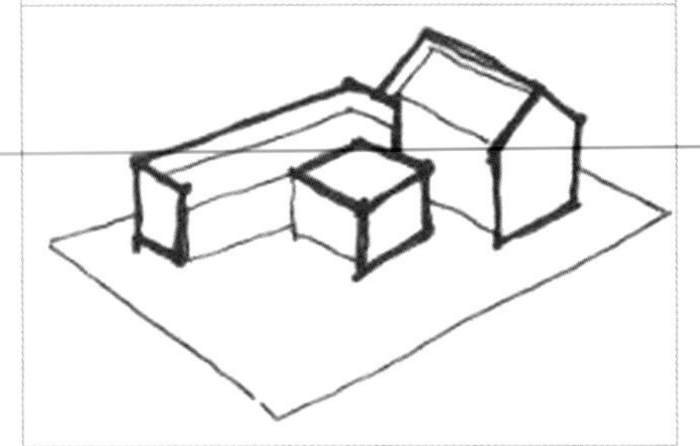

building and to absorb the characteristics of the site, its size, spatial qualities, material and sense of scale.

Having considered the place, choose the type of drawing and the media that will complement the intention of the sketch. A series of quick spatial interpretations using a pencil or pen may communicate movement or light activity. A more considered, intense drawing might be appropriate to suggest a place's important features, such as the detail and colour of materials.

A complex image may call for using a range of media, from pencils – which can layer the intensity of light and tone – to watercolours, which can wash over a drawing and suggest the different areas of interest to focus upon.

In addition, annotation on observational sketches can be very useful as a way to further highlight specific observations to complement the drawing. These notes can explain activities, materials or other considerations that may affect future design decisions within that space or environment. Observational drawings are recording what is in a space already, they are a 'reading' of that space at a particular time and need to communicate as much information as possible.

This sketch of St Mark's Square in Venice traces just the outlines of the buildings along the skyline to describe the varying scales of the building and their roof details.

STEP BY STEP OBSERVATIONAL SKETCHING ON THE GO

Drawing in a city can be enjoyable or it can be difficult. Since a lot of time is spent outside, the weather will play an important factor in determining whether you make a quick sketch or a more slowly executed study. It is important to be prepared: carry a small sketch book and find a suitable place to draw. It may be done while sitting in a café with a great view or while standing at a street corner. The sketch book must have a hard cover as this gives a surface to support the sketching activity and will protect the drawing. Use the best quality paper you can afford and pencils of various types to achieve variety of tone.

1 Start by setting out lightly drawn guidelines. Remember that these guides are to achieve proportion in your sketch, so try to keep them geometric and simple. Try to break down what you see into geometric shapes.

2 Using the guides, start sketching outlines of what it is you are observing.

3 Add detail to your sketch.

Characterization

Another form of observational drawing is to concentrate on specific aspects of a view: the use of materials, light and shadow in a street, edges, boundaries, objects within a street. A number of sketches can be made from one viewpoint to explore and characterize a street scene.

As well as a long view encapsulating the whole street scene, more detailed observations can be drawn to consider relationships of materials and objects, including cars and people. This can suggest the scale of the space. The relationship between these two different drawing types, the zoomed-out view and the close-up detail view can reveal the relationship of the parts to the whole.

Sketches of a city can be taken at street level or from a more elevated viewpoint, allowing a clearer understanding of connections across and within the city. When sketching in the city it is also useful to include other drawings such as plans and sections to further explain the relationships of buildings and spaces.

To design an urban environment the existing context needs to be carefully studied. It reveals clues about the place that can be cultivated in ideas for the development of the city. In urban design, understanding relationship to context is the key to successful integration of new ideas.

Sketching techniques that record spaces as they are or as they are experienced can reveal how the city changes in character. A comparative exercise can be useful: draw in one street or district and then move to another and draw a view and then compare aspects of building, mass, form and density.

A variety of media can be used for sketching a city, but as such drawings need to be made quickly and in the open air, a light pen or a pencil is usually the best option. If you have more time, using colour, pastels, watercolours or pencils to highlight an aspect of a scene can help to focus a drawing.

Sketches can benefit from more detail by adding written notes. Observations can be incorporated in a drawing to explain use of materials or other significant aspects of the view for further consideration.

Opposite
A series of small sketches through an urban route serve as snapshots through a city.

Below
Watercolours can be used effectively to capture a sense of colour and bring a sketch to life.

STEP BY STEP SERIAL VIEWS THROUGH A CITY

This series of images represents a journey through a city using maps, photographs and coloured sketches, and was developed from ideas in Gordon Cullen's book *The Concise Townscape*, in which he describes a series of views through a city.

Underneath each sketch is an abstract diagram of a route through the city and each point of view is indicated on the route diagram. This allows for a clear understanding of the journey, while the sketches themselves explore and focus on a range of experiences. The pen outlines were sketched on top of photographs of the chosen views, and have been coloured with simple washes so that the building outlines can still be read clearly in the sequence.

ROCK N ROLL
5
6
7
8

This page and opposite
These pages, taken from sketchbooks, indicate a range of approaches to drawing. Collage techniques, photocopies, photographs and a variety of media have been used to record ideas and observed experiences. All of these images and observations were used to inform ideas for designing buildings or spaces.

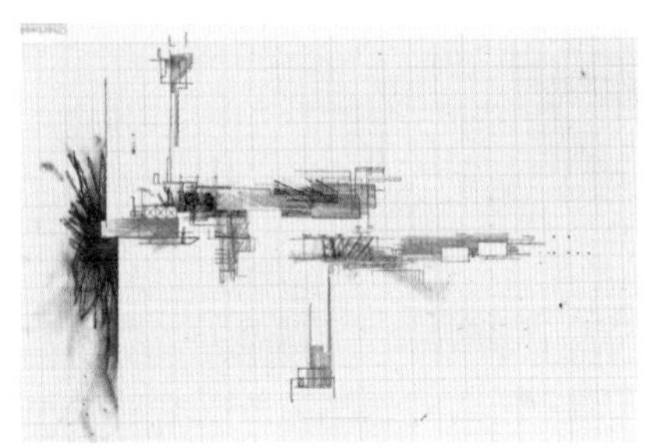

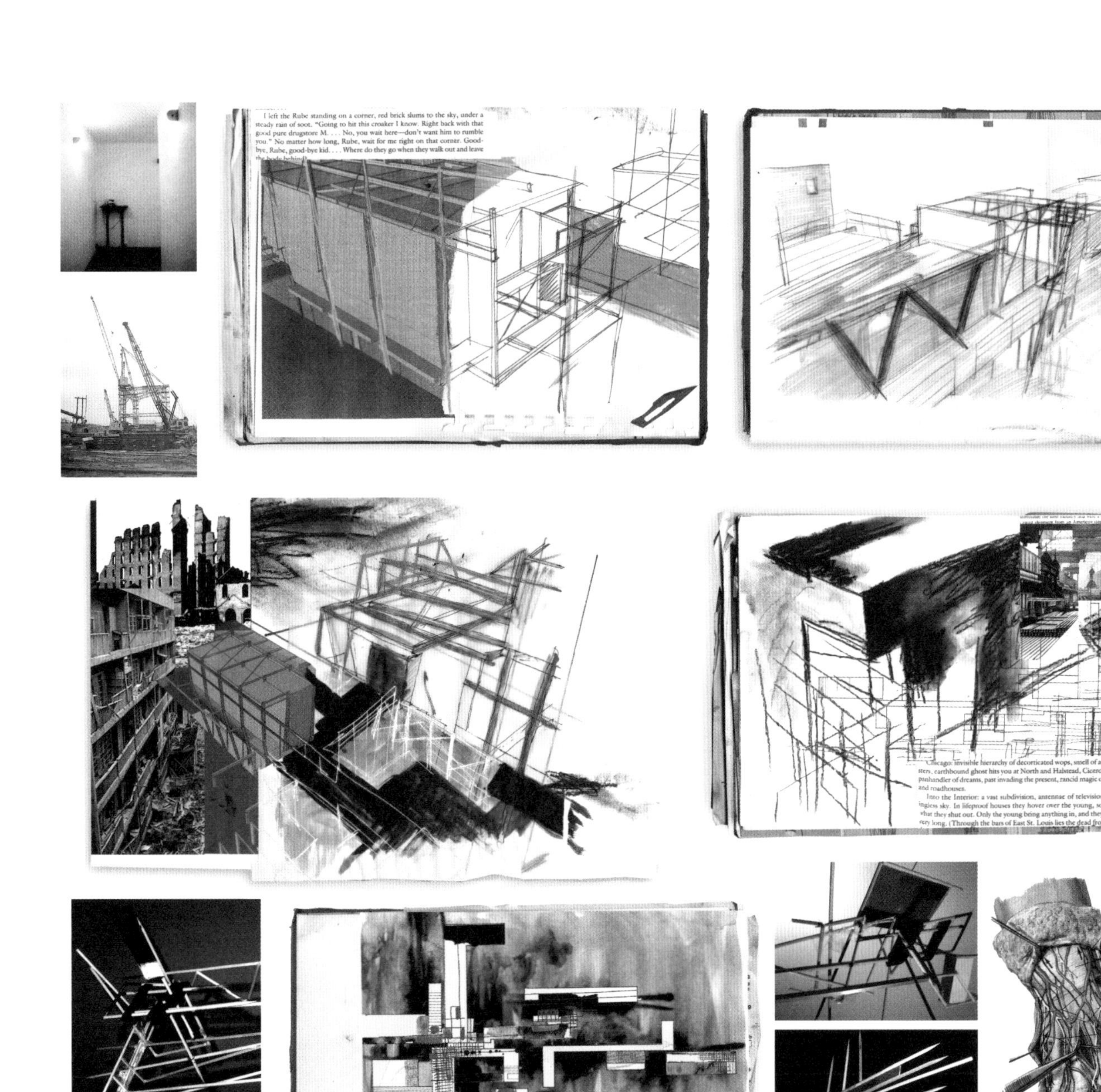
I left the Rube standing on a corner, red brick slums to the sky, under a steady rain of soot. "Going to hit this croaker I know. Right back with that good pure drugstore M. . . . No, you wait here—don't want him to rumble you." No matter how long, Rube, wait for me right on that corner. Good-bye, Rube, good-bye kid. . . . Where do they go when they walk out and leave
Chicago: invisible hierarchy of decorticated wops, smell of atrophied gangsters, earthbound ghost hits you at North and Halstead, Cicero, Lincoln Park, panhandler of dreams, past invading the present, rancid magic of slot machines and roadhouses.
Into the Interior: a vast subdivision, antennae of television to the meaningless sky. In lifeproof houses they hover over the young, sop up a little of what they shut out. Only the young bring anything in, and they are not young very long. (Through the bars of East St. Louis lies the dead

Types of drawing

The conventional range of orthographic drawings used to represent buildings at various scales are also used to describe cities, or buildings in the context of a city environment. Orthographic drawings are measured and drawn to a variety of scales and include plans, sections and elevations.

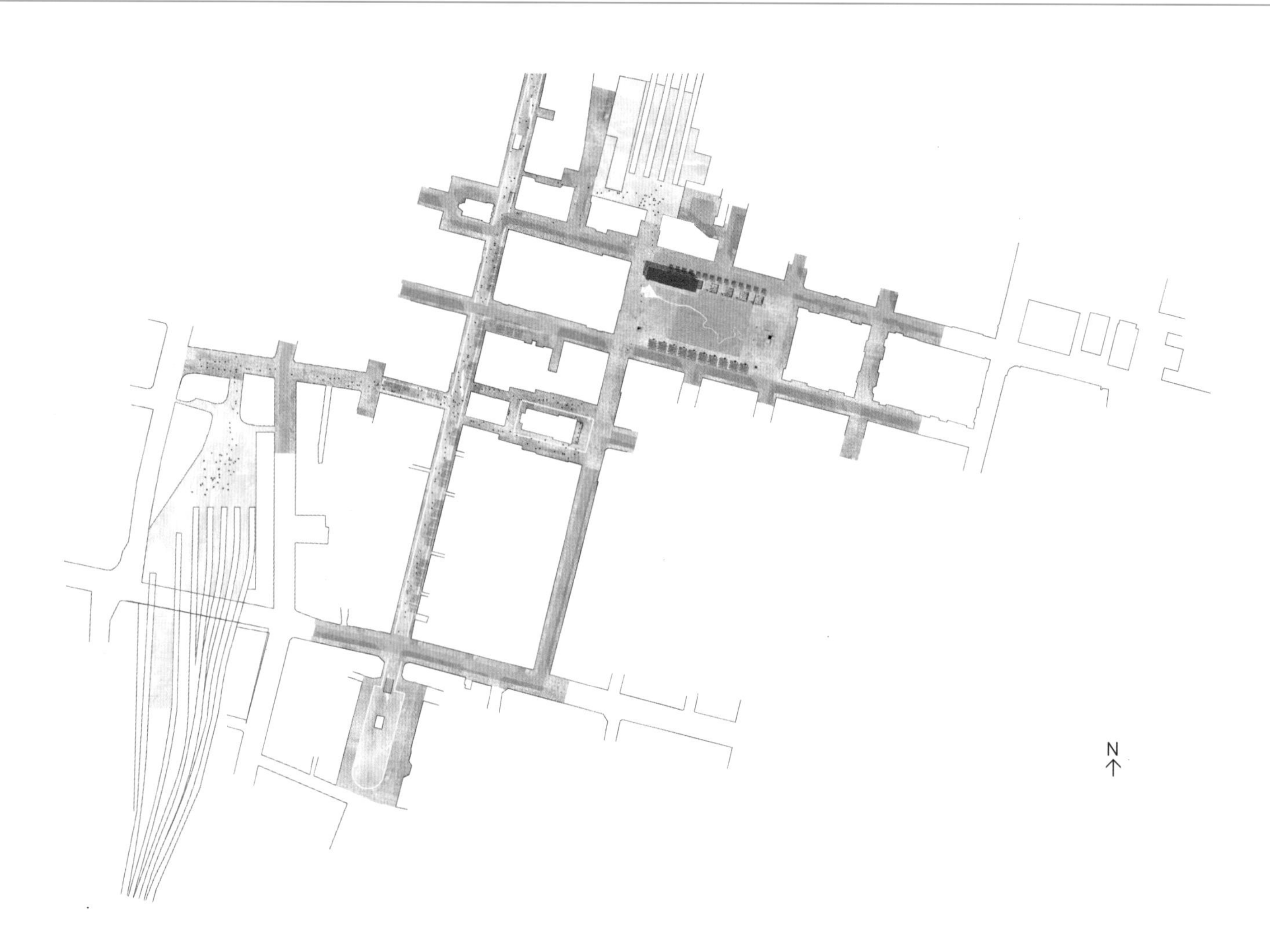

Above and right
This proposal for the competition to improve George Square, Glasgow, by studioKAP architects locates the site by isolating a part of the plan of the centre of Glasgow and relating the space to key routes through the city (above). A more detailed plan of the square itself was also drawn (right).

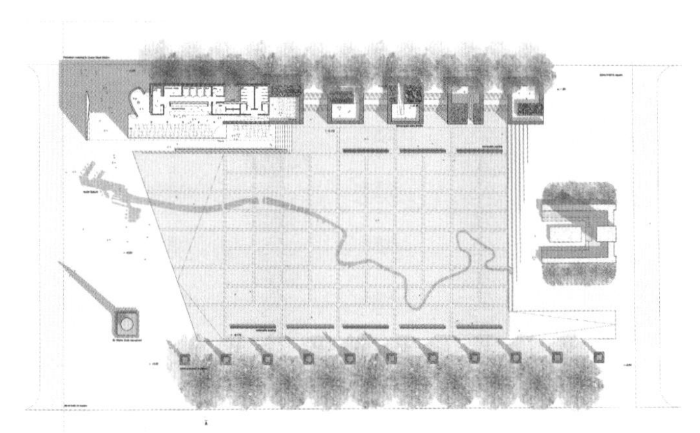

Plan

A plan can take the form of a site location drawing, which places a site within a larger map of an area to locate a building or proposal. The plan drawing allows an understanding of entrances, access, and movement across or through a site, as well as important adjacent locations and adjacent buildings or structures. A plan should indicate orientation, so a north point is essential. It is the convention for plans to be oriented so that north points upwards on the page, although sometimes this is not possible. When gridlines are used, they are normally indicated with north to the top of the page.

Section

A slice across a city allows an understanding of relationships and the relative heights of buildings. This drawing can be a sketch that is not to scale but which helps to describe relative heights, across a street or square for example. Alternatively, the section may relate to a measured plan or map which is part of a survey or accurate drawing of the city.

Axonometric

The axonometric drawing is a useful way to describe a city. It is a view as though looking from above. Generated using a plan drawing or map, an axonometric can show relationships across broad areas of a city, as a physical model does, providing a good overview. It can also be used to explain concepts or make connections across large schemes. Exploded axonometric images allow a scheme to be presented as a series of layers that have been pulled apart to reveal connections within the scheme.

Below

This competition-entry scheme by Rocky Marchant and Ergin Birinci proposes a tower structure for the city of Damascus. The section through the tower is shown in relation to the surrounding buildings.

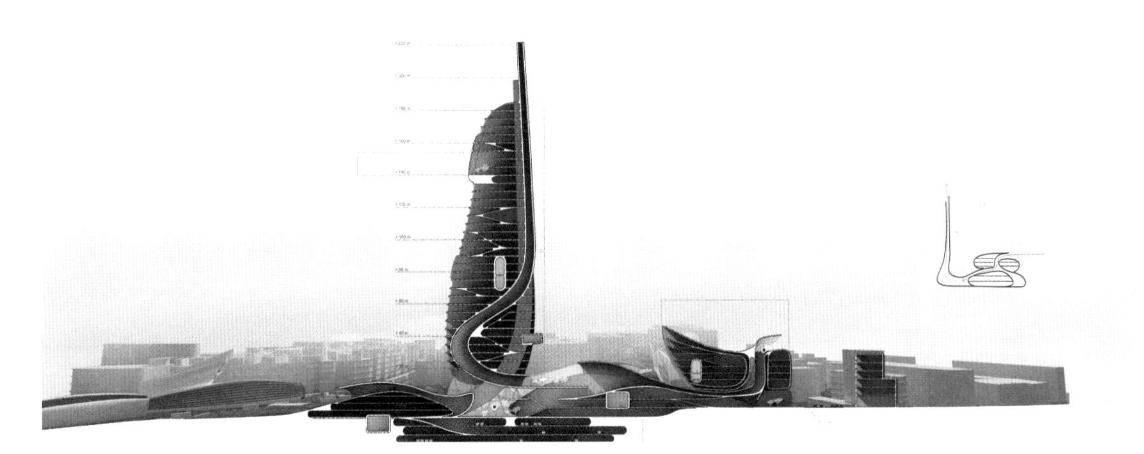

Digital techniques

Manipulating digital photographs with various software can illustrate a range of ideas, making it possible to reinterpret the environment as it exists, adjusting or sharpening the view.

As well as undertaking a sketching survey of a city or site, a photographic survey can also be useful. When photographing a city, similar techniques can be used to those applied when sketching it. A journey may be described; there may be a study of distant views and then close-up views of materials or surfaces. The photographs could be sequenced to tell a story about an experience, how a part of the city has been interpreted. There may be a study of shadow, light, material or form. The advantage with photographs is that they can be manipulated afterwards in various software packages such as Adobe Photoshop to enhance, alter, exaggerate or rearrange a view, which means the image can exist as several views rather than just one.

This photomontage site analysis by Rocky Marchant and Ergin Birinci combines an aerial photograph of a site and then keys in important features with specific images to illustrate details.

Storyboard techniques

A storyboard is used in film-making as an organizational device to help plan a sequence of frames for a film. It is a useful device for both organizing drawings and explaining an experience through a city in a film-like way. The storyboard is a framework and can suggest action or movement between the frames.

Below
This interpretation of a journey through Southampton highlights the main views and buildings on a route that surrounds a key development site, as well as documenting pedestrian and vehicle activity.

Bottom
The details of the buildings are described in this set of pencil sketches illustrating a journey around Portsmouth.

STEP BY STEP DERIVE

The idea of the *dérive* or 'drift' was developed by the Situationists in Paris in the 1950s. Guy Debord was interested in new ways to explore and describe the city without using conventional scales maps. 'Drifting' allows someone to explore and discover new spaces and places. The city can be understood as a collection of experiences: considering the implication of material and space or the interrelationship between colour and light. To observe and record these differences is an excellent way to extend your knowledge of materials, not only the range of materials that is available but also the different methods of applying and assembling the materials.

1 Start walking in a new city. Don't use a plan – just allow yourself to 'drift'.

2 Record views with a camera or sketches. Try to create a photographic diary. Look at a view of a street and then zoom in closer to see the detail and materials.

3 Look at the view and record experiences, it may be the effect of light or shadow on the walls.

4 Record colours. Look closely at the juxtaposition of colours and the effect of light on the surfaces.

5 Combine your freehand sketches and photographs to create different sorts of drawing. The same view could be used to describe the material quality, the light quality and the spatial experience of a journey.

Painting and collage

Some of the earliest visual records of the city are paintings. A painting communicates an understanding that can be momentary, connected to an experience. It may be planned to set a scene of everyday life or it may connect to an idea of a place. It involves interpreting atmosphere, colour, light and material. The term painting refers to a single image that uses colour of any sort on a fixed background to interpret a view of a place. Traditional painting would involve oils and canvas, watercolour and paper; today the media are more varied. Painting is very much about preparation and intention; it is still an important way to describe the city, necessitating careful planning and the detailed consideration of subject and technique.

When painting any subject, it is useful to use a sketchbook to test and develop ideas, to plan the painting. The sketch needs to be carefully constructed, with notes to suggest what aspects of the scene or view the image is going to encapsulate. When painting views of cities, initial decisions about the viewpoint need to be taken; the direction of the sun and shadow will have an effect on the view. Painting outside and experiencing the light changing across a view of a city or square can add to an understanding of the place. Taking time to choose the position or viewpoint, to compose the frame

Above
Serial views through the city act as storyboards, creating narratives within a sketch. This view shows the boat museum on the quayside at East Cowes, Isle of Wight, by Panter Hudspith Architects.

Right
This atmospheric street scene of Lincoln by Panter Hudspith Architects shows a view looking up Danesgate, with Lincoln Cathedral providing a focal point.

Left
This series of images shows an interpretation of a journey through a city. Views and experiences of the journey have been interpreted as almost abstract images, highlighting aspects of light and texture.

Below
This collage was created by layering photographic images of views of a building, mixing digital images of the elevation with close-up views of the entranceway and the surface of the wall. Figures were superimposed on the image to give a sense of scale and activity.

Watercolours are used in this image to create a plan of an urban route and at the same time to evoke the experience of proceeding down that same route.

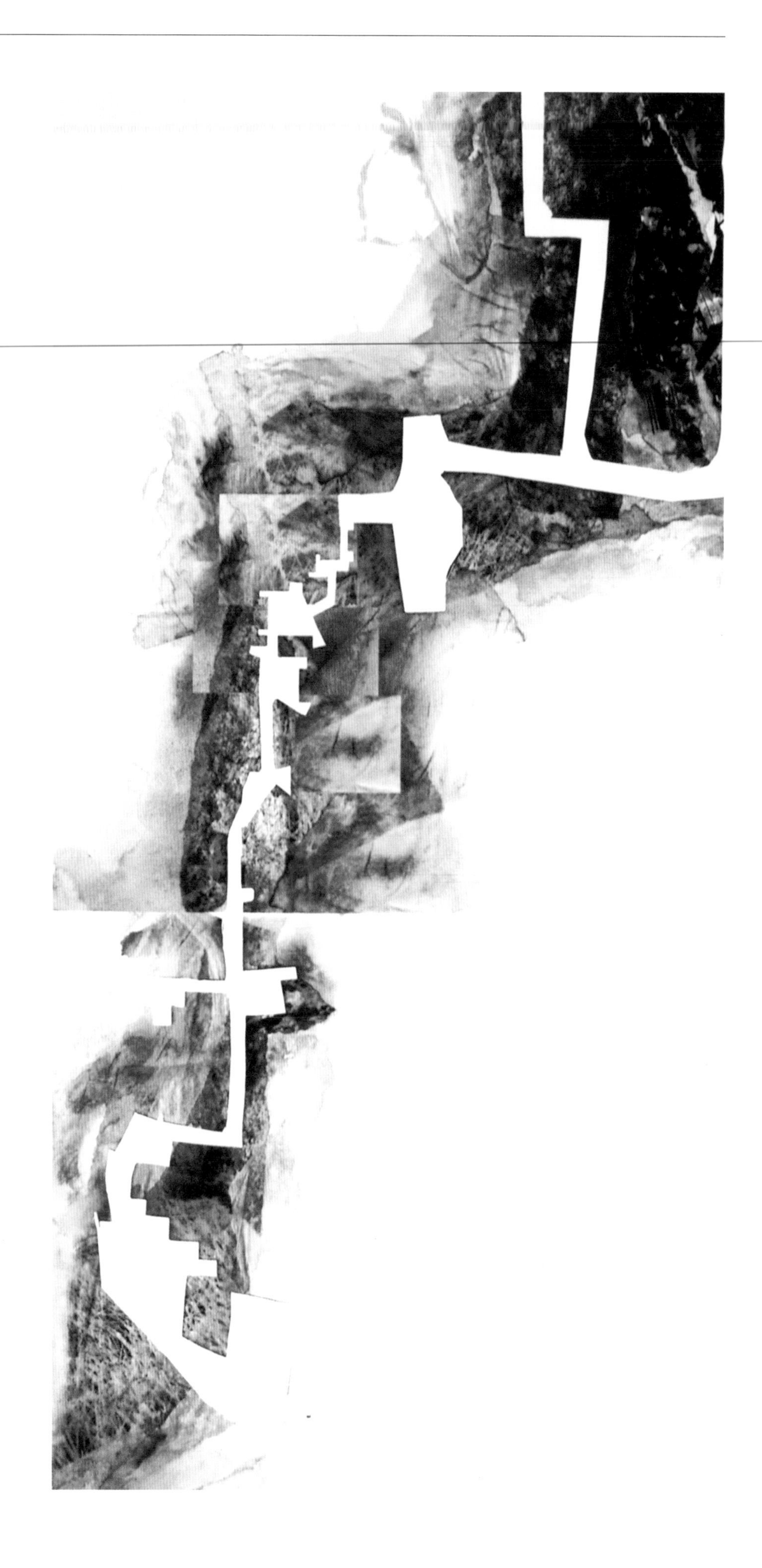

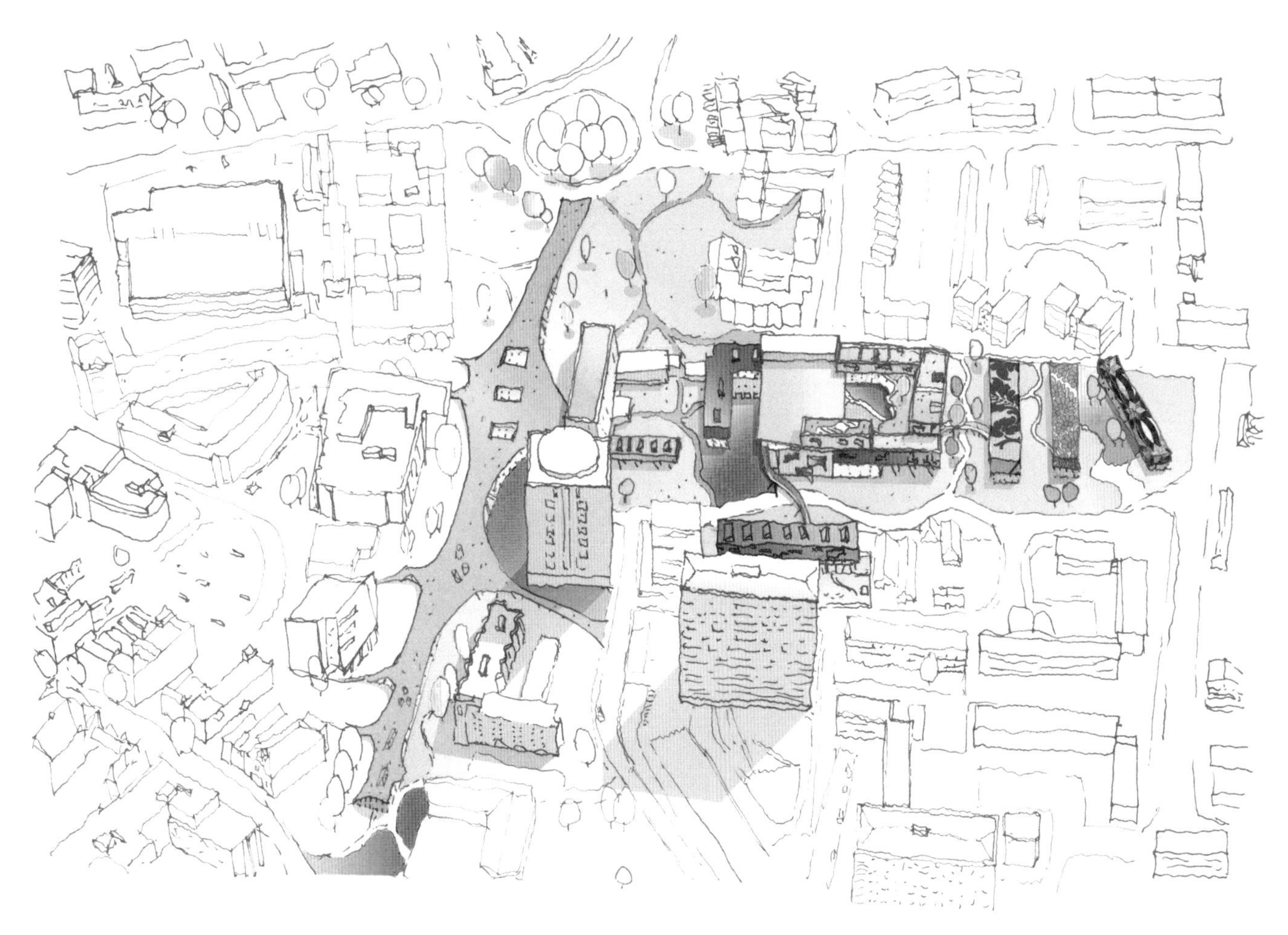

The drawing clearly shows new and old urban qualities by keeping the existing urban fabric monochromatic and using paint only on the interventions.

and the subject, are all part of focusing attention within the image. As with using a camera, the frame of the view is key when planning a painting or a drawing, deciding what elements of the view need to be encapsulated.

To create an impression of a place once time has been taken to absorb the view, and to determine the intention of the painting, important decisions need to be made about the medium. The simplest way to start is to use a sketchbook with good-quality paper, and to outline a background, then introduce colour to interpret the view. Your approach may be as simple as identifying light and shadow. Or it may concentrate on texture of materials and surface. If the image needs to be built up with a certain opacity, then use watercolours to layer colour. If a solid block of colour is needed use acrylic paints. Use oils to incorporat texture into the piece. Pastels have a softness and allow for blending of colour. It is useful to experiment with colour and start to test the medium to see how it reacts in different situations.

A sturdy sketchbook is all that is needed to start to draw. Other bases may be used for the painting: simple pieces of timber, canvas boards or panels. If using a heavy medium such as oil, a robust well-prepared surface is

DANCE

necessary to hold the paint. Lighter materials such as watercolour can be applied to a good-quality paper or similar surface.

An initial idea can be realized as a drawing, followed by the application of watercolour or paint, and then further developed through scanning or digital photography and adapted using software such as Photoshop. An interpretation of an idca that dramatically incorporates aspects of colour and light, tone and shadow can result in a powerful image, and it can exist as an artistic representation outside of the proposal.

Below and opposite
These serial views of a proposed building within an urban context were created using a simple yet effective drawing technique which is crisp, tidy and ideal for professional presentations.

Below
A painting can be used to represent and analyse a city in an original, creative and abstract way.

Bottom
A computer-rendered image with a watercolour-like finish by Richard Murphy Architects. The image shows a proposal for practice rooms, a foyer and an auditorium at Jesus College, Cambridge, as seen from the Fellows' Garden.

STEP BY STEP WATERCOLOURING A SKETCH

Watercolour adds depth as well as colour to a sketch and can highlight specific aspects of a view. Partially colouring a sketch can be a useful way to emphasize certain parts of the drawing. The best watercolour images take time – the colour is layered and the intensity of the colour is developed through washes that build up the image.

1 Start with a sketch.

2 Add watercolour to the sky. Use a lot of water to make the paint bleed and dab the paper with paper towel to give it an attractive faded texture.

3 When the sky is dry, paint one of the buildings.

4 Finally, add shadow and detail to the entire painting and let it dry.

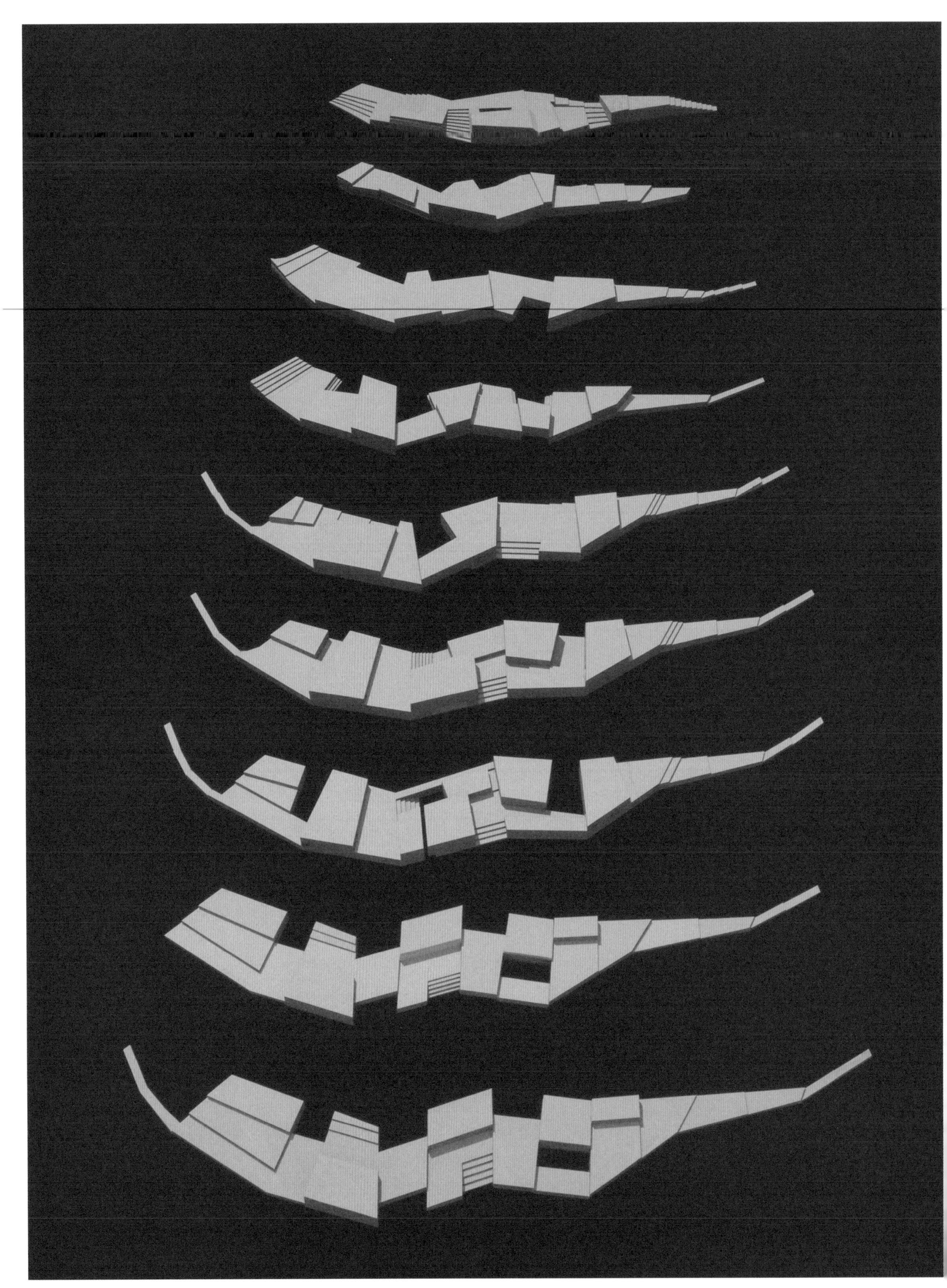

THE CITY AS DATA

Analytical tools

There is a range of approaches to describe the existing and proposed context of cities, embracing various mapping and measurement techniques and others that are more abstract, based on interpreting information.

Much historical or statistical data about the city can be represented by maps, charts or diagrams – information such as density of population, uses or functions of urban environments, heights of buildings. Climatic data such as sun paths and wind direction can be set out and described visually. The city as data investigates the various visual methods and techniques available to transform complex information about the city into easy-to-interpret images.

The ideas of *genius loci,* as suggested by Christian Norberg Schulz (1926–2000), help us to understand the urban environment. These refer to the sense of place, which can be individually interpreted through painting and drawing. However, there are also ways to measure and record cities using mapping techniques.

This section explores the analytical tools that can be used to describe urban spaces and places.

To analyse information requires an understanding and then examination of a subject. The analysis needs to be presented as a set of separate pieces of visual information in order that it may be properly interpreted. This may be done with drawings, photographs, diagrams or maps. All these types of representation have limitations and advantages; some information needs to be carefully pulled apart to be clearly presented and understood.

TIP GOOGLE EARTH

Programmes such as Google Earth create an opportunity to explore a city and understand its context without sourcing maps. These representations can be accessed at many different scales and can be used as a basis for axonometric images or just to inform site analysis.

STEP BY STEP ANALYSIS THROUGH PHOTOS AND DRAWING

An urban site or location can be analysed by using a range of photos that explore different aspects of the site. Using a carefully chosen set of photos, the images can be drawn over to highlight particular points or characteristics of the area.

1 This photo relates the urban square to visual markers beyond the space (such as the minaret in the distance).

2 A photo was taken of an existing building on the site and then a sketch of a proposed new colonnade structure was layered over it. The sketched colonnade mirrors the forms of the colonnade existing elsewhere on the site.

3 This perspective view of the covered colonnade has a sketch layered over which highlights the form of the columns and the arches.

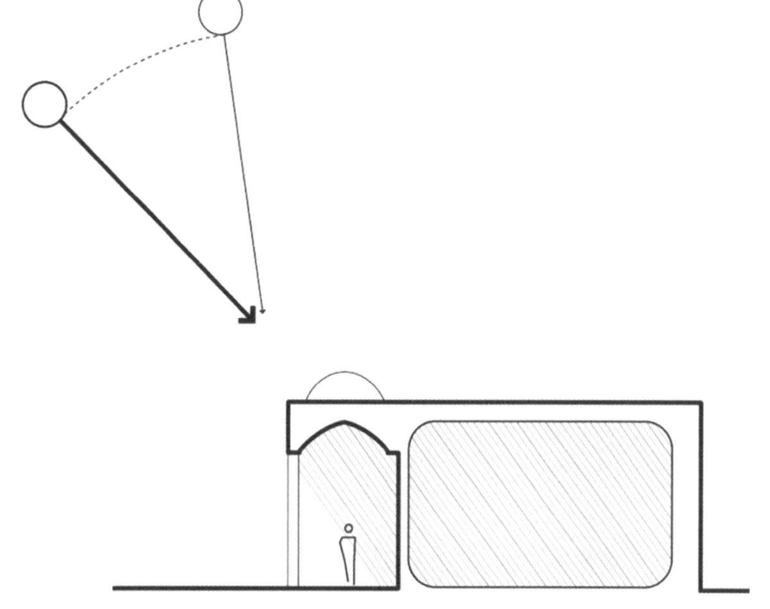

4 A section diagram through the building explains how shadow affects the spaces within the building and how the colonnade provides shade when the sun is very high.

Below
This drawing uses a map of Brighton as a starting point for analysis. The map is layered with colour to identify building use: the proposed new development is represented by a layer of cork while the open space coloured grey. Routes are overlaid with string to suggest connections across the site.

Diagrams

The simplest way to explain complex information in a clear and concise way is with a diagram. Colour can be added to illustrate a series of ideas. Indeed, a city can be reduced to a set of diagrams to explain aspects of geometry, axis and route. A diagram can be used to explain an idea as a plan, but also as a section through the city. The difference between the sketch and the diagram is the reductive nature of the diagram; it has a minimum of lines.

The diagram may be a trace over a map or plan that highlights key pieces of information, such as route and access. Or it may be drawn completely randomly to suggest a concept or idea. Diagrams need to be kept simple to clearly explain an idea or set of ideas. Additionally, text can help to elaborate an idea.

The city context needs to be described in many different ways, sometimes an analytical drawing or diagram can be part of a series of drawings that need to be considered sequentially. The drawing may have many layers applied to it, colour to add clarity, or text to elaborate an idea or a point. For masterplan drawings, text overlaid on a plan or perspective can focus on a key point or idea.

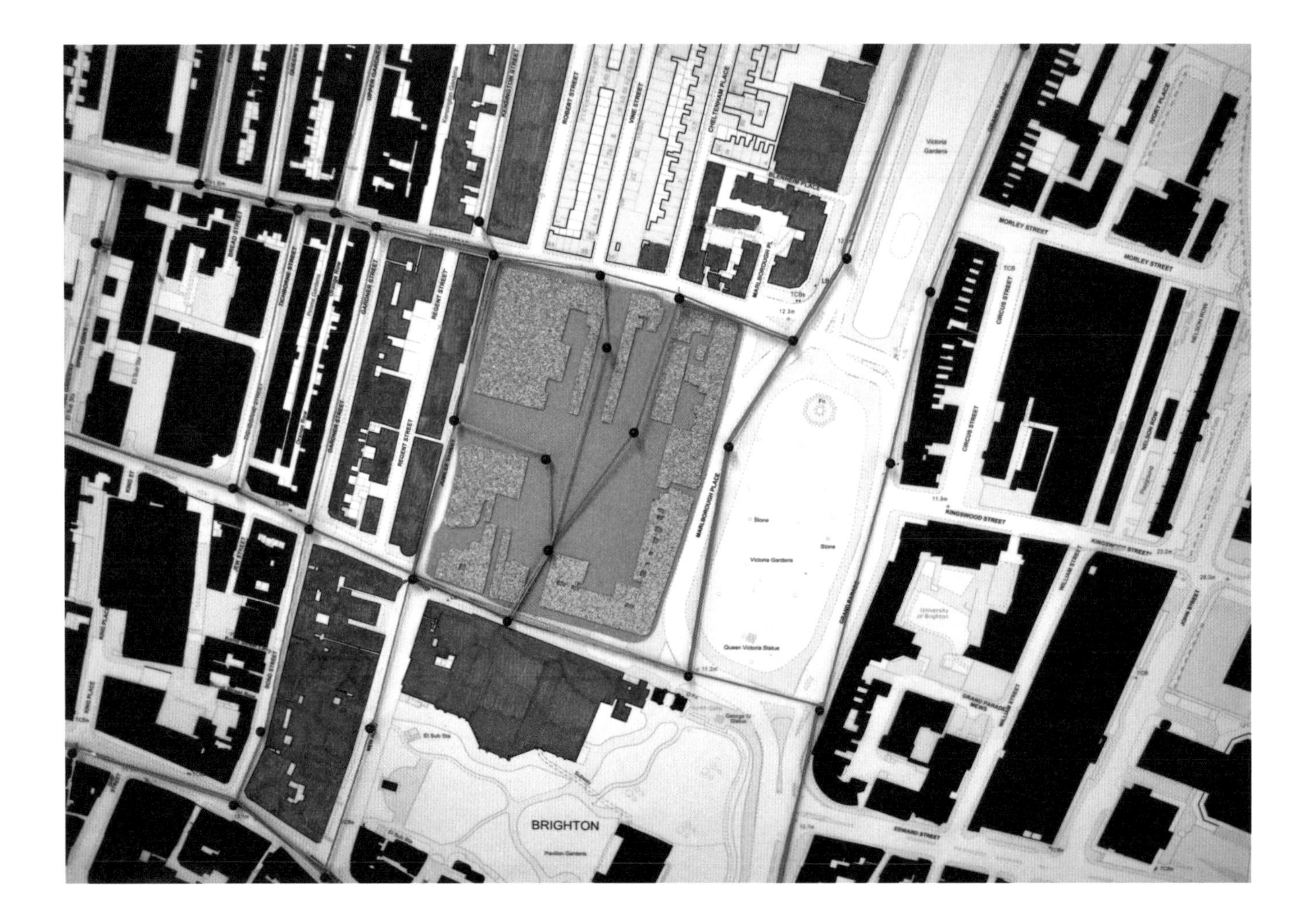

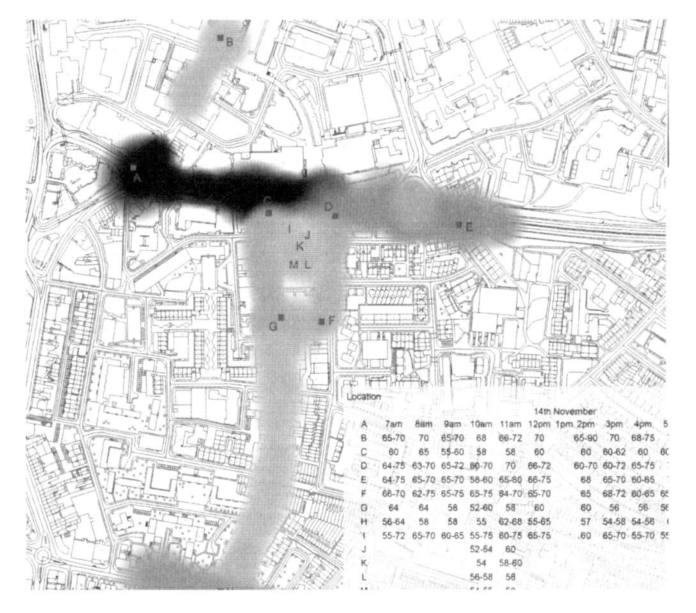

Above
This map uses a colour gradient to analyse noise levels in an area of Portsmouth.

Above right
Colour is used to highlight zones of activity within the city.

Below
On this map colour is used to analyse and represent building heights.

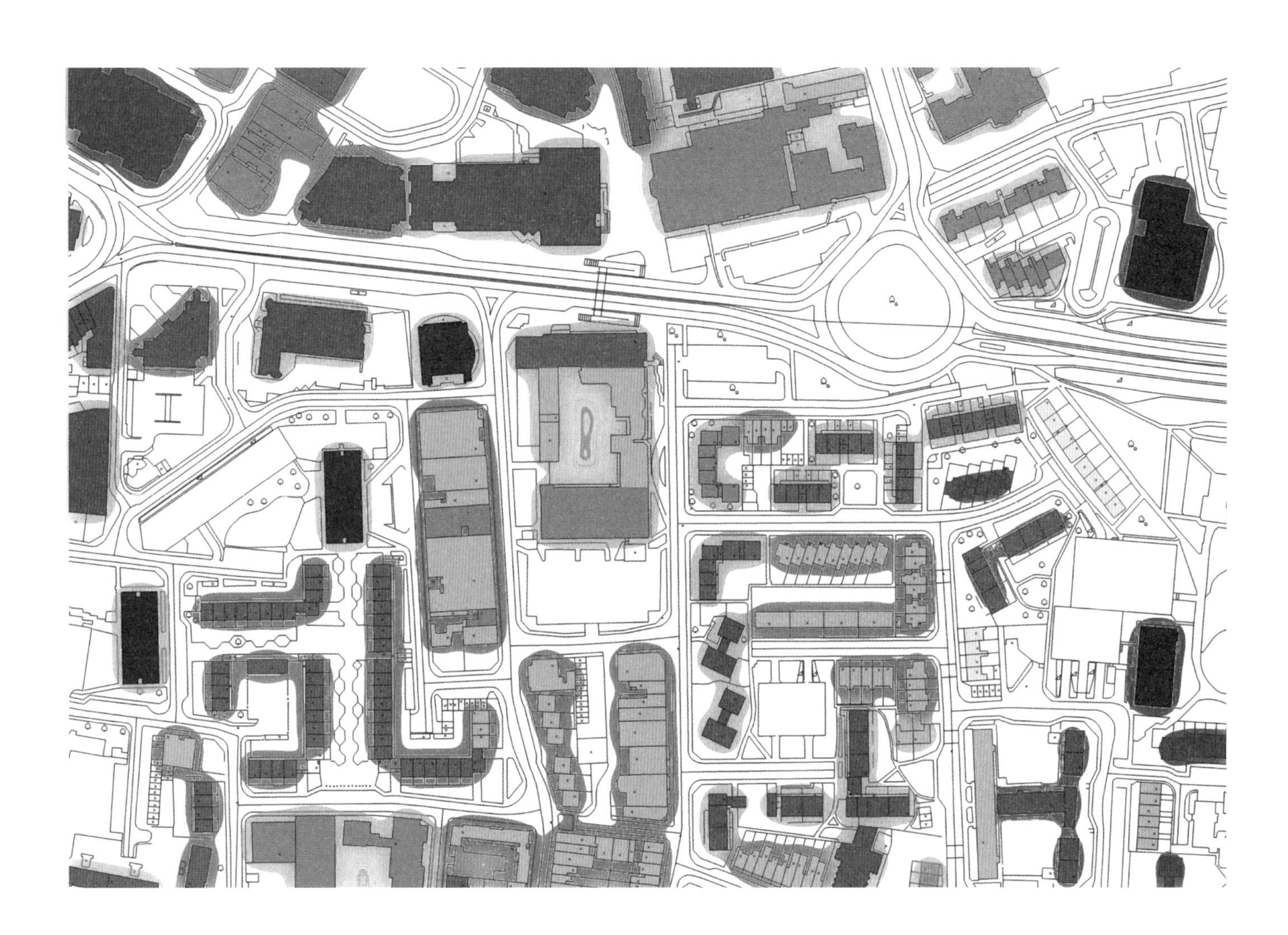

STEP BY STEP MASSING ANALYSIS

When first considering a site, a set of analytical three-dimensional sketches can help to explore ideas about the site that inform the concept development. The following images show how certain ideas and objectives were explored.

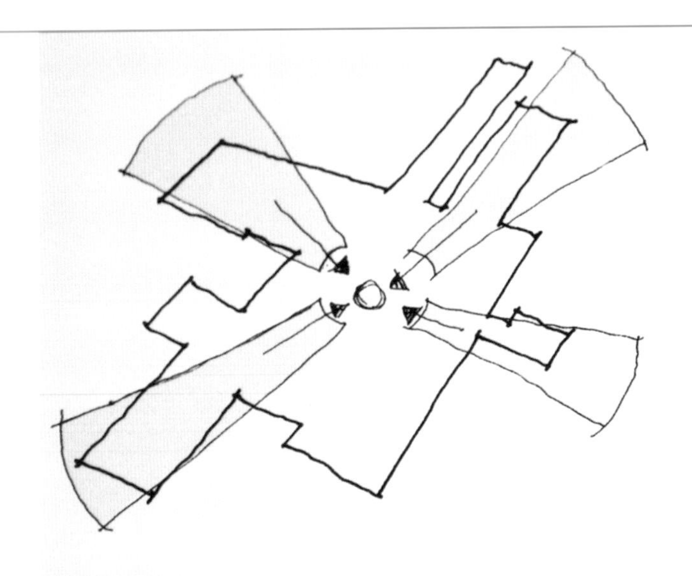

1 Opening the site and increasing access though the site.

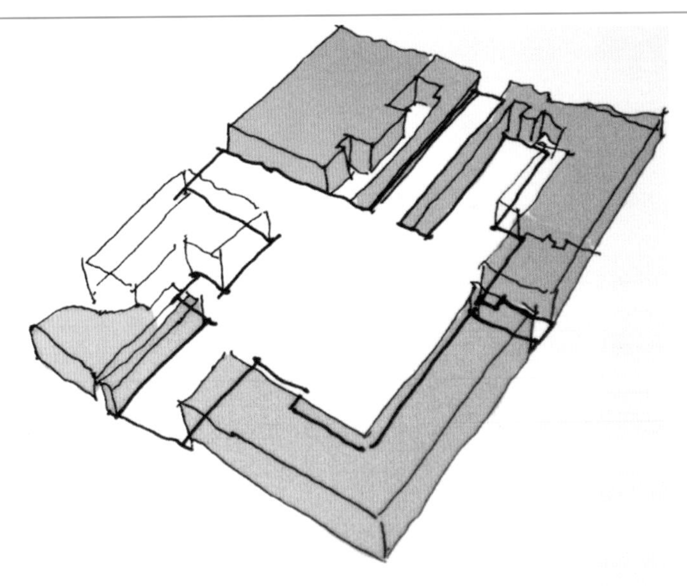

2 Considering the wider urban context and uses of the existing surrounding buildings.

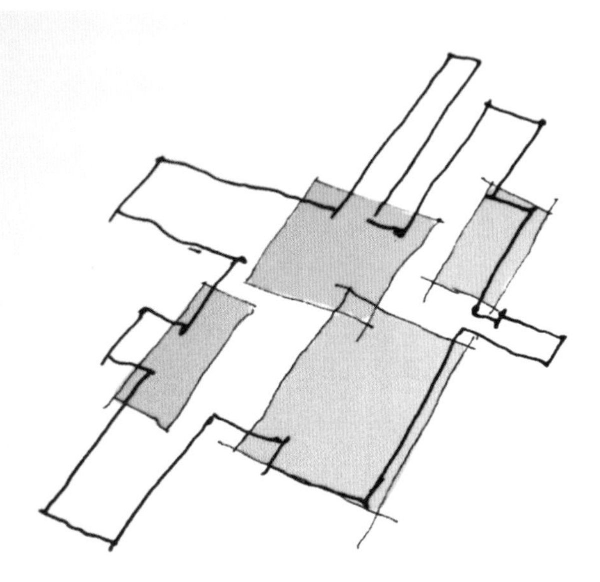

3 Considering the urban context to determine possible spatial arrangement of a proposed scheme.

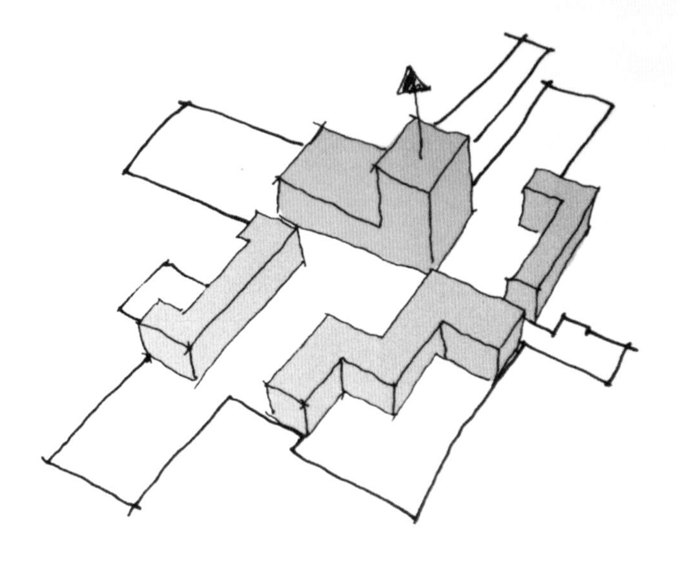

4 Creation of blocks defined by external spaces and exploring the implication of vertical massing.

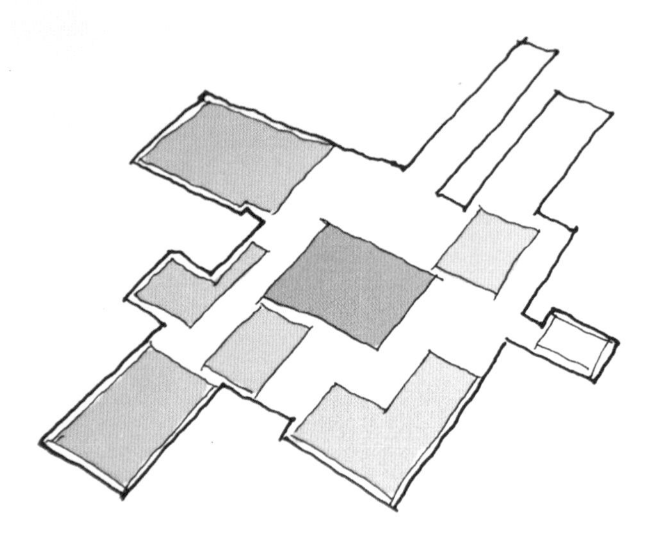

5 A series of public spaces leading to a main central square, defined by a vertical element.

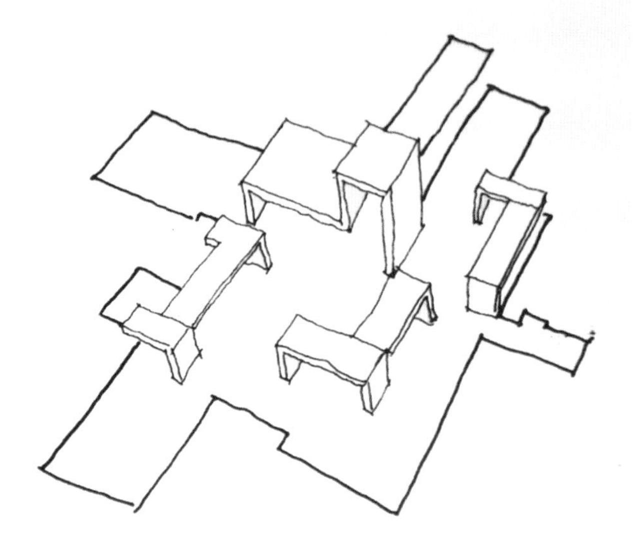

6 External spaces and building forms defined by planes.

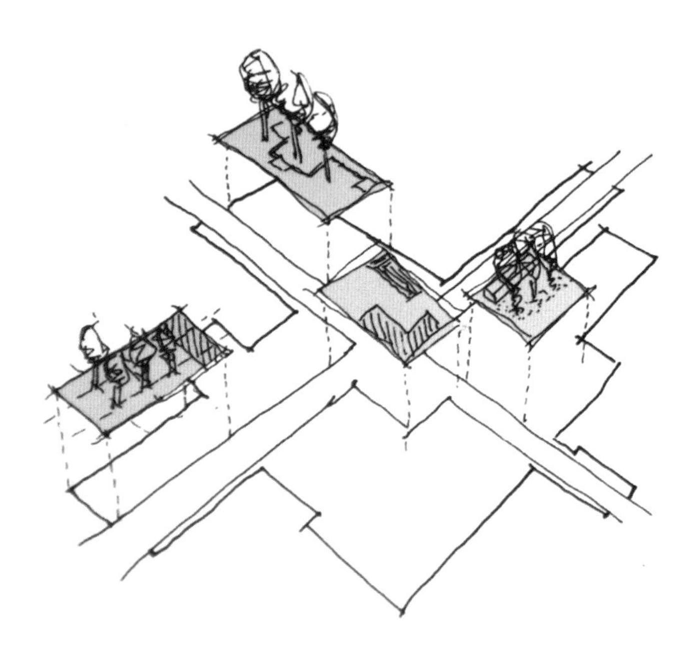

7 Landscaping the public spaces and the use of the 'street' to connect the spaces.

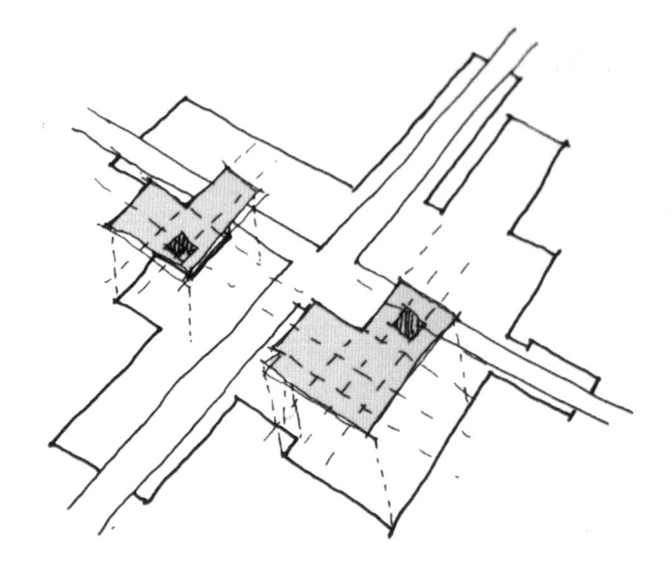

8 Reflection of internal layouts on formally defined spaces.

When starting a site analysis, a map of the city will aid thinking and provide a base for a drawing. Analytical drawings can begin with a map of a part of a city, which can then be traced over to isolate particular aspects of the city's organization. A series of maps at different scales can be useful. There may be connections or routes that need to be identified at the scale of the city, whereas other site features can be connected to the immediate site using a different scale map or plan. This could start with simple organizational systems, such as geometry, lines of connection or axes within the city. Historical layers can be identified, defining important limits. Topographical features such as rivers and hills can be isolated. Boundaries can suggest ownership, site limits or control zones.

Separating all this information is important to allow the city to be read as a series of layers. The elements can then be examined to allow a better understanding of the composition of the place. Analysing a site is about reading all the information that the site offers as clearly as possible. This can be achieved using maps, but three-dimensional drawings such as axonometrics and isometrics can also explain these ideas, and exploded drawings can pull apart information to allow the 'layers' of a city to be read and understood.

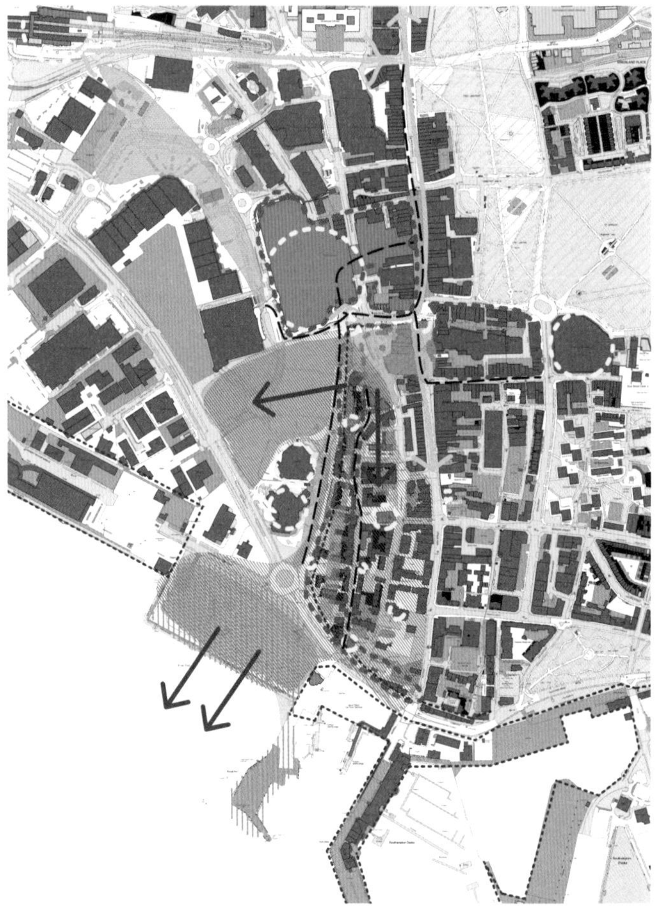

Above
An Urban Baseline Study of human activity patterns and urban design characteristics in Covent Garden, London. Studies such as this, which was created using the Space Syntax technique, are employed by architects for the generation and evaluation of design concepts.

Right
Opportunities and constraints: this image shows a quick analysis of urban features using a figure-ground map as a base.

Visual notes

Visual note-taking is a way to record ideas about a journey or experience in a city, allowing an analysis of the information within the city as it is encountered, a mixture of sketches overlaid with text. This sort of information can later act as a prompt for important observations or be added to a drawing to indicate particular ideas. When experiencing a site for the first time, it is useful to walk around it noting down important features and observations, drawing small sketches to record building heights, form and scale, and then using a layer of text over the drawing to explain particular points of reference.

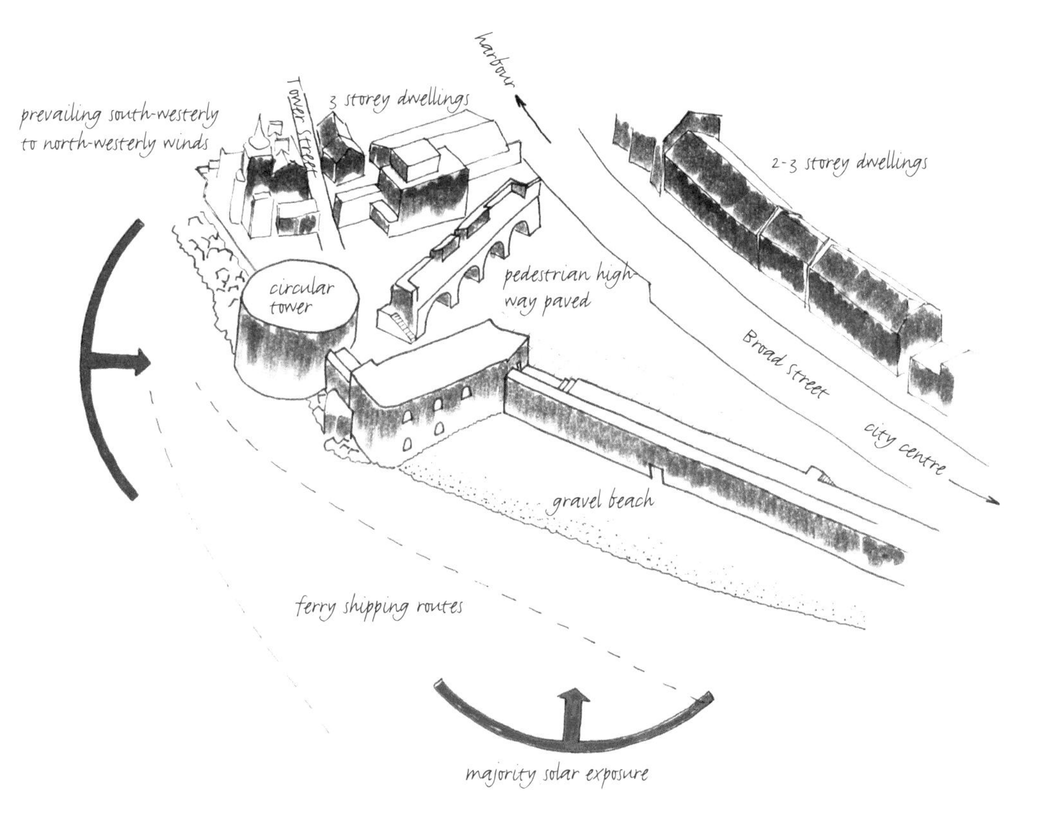

Left
A sketch identifies key aspects of a site and uses text to help explain other important site factors.

Below
Graphic symbols are used here to highlight activities taking place in this section through the city of Southampton.

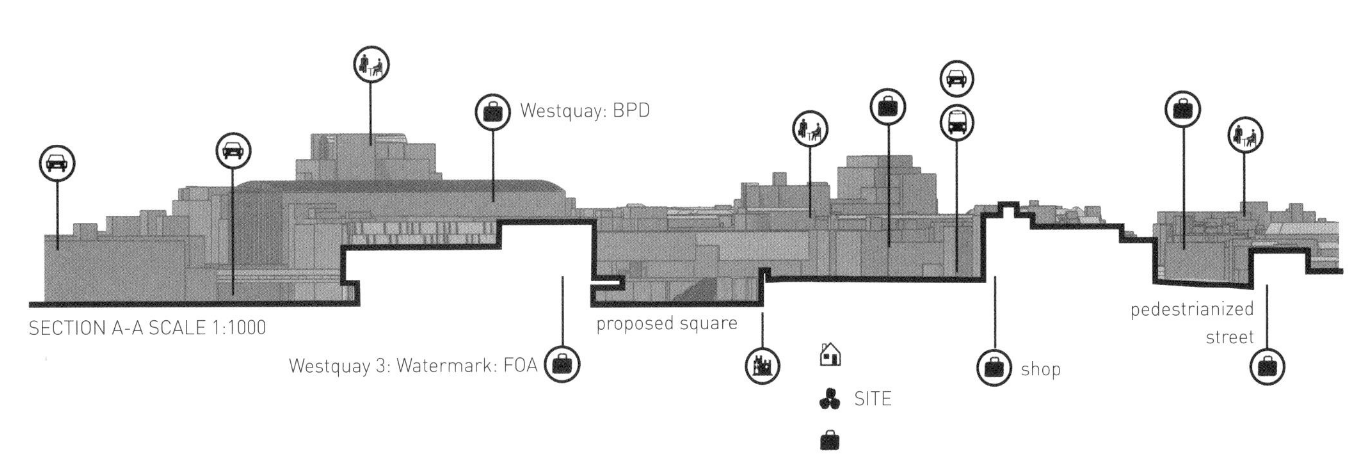

Below
These figure-ground maps describe different aspects of a site as a series of information layers, indicating buildings, boundaries, route connections and land use.

Diagram sequences

A range of analytical drawings shown together can be useful for understanding the evolution of a city or masterplanning concept. Drawings at the same scale allow for the comparison of ideas or for a concept to be broken down into simple stages.

These types of images are essentially a set of maps or diagrammatic representations of a place, which build to create a coherent whole.

Such maps might use the figure-ground technique of illustrating built form separately from space, or they might use colour to identify particular aspects of a concept.

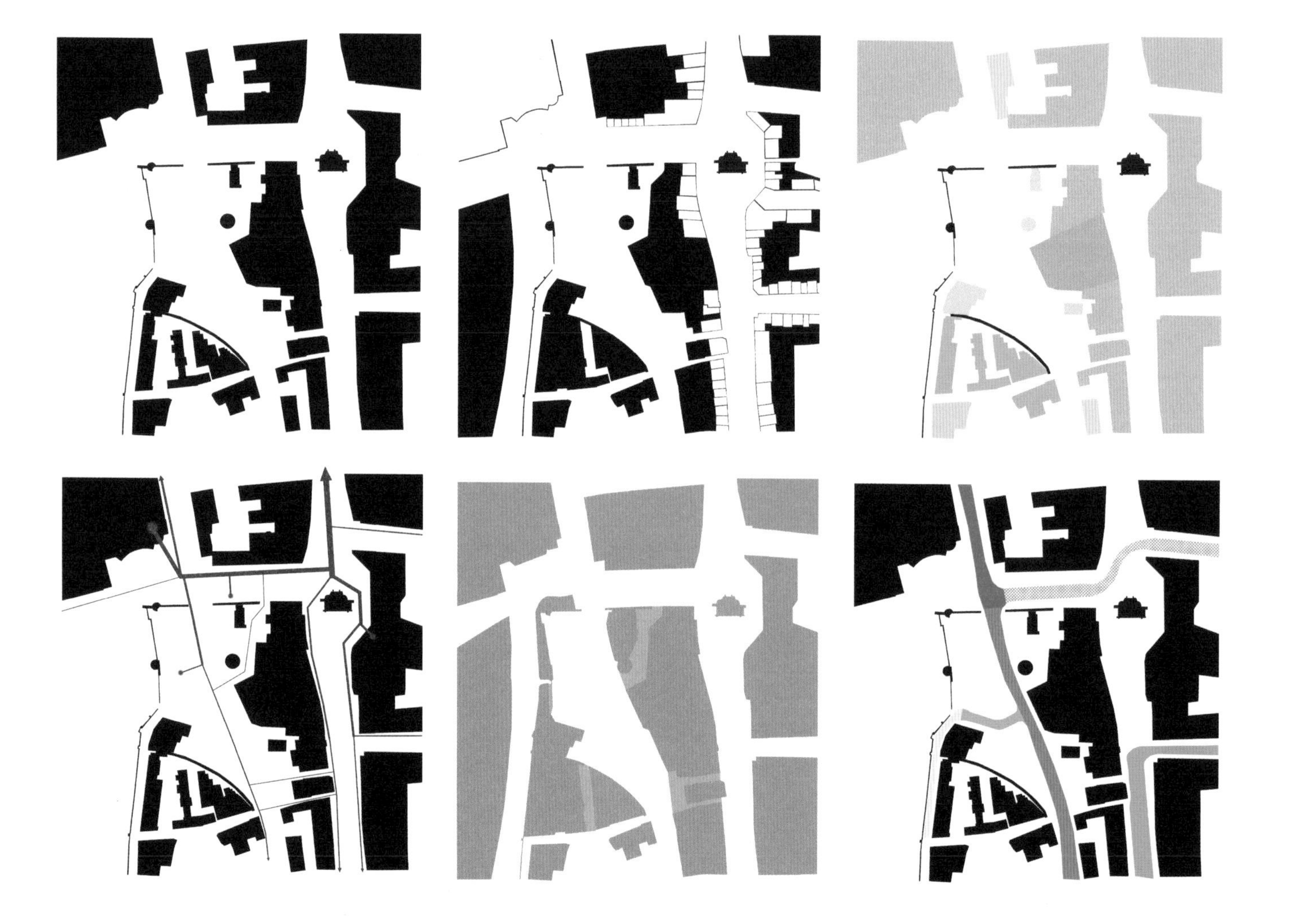

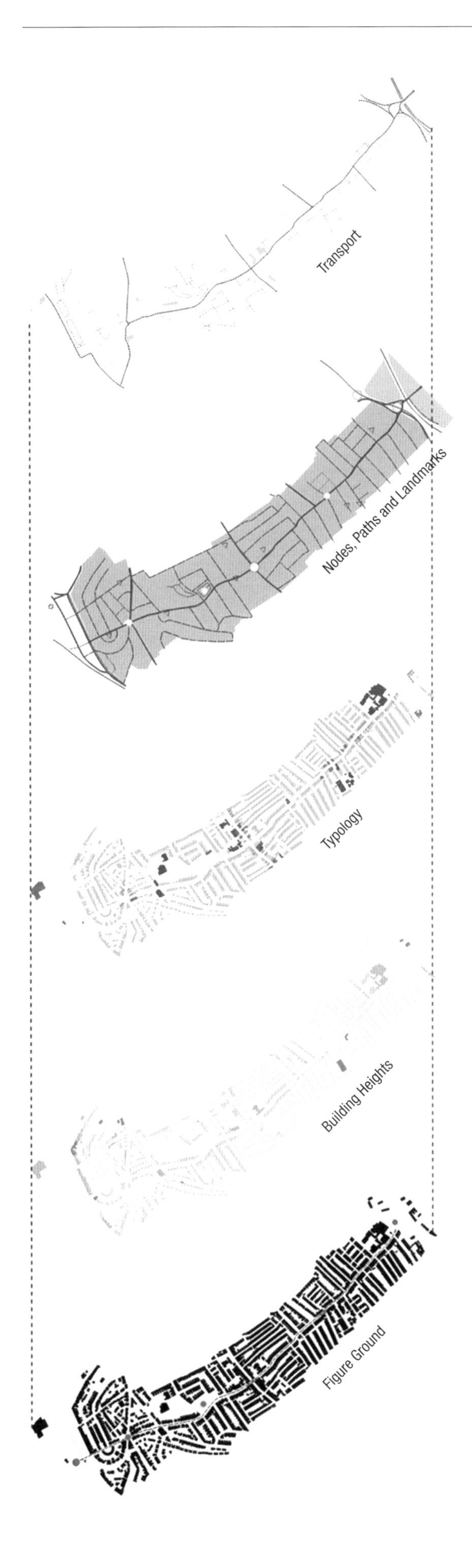

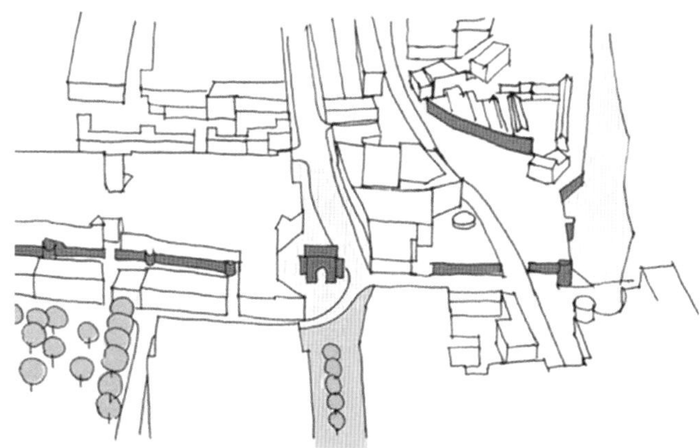

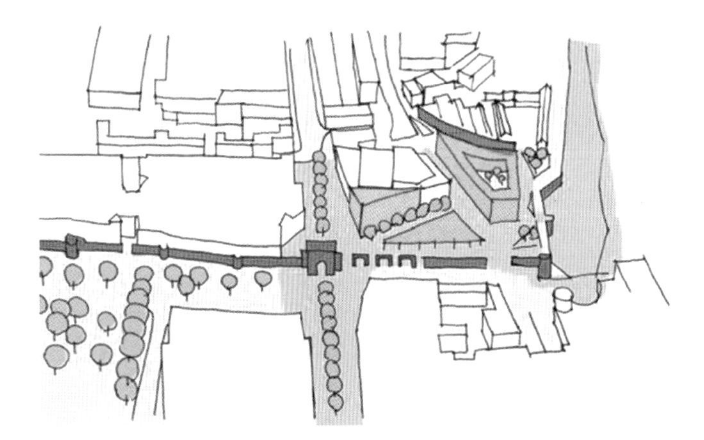

Left
This figure-ground plan has been exploded in order to highlight key elements.

Above
This series of images demonstrates the use of aerial photography to aid urban analysis.

STEP BY STEP ANALYSING A SITE

To achieve a successful site analysis drawing, take an existing map, place a piece of tracing paper over it, and start sketching.This illustration comprises different analyses of the same site. The key is to create a series of diagrams, each with a different purpose. Analyse route, shape, typology and environment. Use different colours to make your analysis easier to understand. The diagrams should be simple to convey your analysis effectively and quickly.

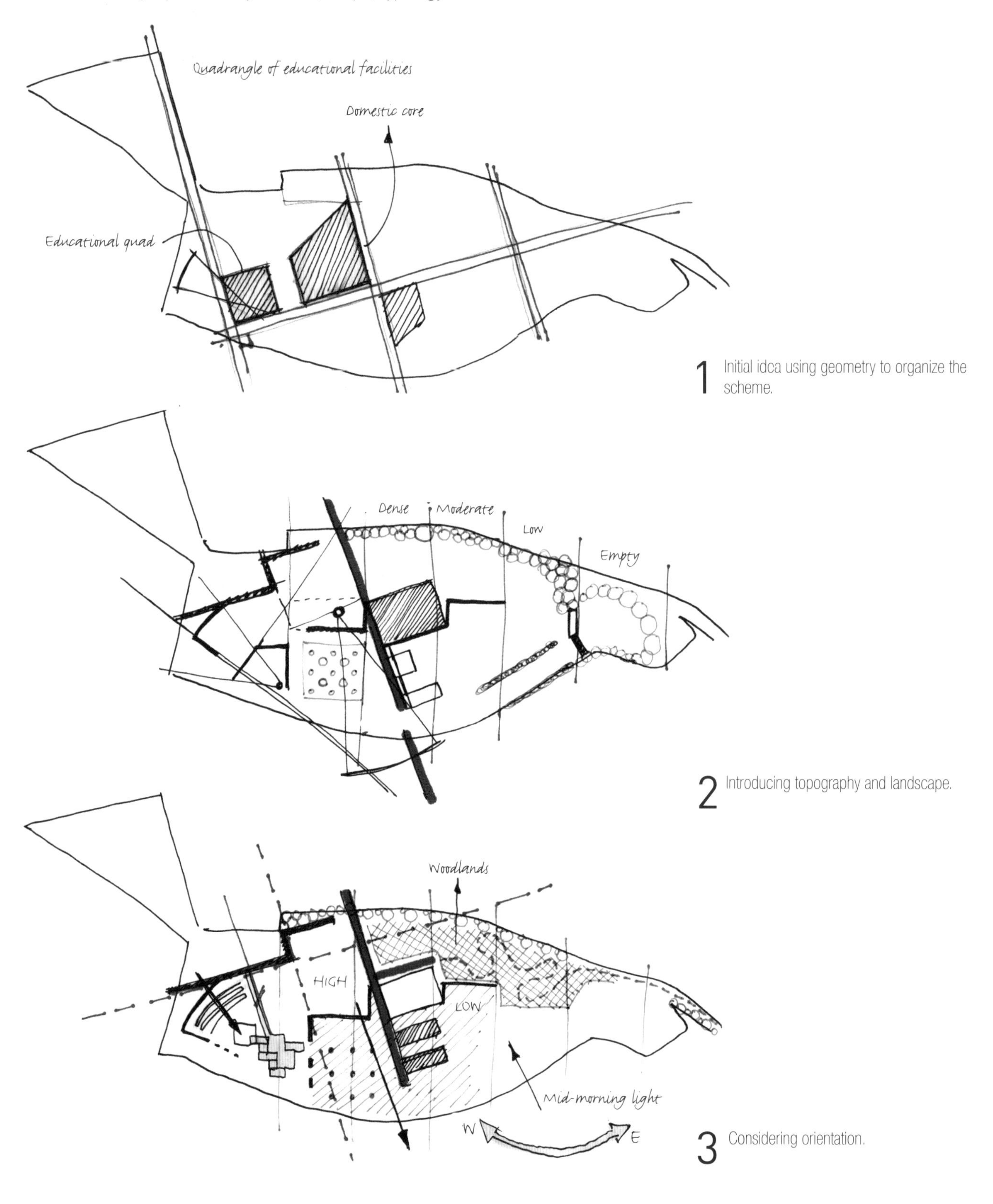

1 Initial idca using geometry to organize the scheme.

2 Introducing topography and landscape.

3 Considering orientation.

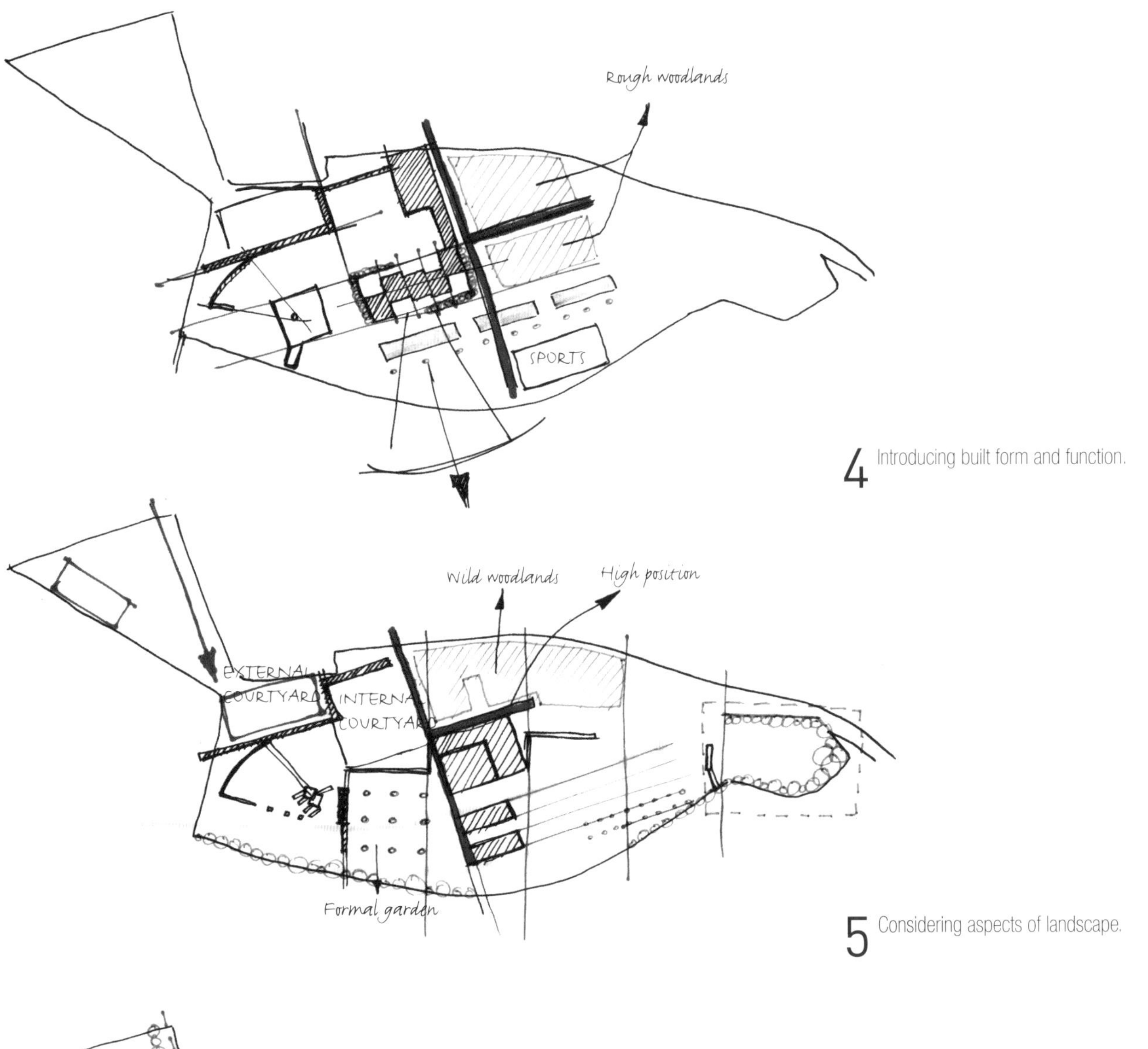

4 Introducing built form and function.

5 Considering aspects of landscape.

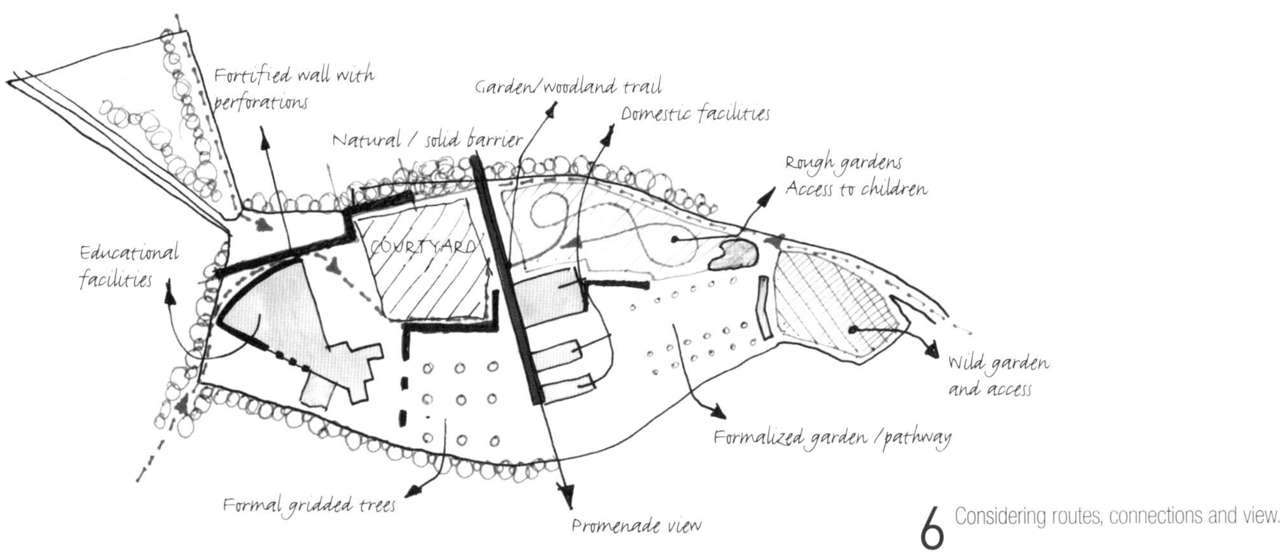

6 Considering routes, connections and view.

Below
Playful use of colour on an existing photograph not only brings this image to life but also serves to highlight the boundaries of the buildings.

Outline and photography

A photograph is a useful starting point when breaking down the elements of a site in a way that is easy to understand. The original photograph can be drawn over in Photoshop to highlight important aspects of the site. This technique may be used to frame particular points of interest or details, or it may be used to identify particular buildings or sites for consideration or development. This use of outline is a simple but effective device that can transform a photograph into a tool for focusing attention on particular considerations of a view. Different colours can be used and linked to a key, for example to identify ownership or land use in a city.

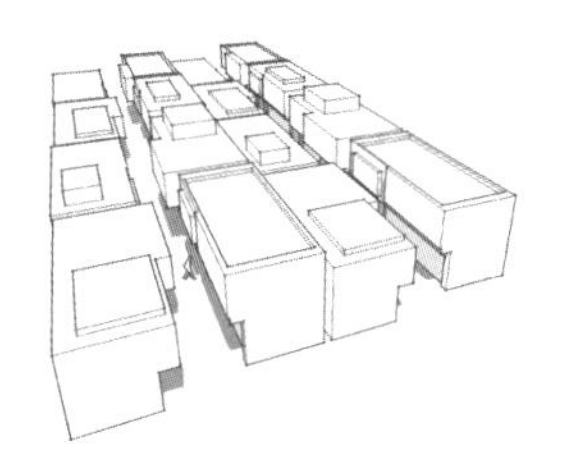

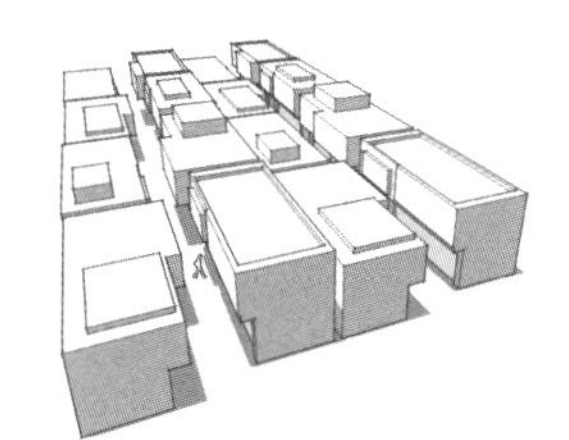

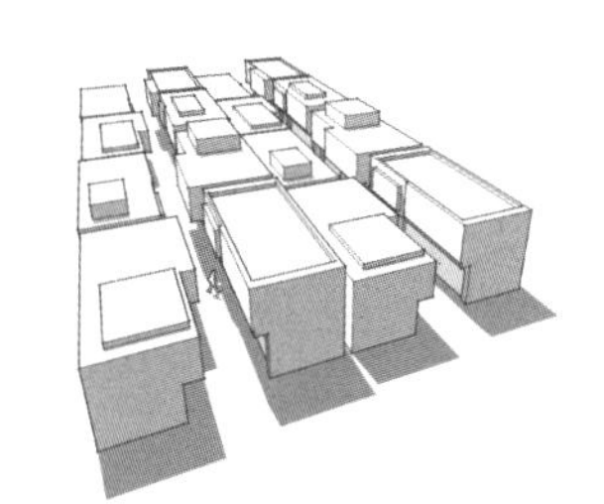

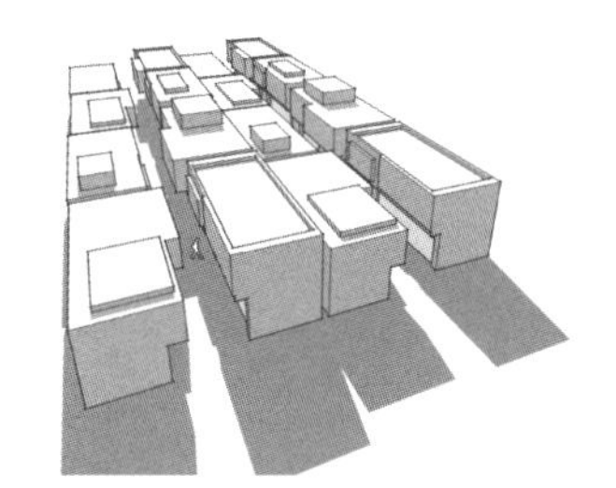

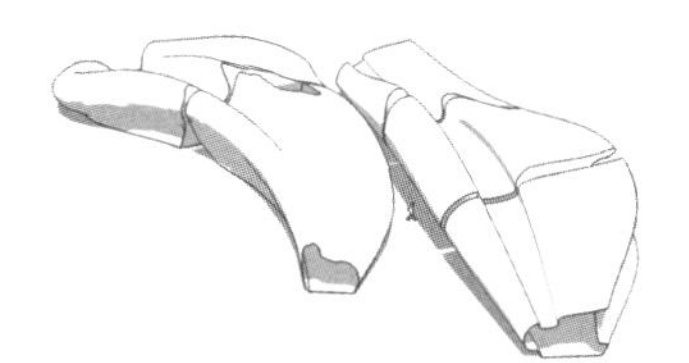

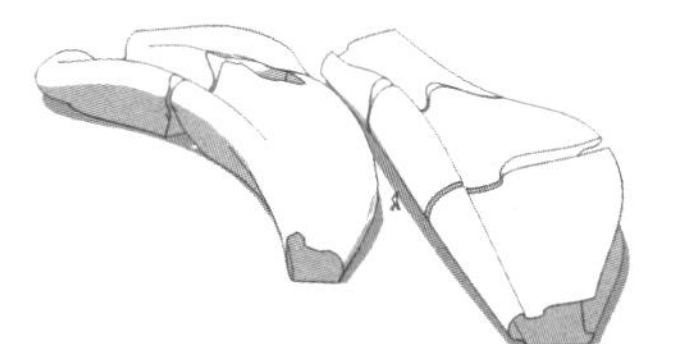

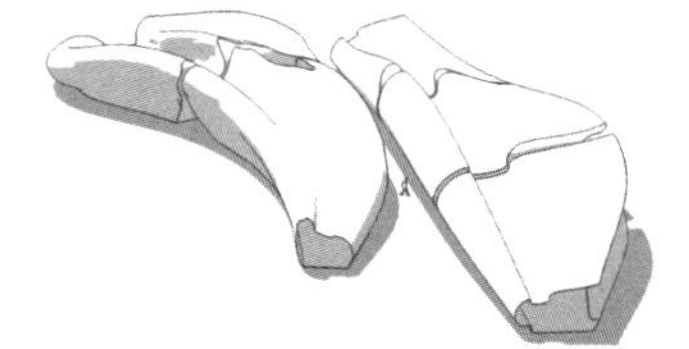

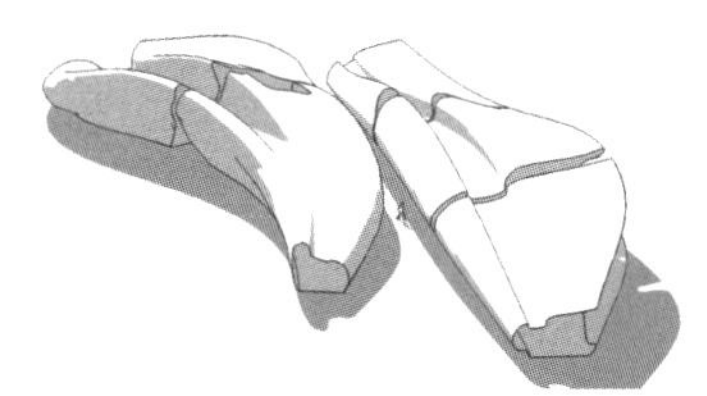

Above
This sequence of images shows an analysis of a souk in Damascus and shade conditions. Elements of the photographs are outlined to highlight the traditional strategies for blocking direct sunlight at street level to reduce heat. The first set of drawings investigates the shade conditions at specific times of the day in the old souk, and the second set illustrates the shade conditions of a proposed modern souk development. Both drawings are oriented in the same direction and shade readings were taken at the same time of year.

Mapping

It is not down in any map; true places never are.
Herman Melville, *Moby-Dick*, 1851

A painting does not normally indicate a plan of action, neither does a sculpture, nor a perspective drawing, but a map always predicates an action. If historical, it records an action, and the it allows viewers to locate themselves in relation to a place or point. All maps are forms of abstractions; they make a connection between the imagined and the experienced. A map is a visual representation, but it describes something which cannot be seen; it is an abstraction of reality.

When we consider our cities and their evolution and development, we always look to the map as a reference. The horizontal surface of the map records the relationships between spaces, places, streets and buildings.

To 'map' an area is to use a set of data to represent an idea of that place. The data available can vary from physical information – measured buildings, streets and squares – to density of population. Mapping can also describe functions in different environments.

Right
A plan of Munich by Space Syntax, which represents the city as a series of coloured blocks.

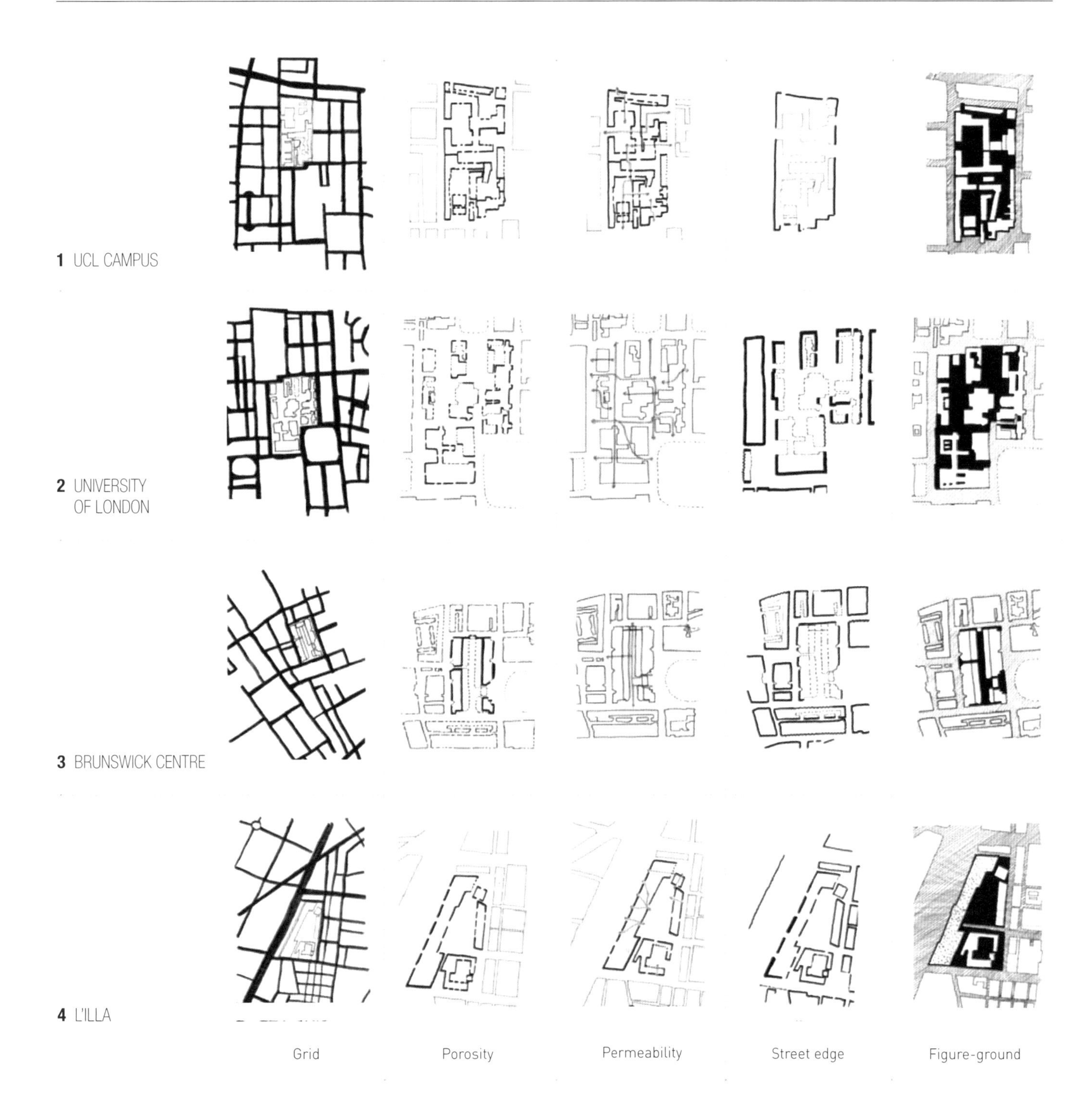

Above
In this study of the Fitzrovia and Bloomsbury areas of London by S333 architects the drawings analyse the performance and organization of university campus systems at the urban block scale.

Typology

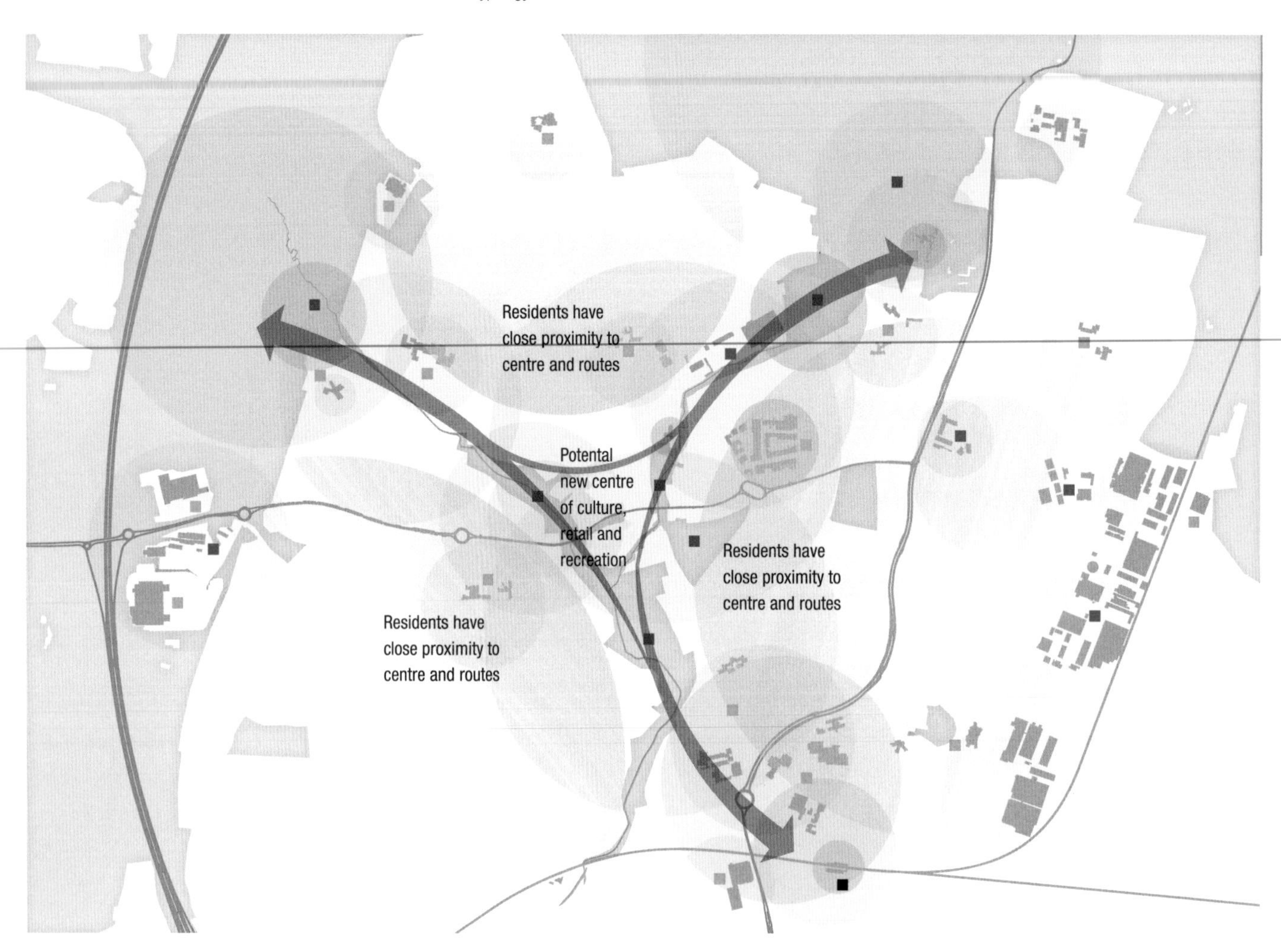

A map is a lens through which the viewer can read the interpretation of the map-maker's view of the world. Maps once made become images, part of a broader cultural description. They are an account of the physicality of the place and record its memory and cultural history. A map represents a moment in time and a particular impression of a place. It can be selective with information and tell a story in a particular way. A map can describe journeys, functions in a city, open spaces or areas of light and shadow. It can map whatever information needs to be described.

Maps function as cartographic lingua franca allowing mental geographies to be constructed.

J. B. Harley, 'Deconstructing the Map' in *Cartographica*, Vol. 26, No. 2, 1989

In creating a map, the map-maker needs to be clear about the journey he wishes the map-reader to take. There needs to be a sense that the map will give concise information to allow wayfinding from one point to another and to afford along the way useful encounters.

Maps are recording systems and in the context the city are a way quickly to communicate complex data. A map may be a two-dimensional representation of a journey or data that is presented in visual form.

The Situationists, formed in 1957, were a group of activists who used psycho-geographical approaches that allowed an impression of the space to determine an urban environment. Guy Debord (1931–94), the self-proclaimed leader of the Situationists, challenged the idea of the city as a real physical environment (see page 22). The group produced maps that paid little attention to scale and used experience to suggest journeys and connections, the notion of the *dérive* or drift through a city. This idea of wandering through the city without a predetermined plan was also connected to Charles Baudelaire's (1821–67) concept of the *flâneur*: he theorized about Paris and the city, considering it a large house for someone to wander through and experience, in which the streets were analagous to corridors and the restaurants to dining rooms.

The art of losing oneself in the city was not only a physical journey, but also an attempt to escape from reality.

Cognitive mapping: perception and knowledge

The term mapping can be seen as the process of engaging with a place. Many artists who need to understand the context of a place will map their interpretation of the environment, which may mean assembling a set of information that provides the basis for a piece of artistic work.

A method called cognitive mapping was used by American psychologist Edward Tolman (1886–1959) to analyse the behaviour of rats in a maze. He had observed that behaviour is learned through trial and error. Maps are used to illustrate behaviour. Mind maps are diagrams used to describe ideas and can assist with problem-solving and decision-making. They are an abstract map of a situation. The information is arranged according to availability of certain information which may be associated with memory or process, function or activity.

Other sorts of maps include concept maps which help to represent knowledge and information in particular ways. All these mapping techniques deal with connections between situations, places or ideas. The process is important. Maps can also be laid over each other to allow information from one mapping exercise to inform another.

Opposite
Arrows are used to demonstrate pathways through the urban environment.

Below
Photomontages such as those shown here can be a useful device for analysing the rhythm of façades in the city.

Figure-ground mapping

Below
An inverted figure-ground shows negative space more effectively.

Maps of a city or place need more detail than just the lines that denote edges and boundaries. A figure-ground map allows a description of different spatial conditions suggesting density or urban space using measured drawings and plans drawn to scale.

The traditional figure-ground map identifies the buildings as solid blocks separated by spaces. This allows for the buildings and spaces to be read clearly to get a sense of the density of a place. It is a reading of the figure (building) against the ground (the spaces between).

This exercise is best done with the buildings indicated as solid in one image and the spaces read as solid in another – that is, with the elements reversed out.

The figure-ground drawing is an abstract sort of map, but is normally drawn to scale. It has many uses and allows an understanding of a city as a complete place, or as a series of discrete maps.

This technique can be developed to identify and characterize different sorts of spaces – to distinguish between public and private spaces, for example – or to make a three-dimensional map or model, which can give depth to the drawing. The analogy for this exercise is the photographic negative, which, as a process, reveals new ways to see or understand a site or place.

TIP FIGURE-GROUND SCALE

It is important to verify the scale of a map when printing it out. It is all too easy to select 'fit to page' or adjust the compression when exporting. Take a simple dimension of the computer screen and check it using a scale ruler on the final printout.

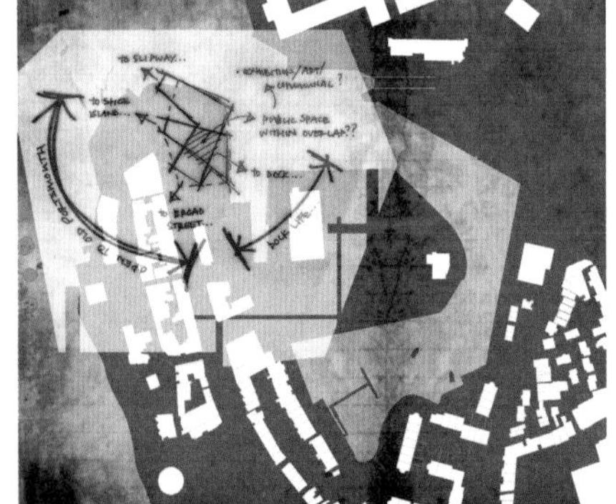
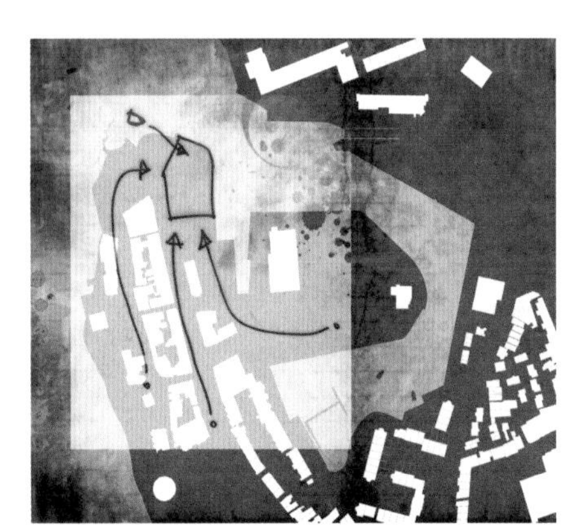
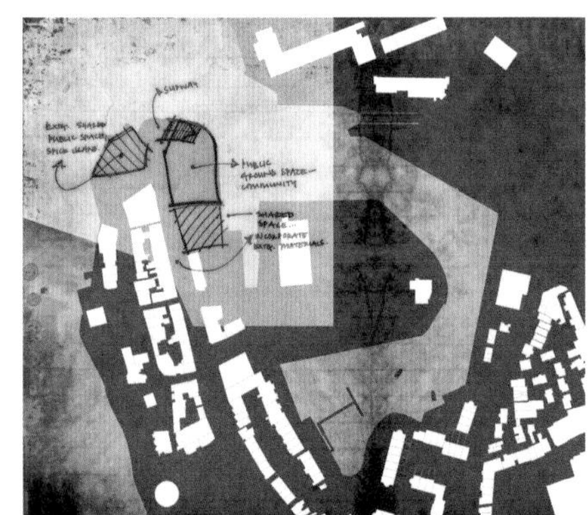
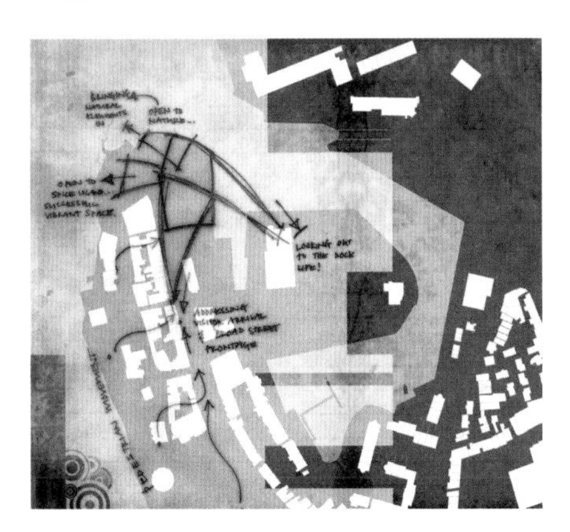
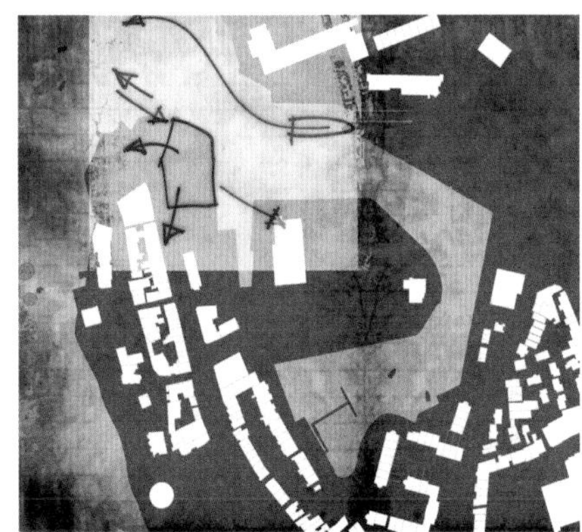
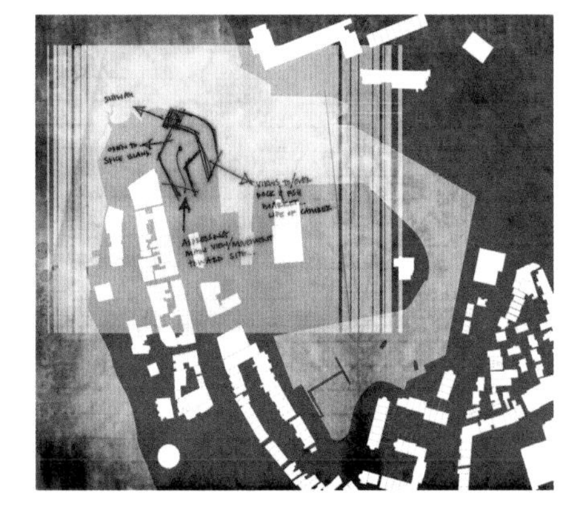

Below
S333's scheme for the Bircham Park North West Quadrant masterplan in Derriford, Plymouth, demonstrates an understanding of the role of collegiate spaces in the forming of clusters and mixed-use urban centres. The architects' approach promotes ideas of connectivity and the benefits of green space.

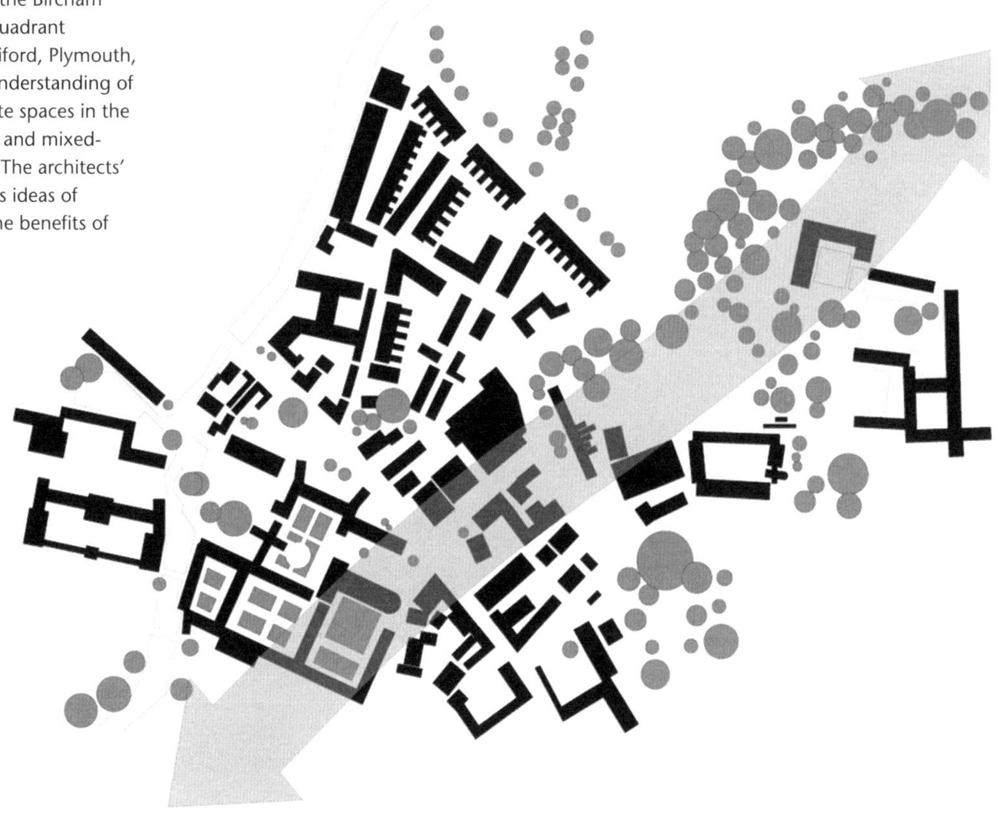

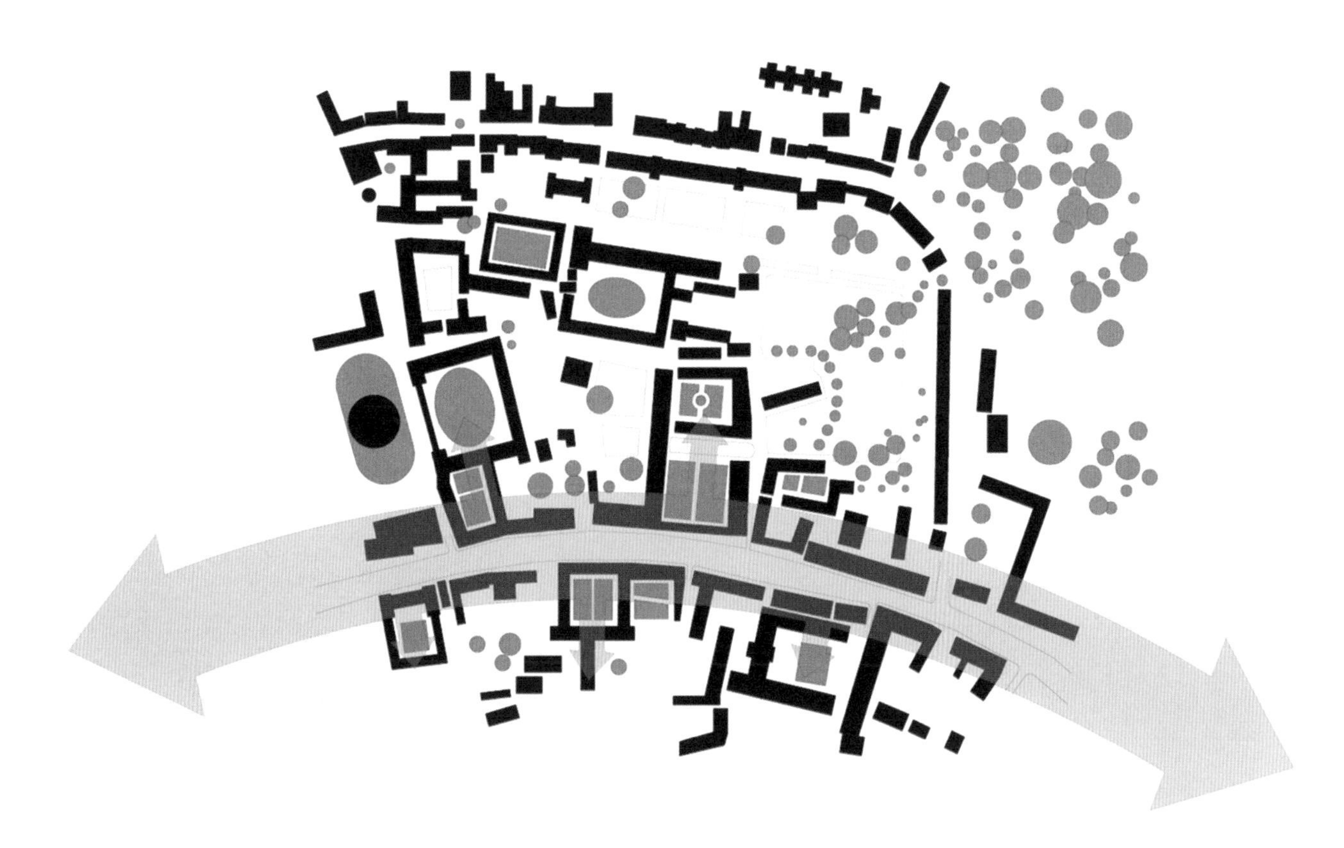

Above
A series of urban prototype figure-ground drawings of Hulme, Manchester, by S333. The historical extremes of either too much or too little public space and the typological homogeneity of the area were resolved through a new differentiated network.

Right
A physical model showing key topographical elements and buildings in figure ground.

STEP BY STEP CREATING A FIGURE GROUND

This process requires the study of accurate maps of the area. This can be done on a computer or as a hand-drawn exercise. The figure ground can also be developed as a three-dimensional model impression.

1 Lay a piece of tracing paper over a map and trace the outline of street edges and buildings.

2 Start filling out the buildings you've just traced with a black pen. When that is done, your figure ground is complete. Be clear about the aspects of the city you want to identify as 'space'.

Conceptual field

The term conceptual field refers to a development theory that establishes connections across different areas of knowledge.

The drawings, sketches, plans and sections that we use to depict cities can be combined in the form of either a measured drawing to scale or a sketch to make connections across an urban environment. The conceptual field slices through a city and within that slice reveals the concept of the city, and connections across and through it. It may reveal the connection between a shopping area and a residential quarter. There may be aspects of scale in a city, for example one area with high-rise buildings and another with low-rise buildings. A drawing of this sort identifies the key concepts and links them with a sketch which may be annotated. This drawing can reveal ideas that cannot be understood from looking at a map.

Below
This site section by Re-Format architects slices through a proposed residential scheme in Nottingham to reveal the relative heights of the buildings.

Bottom
This proposal for a university campus scheme by Design Engine cuts across a range of buildings to reveal the relationships between the structures and spaces across the site.

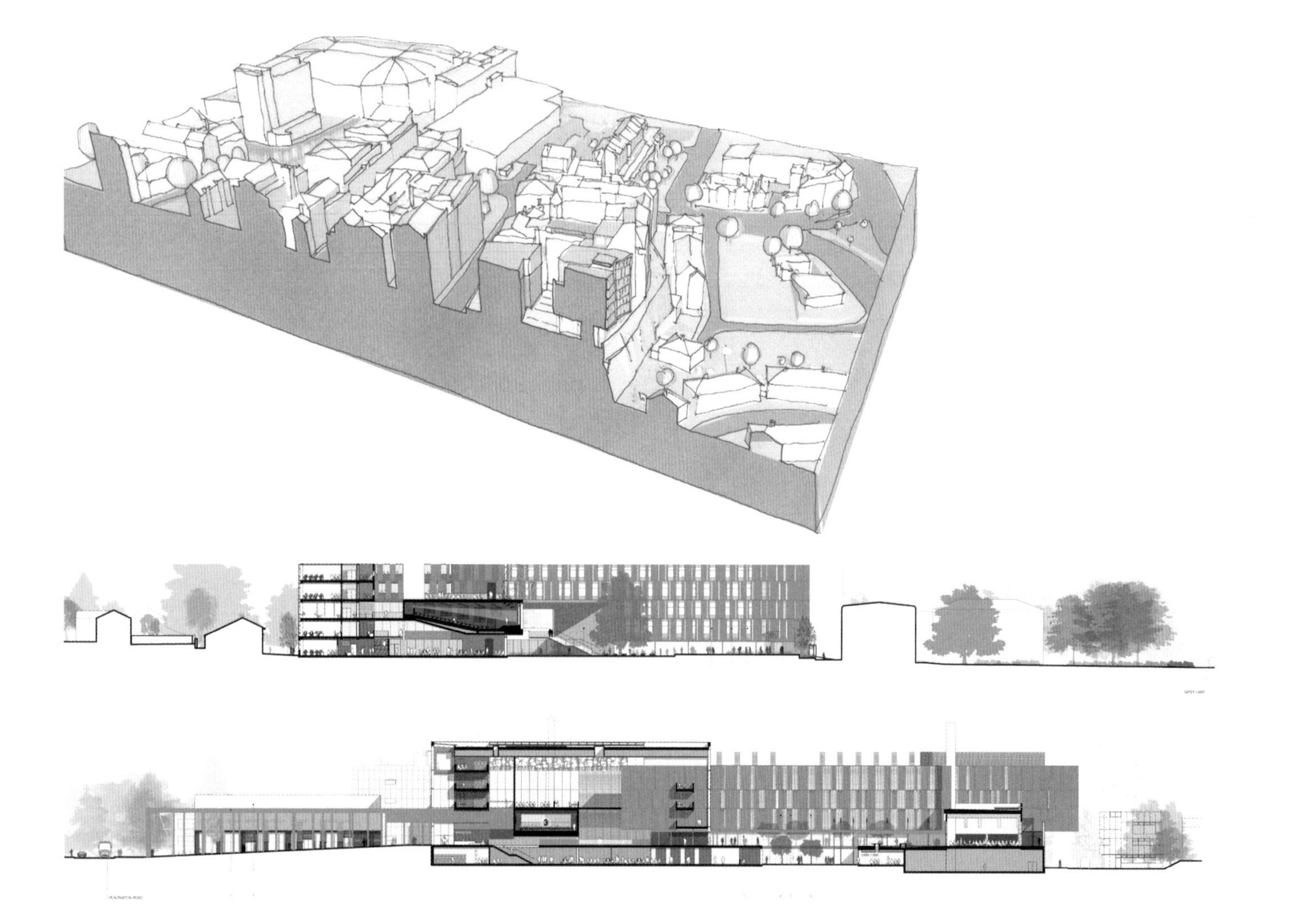

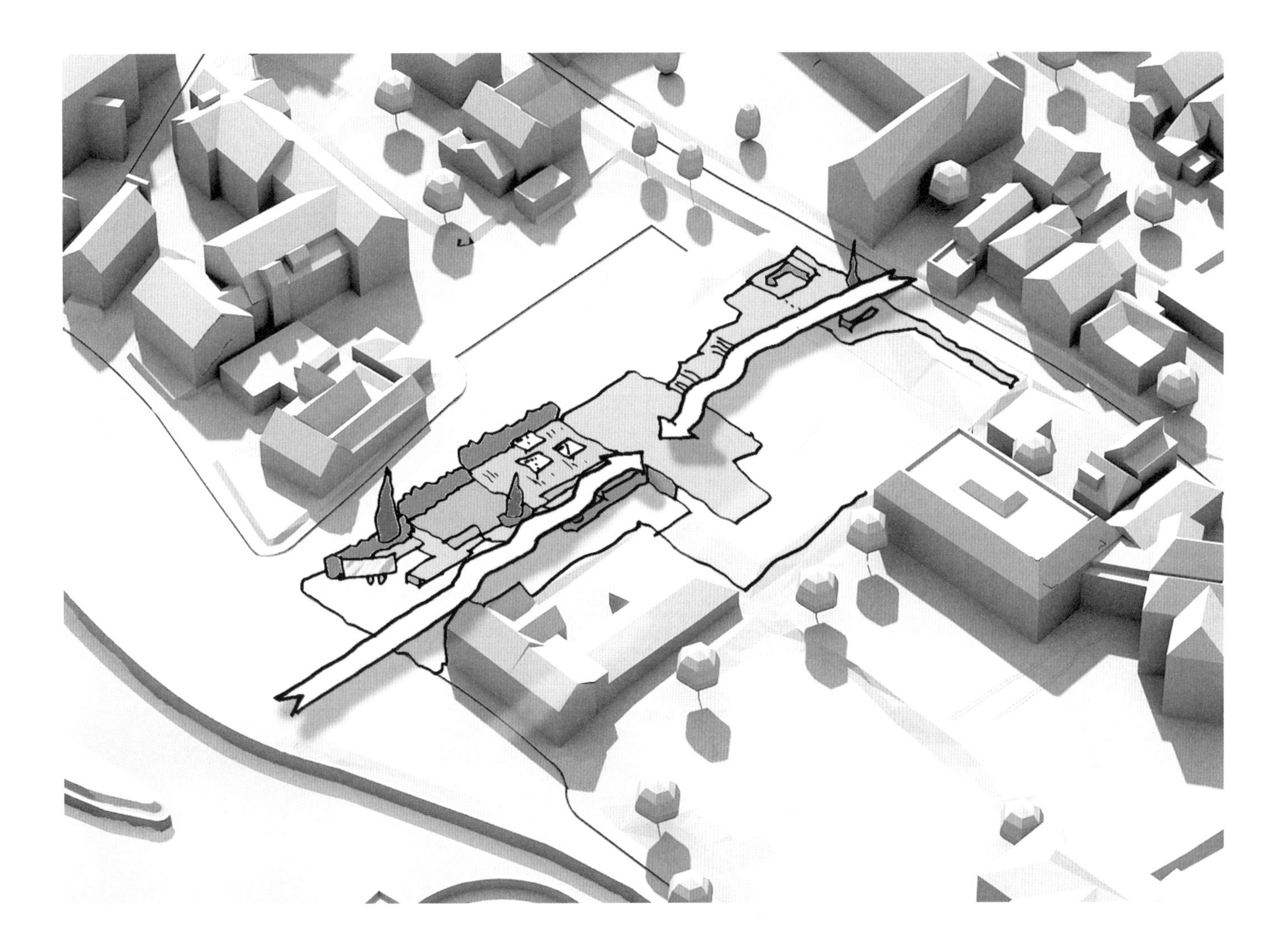

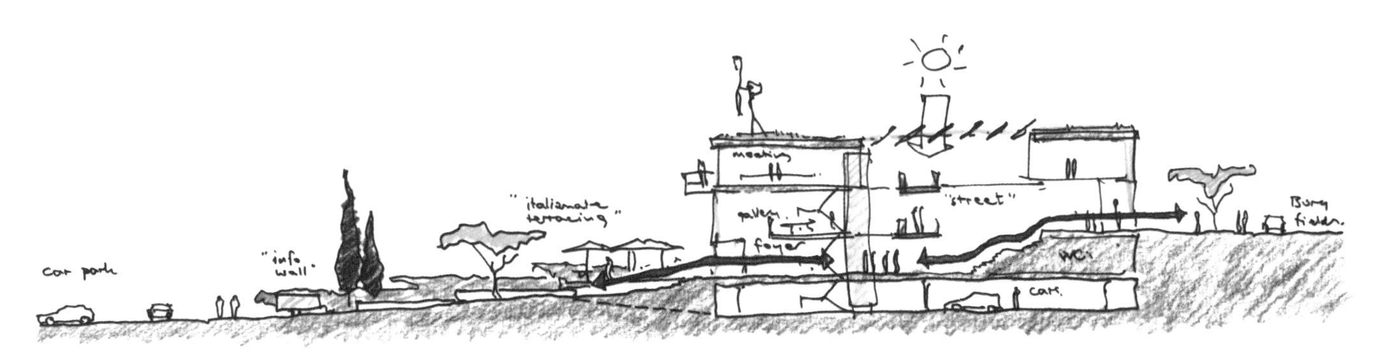

Top
This sketch of a church project in Guildford by Re-Format architects has been overlaid onto a CAD model of the site to suggest how the proposed scheme will relate to the surrounding buildings.

Above
A long section sketch drawing for the same project indicates the relationship between the scheme design and the urban context.

Digital techniques

Photography can be considered a form of mapping. A way of recording the environment, it can be observational, absorbing aspects of the world around us and capturing change over time. A photographic record is an important part of documenting and understanding a site. Aerial photography is part of that documentation: reading a city from above offers the possibility to make observations and connections and to understand the connections in a broader context.

If a series of aerial photographs are taken and examined over time, cities can be assessed in terms of metropolitan growth and change. Aerial photographs enable visualization of density and comparisons of different parts of a city.

This page and opposite
In this series of photographs of a souk, a layer of tone and colour was applied digitally to outline important architectural details and draw attention to particular aspects of the route through existing buildings. The photographs were then used to create a simplified computer model of the souk, in which daylighting effects are explored.

Photographic recording of spaces and places can involve a variety of techniques more commonly applied in other disciplines to interpret the city experience. Collage and sequential cinematic imagery, borrowing techniques from film-making and storyboarding, can explore the idea of movement through a series of spaces.

When first visiting a part of a city, making a photographic survey of the city is important to find out about the character of the place. The aim may be to capture a journey, to create a collage or to record a series of views. Images can be taken to identify various aspects of a place, such as use of materials or building form. Photographing an urban environment requires similar careful observation as that needed to sketch it. The images can be used to create photomontage impressions of ideas for buildings or design ideas for various parts of the city.

Manipulating digital photographs with various software can illustrate a breadth of ideas. Images can be enhanced or extended to become part of a greater presentation.

A photo image can be drawn over to highlight a particular aspect of a view. It can become part of a collage of a design proposal, or be used as a photomontage to suggest how a part of a city or scheme may be developed.

TIP SERIAL VIEWS

It is sometimes hard to find the time or a suitable position to stop and draw on a hurried architectural city tour. It can be useful to take a set of photographs and use them later as the basis of drawings.

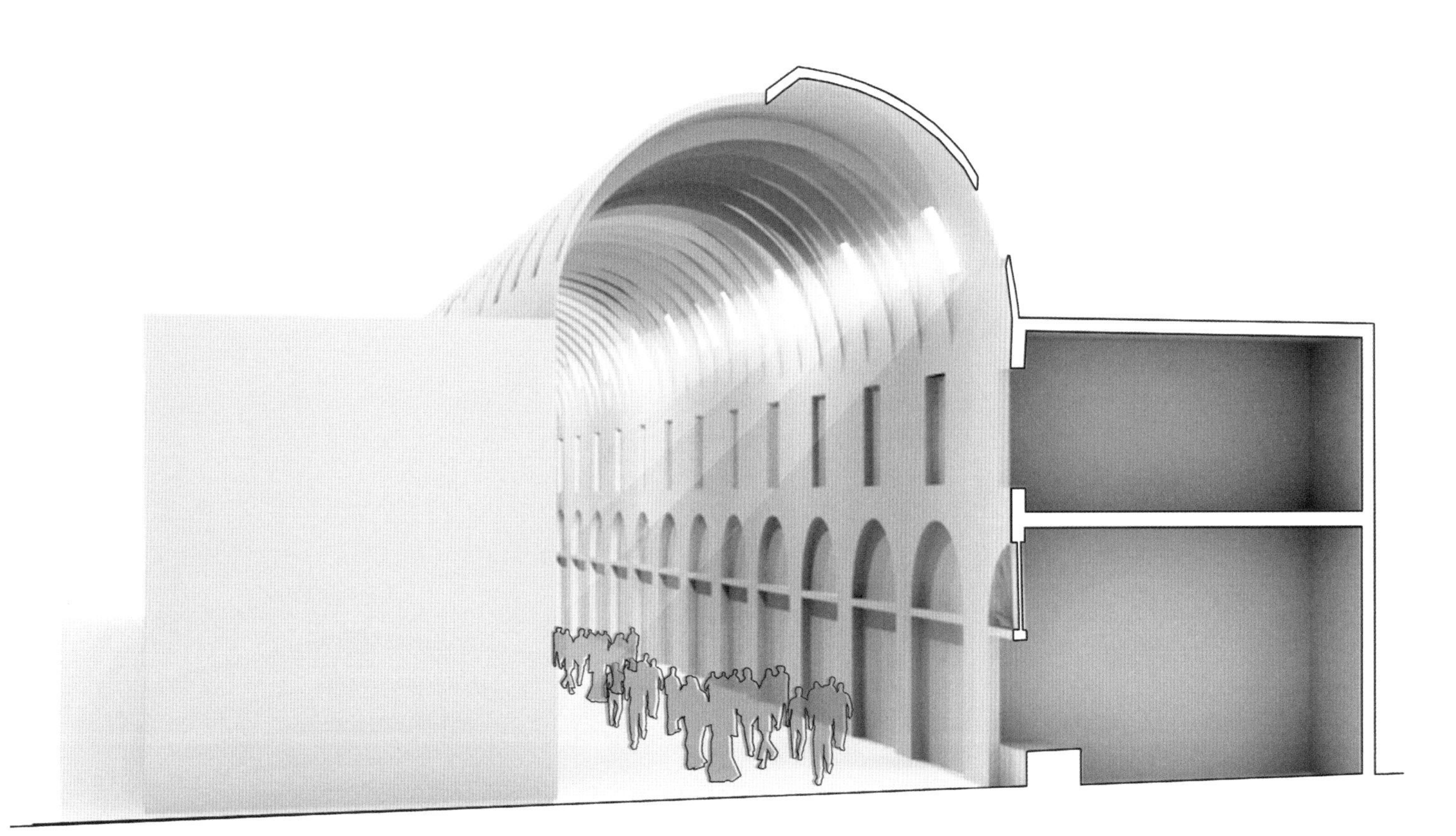

Similarly, film is a good way to record activity in the city. Using film allows a range of experiences to be explored: distances through spaces, moving light, shadow and the dynamic of a place.

Many mechanisms used in film-making can be used to describe urban space. In particular, the storyboard is a framework that allows a film-maker to plan a film as a sequence of images to create a narrative through space over time. Storyboards can explain an interpretation of a journey through a city as a real or imagined experience.

Above and right
These images were part of a series of studies presented as part of a planning application for a new residential development in Albany Mews, Edinburgh, by studioKAP. The architects used digital photographs and CAD images to indicate how the scheme would connect to the site.

STEP BY STEP ENHANCING DIGITAL PHOTOGRAPHS

Using Photoshop, an image can be edited to highlight various aspects, from the tones and shadows of buildings to the background that frames them. A quick and effective way of enhancing a digital photograph of an urban space is to make it monochromatic and add just one colour – in this example, the buildings are monochromatic against a blue sky.

1 Open the picture in Photoshop.

2 Change the saturation of the picture to make it monochromatic.

3 Then play with the brightness and contrast to get a stronger image.

4 Finally, create a new layer and add colour to an element of the photograph – in this case, the sky – to make the buildings really stand out.

Models

Below
Urban models such as this example (which is shown from several viewpoints) are useful for providing a contextual base in which individual schemes can be tested.

An important consideration when designing a building or a larger-scale urban design project is the stage at which a model is most useful. The answer is that it is useful at all stages of the process. It is analogous to a drawing as a tool to assist in design. In the initial stages of understanding a site or a piece of the city, a model indicating scale and form can be quickly made to clarify what exists. It can then be used through to the final stage of the scheme, when it can serve as a presentation model, illustrating a fully developed idea.

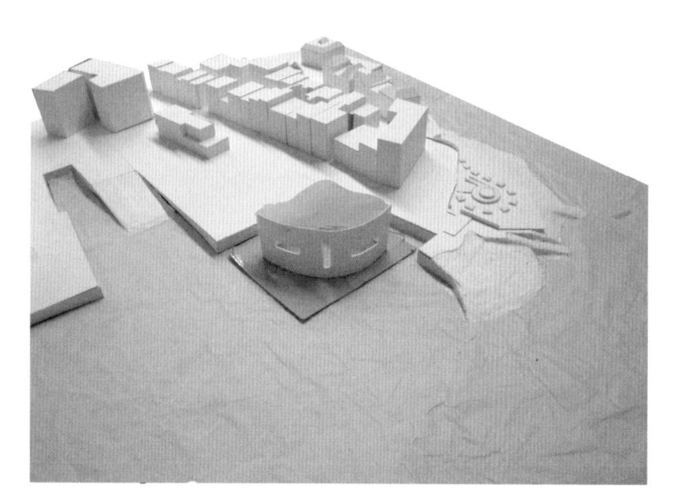

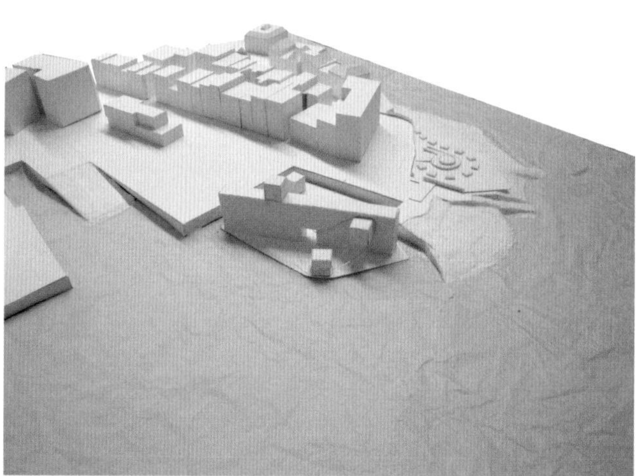

Models are easily understood by those not trained as designers and they represent an important way of describing an idea holistically. In particular, they enable connections across cities to be easily understood, and larger systems such as streets, routes and scale of buildings to be cross-related. A model does not have to be sophisticated; it may just need to communicate the idea three-dimensionally. Sometimes a quick cardboard model can suffice to express a proposal and to test thinking at a particular point. One can then move onto another model and another idea. A collection of models like this is part of the process of design and development.

As with any form of drawing or recording, the purpose of the model must be clear in advance. It may communicate spaces and forms. There may be aspects of connection or communication that need to be described. Once this is determined, then decisions about the technique and the scale of the model can be made.

Physical and CAD modelling can describe a space as it is and can also be used to analyse a place in terms of its history and evolution. The physical model can be a working model which has certain elements as fixed points and design features that can be interchangeable. This allows for evolving ideas to be quickly understood and demonstrated.

Physical modelling is an effective way to represent the city as it is and as it will be. It is accessible, and it allows visual connections as well as an understanding of scale and how parts of the city relate to the whole. A large city model can be about massing, building shape or form, or may be quite abstract. Many models are used as part of the design process as well as illustrating final ideas.

A number of cities now have a city model as the centrepiece of an exhibition to demonstrate their commitment to future development. Paris has a city model at the Pavillon de l'Arsenal, London has one at the Building Centre. These models are an important aspect of explaining how the city is evolving and they allow all development to be placed in a broad context, reflecting the ever-changing nature of the city.

The model is the key communicating device for an urban idea. It has a presence and can be investigated and understood at many levels. It allows an understanding of massing, form, relative scales and heights, views, vistas and connections. There is a personal engagement with a model which allows the viewer to feel part of the process of developing of the idea.

Below
Computer modelmakers Zmapping use a special software programme to create interactive three-dimensional models of cities. Proposed schemes can be imported via other software programmes and viewed within these models. The images shown here are two views of a model of Brisbane generated using digital map data.

Below
Black-and-white photography and shadowing has been cleverly used to bring out the massing of the urban context.

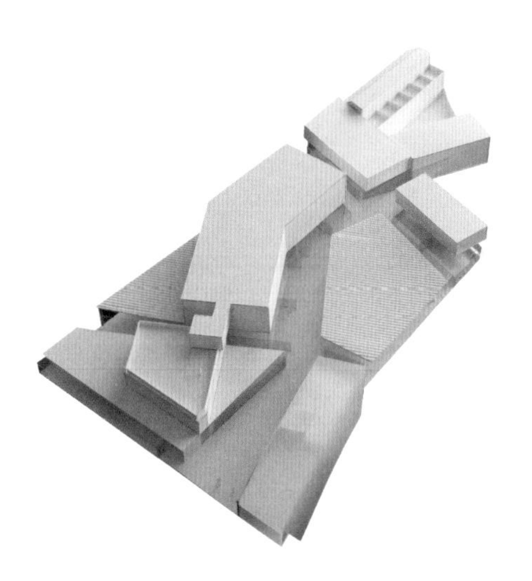

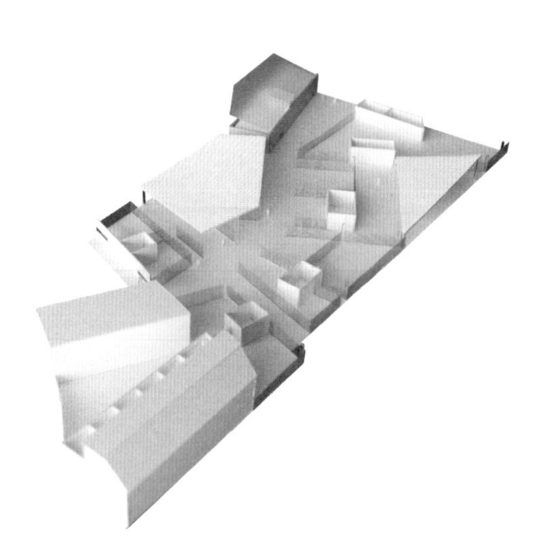

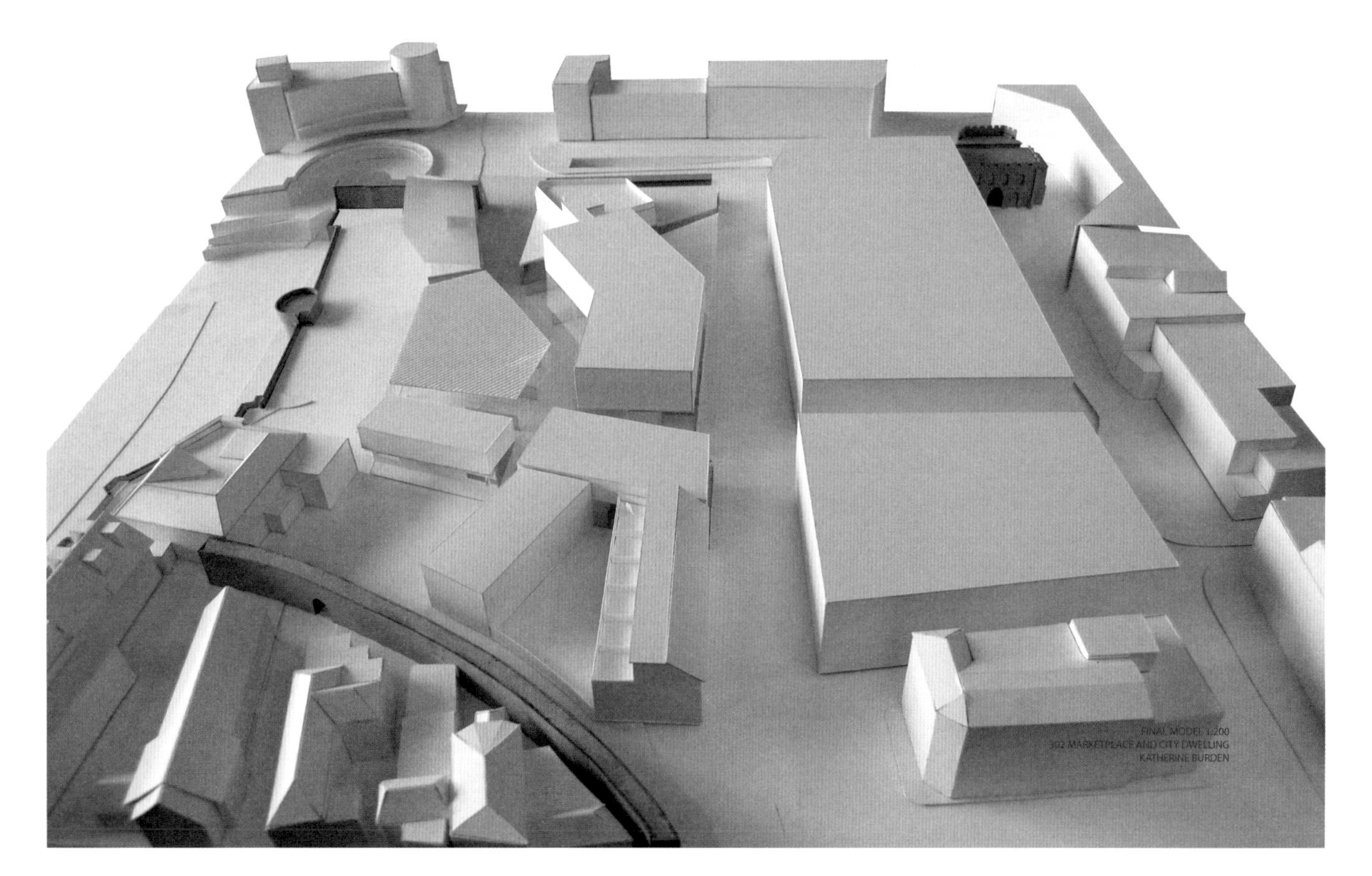

Materials for modelmaking

Physical models can be created out of anything from recycled cardboard to more sophisticated materials that need laser-cutting for precise results.

Most physical models need a base board that may be wood, such as plywood or particle board, or a lighter material such as plastic or card. More ambitious schemes may use other materials such as acrylic, metal or plastic.

Urban models need quite a lot of thought to achieve differentiation between existing buildings and space and proposed buildings and space. Using different materials to highlight this distinction is helpful. A good solution is to have the main model made from a neutral material, such as white board, so it appears as a blank canvas, then to insert the proposed idea in a distinctively different material. The use of materials such as acrylic can also allow light to be used in a model to illuminate various parts of a city or a building.

Processes for modelmaking have developed enormously. A simple way to start a city model is to lay a scale map or plan onto a base board and add elements to it. City models can be made using many different cutting techniques; laser-cutting equipment can be employed to achieve precisely detailed buildings based on a digital drawing.

Foam board can be used to quickly achieve effects for a city model. Use a hot wire cutter to cut forms from various foam boards to produce simple block forms. Large-scale areas of the city can be realized quickly by using woodworking machines to cut simple blocks to suggest building forms.

Above
This model, made by Amodels, of S333's proposal for Bircham Park, Derriford, Plymouth, shows the key concept: an urban structure founded on a landscape of courts, streets and parks.

Left
Cardboard is an excellent material for producing sketch models.

Massing models

To understand the relative scale and size of buildings, massing models can be made using basic information to allow an overview of a city or part of a city. They describe the mass or volume of buildings in a place. This model type is particularly useful in the early stages of design to convey a sense of the density and scale of built form in a city.

A massing model can be made as a CAD model using software such as Google SketchUp, or as a physical model using block materials such as wood or foam. It effectively reduces the city to its simplest form, a series of blocks.

The massing model allows the size of the built form to be understood, and also allows consideration of the spaces between the built form. Such models can vary in scale; they usually relate to Ordnance Survey maps and, depending on detail, may be at a scale of 1:1250, 1:1000 or 1:500.

A massing model can be built initially to indicate existing massing on a site or in part of a city and later used to demonstrate a range of proposals for density or massing at the early stages of design to communicate the implications of scale and form.

Below left
This image shows the use of block massing. The scheme is modelled in the same material as the surrounding context to create a uniform finish.

Below
CAD software can be used to create massing models for exploring the relationship of a proposed scheme to an exiting site. This CAD model tests an idea for a project in a dense city site.

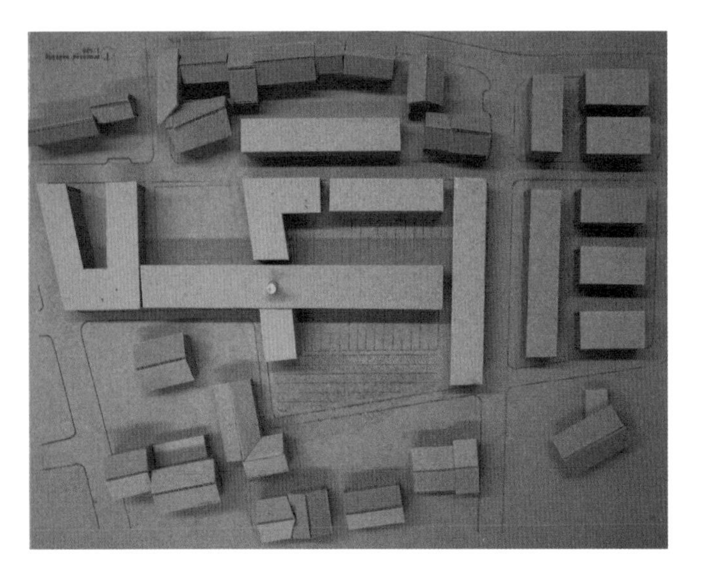

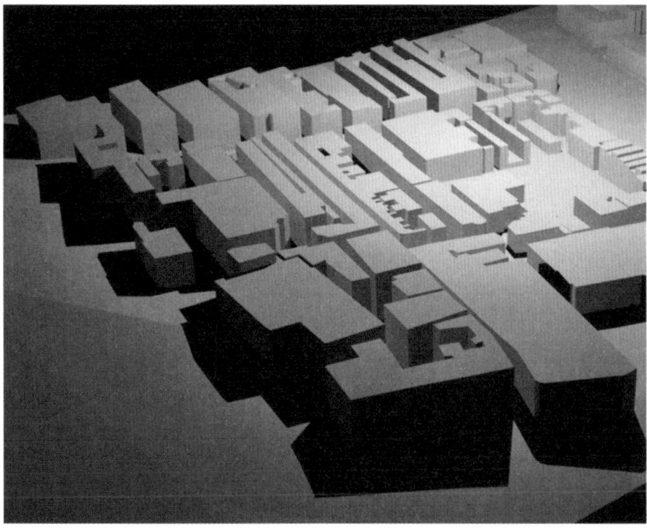

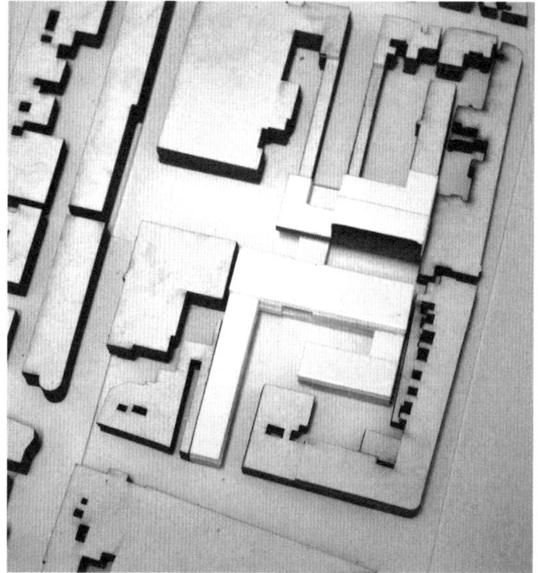

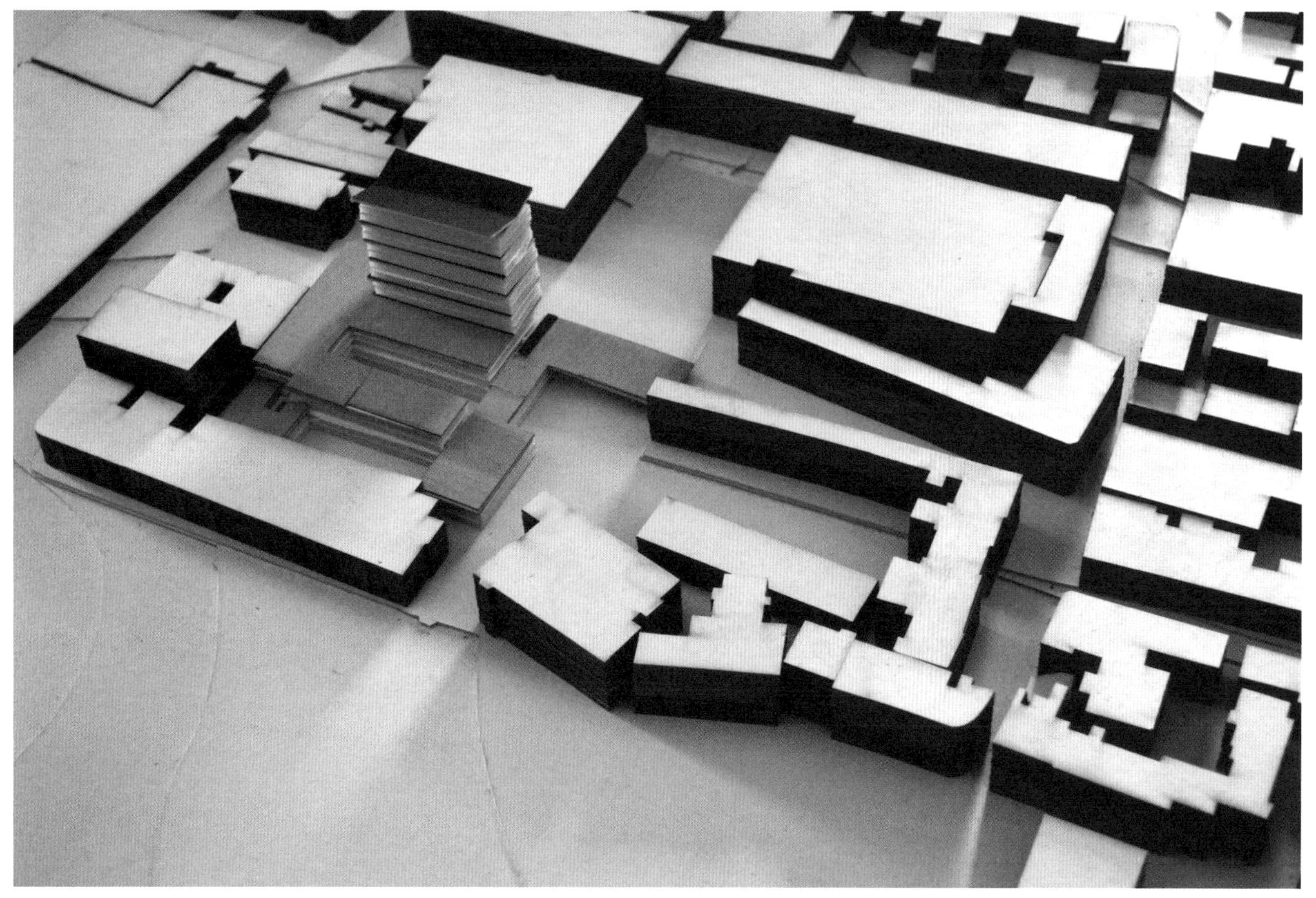

This page
These models describe a series of proposals for a project in Brighton. The scheme was modelled at a scale of 1:500 to investigate the impact of massing on the site.

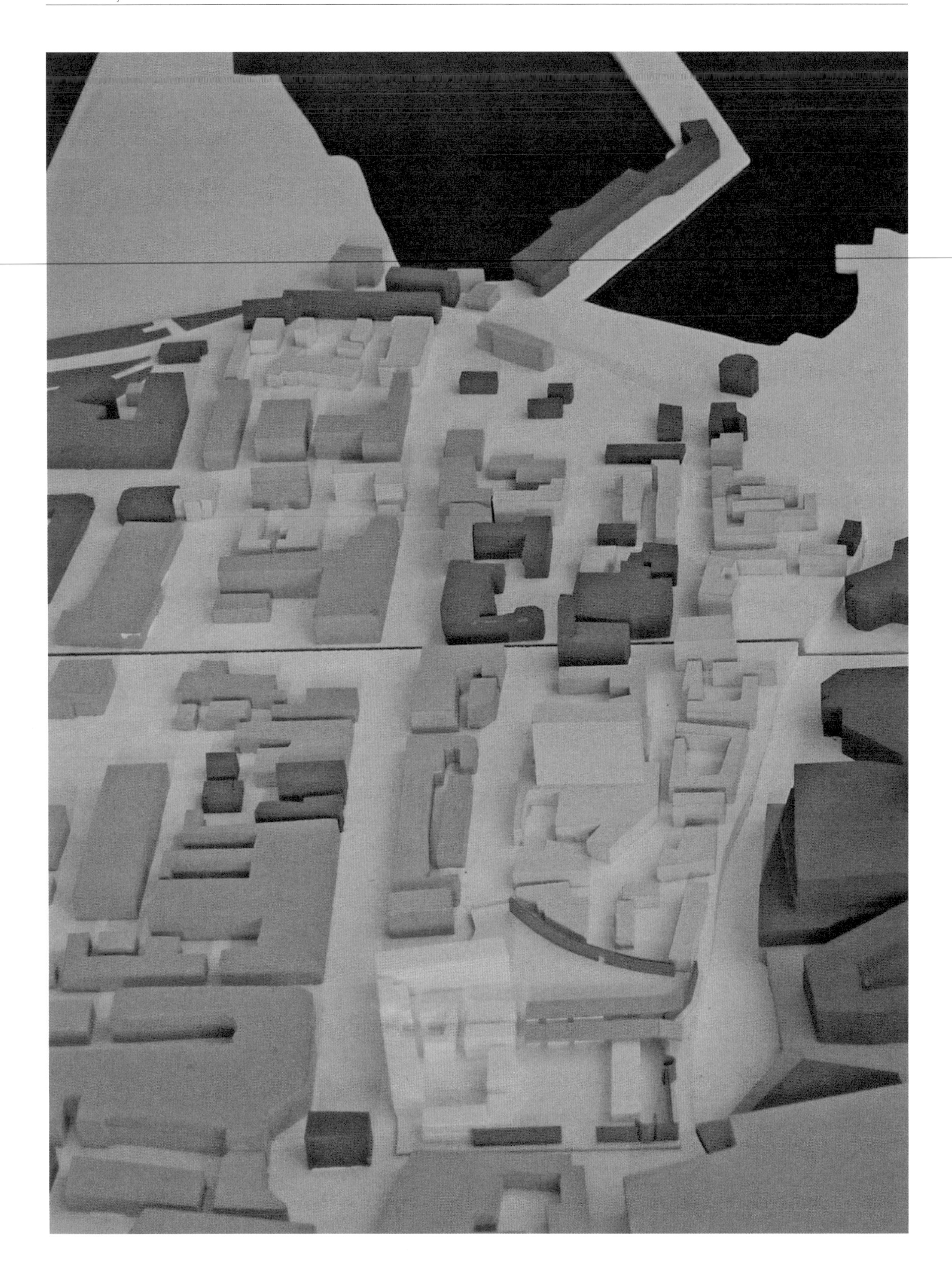

Opposite
Even in a monochromatic scheme the use of varying shades can bring analytical depth to a model.

Below
This urban model of a district of Amsterdam uses a grid as a reference and presents an abstract view of a site for redevelopment.

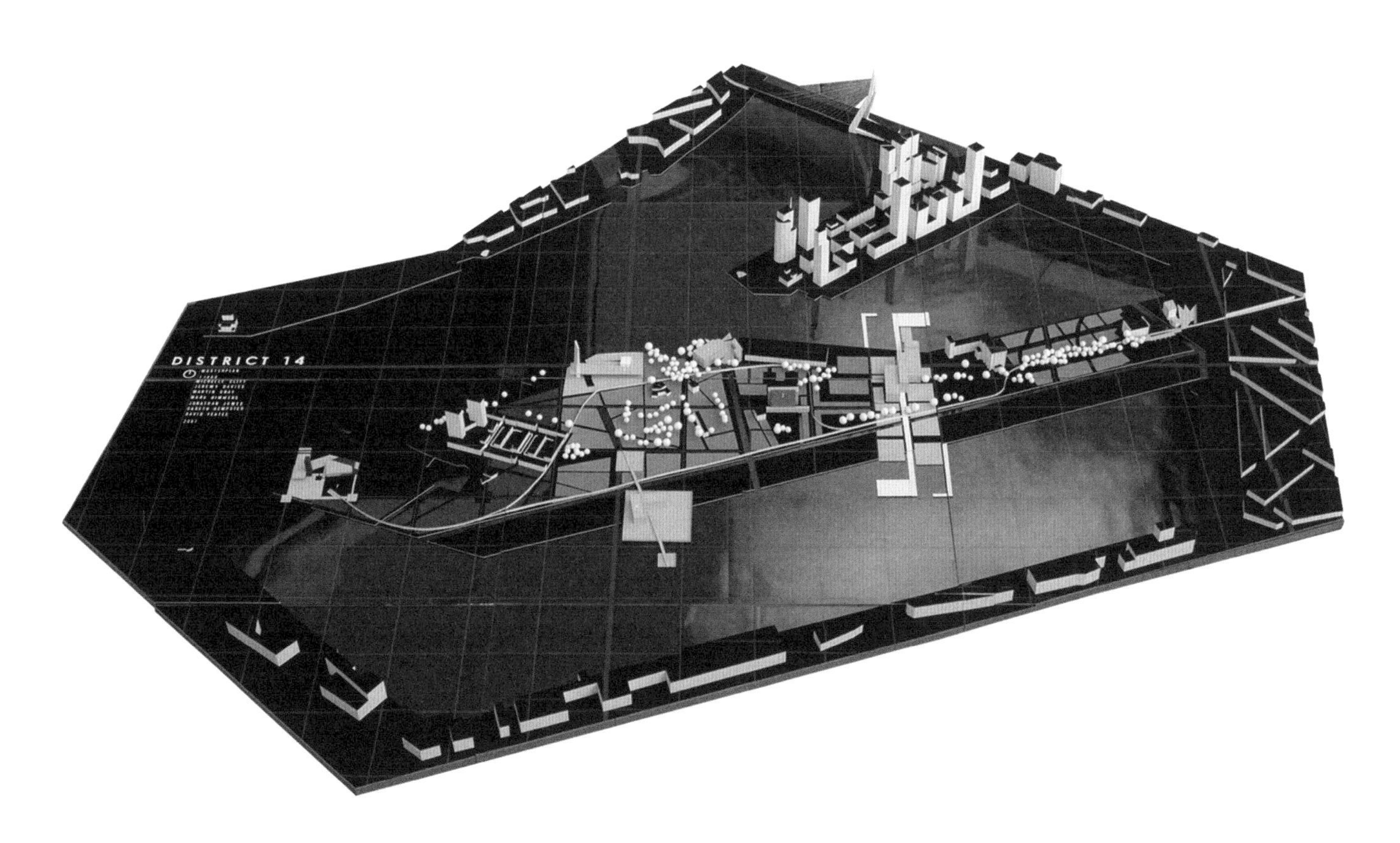

TIP MASSING MODELS

Using two different materials in a massing model makes it simple to differentiate between existing and proposed elements. In this example the proposed new development is represented by the opaque resin volumes on the far right.

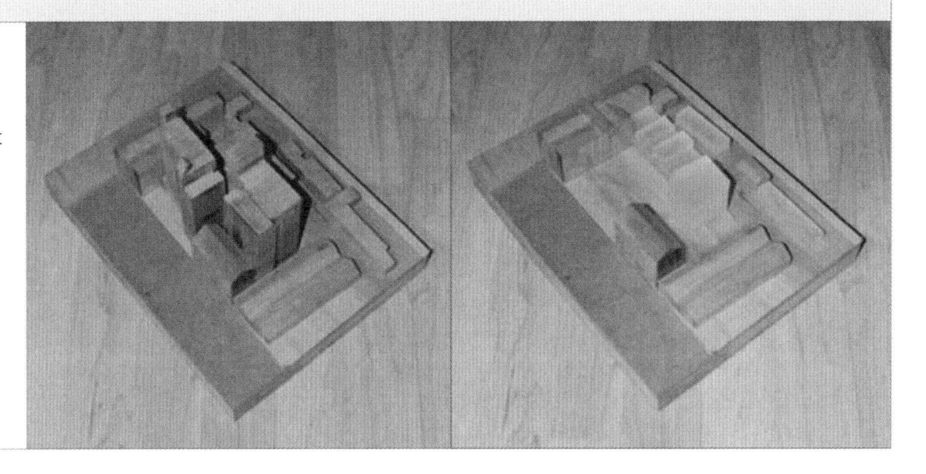

Process models

Designing a part of a city is a complicated process involving consideration of a number of factors and so it takes time to evolve. It is important to have a range of models which explain the development of the idea, how it has grown and shifted. These process models may connect to a site or a piece of the city. It may be that a particular model is photographed as it changes and these photographs are the recorded process, or that models made at various stages are retained. Early models will concentrate on form and the implication of that proposed form on the urban space around. These models are useful for the designer, but also explain the evolution of the design to the client, recording various thought processes and stages of decision-making.

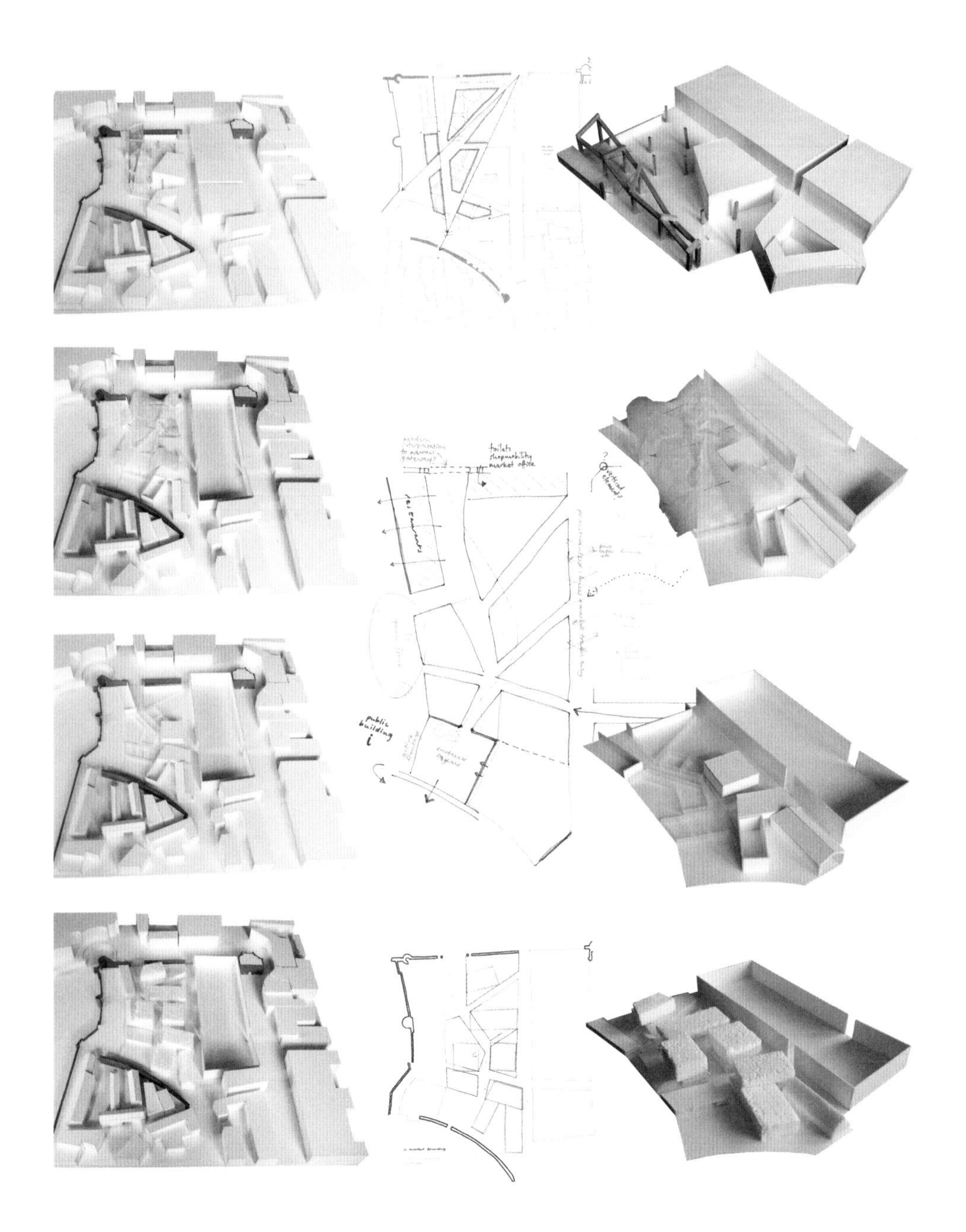

Left
Sketch models can be useful for analysis. Certain elements can be changed as required and the results repeatedly photographed.

Opposite
Process models of the Cantera Cultural Centre, Estepona, Spain, designed by David Chipperfield Architects.

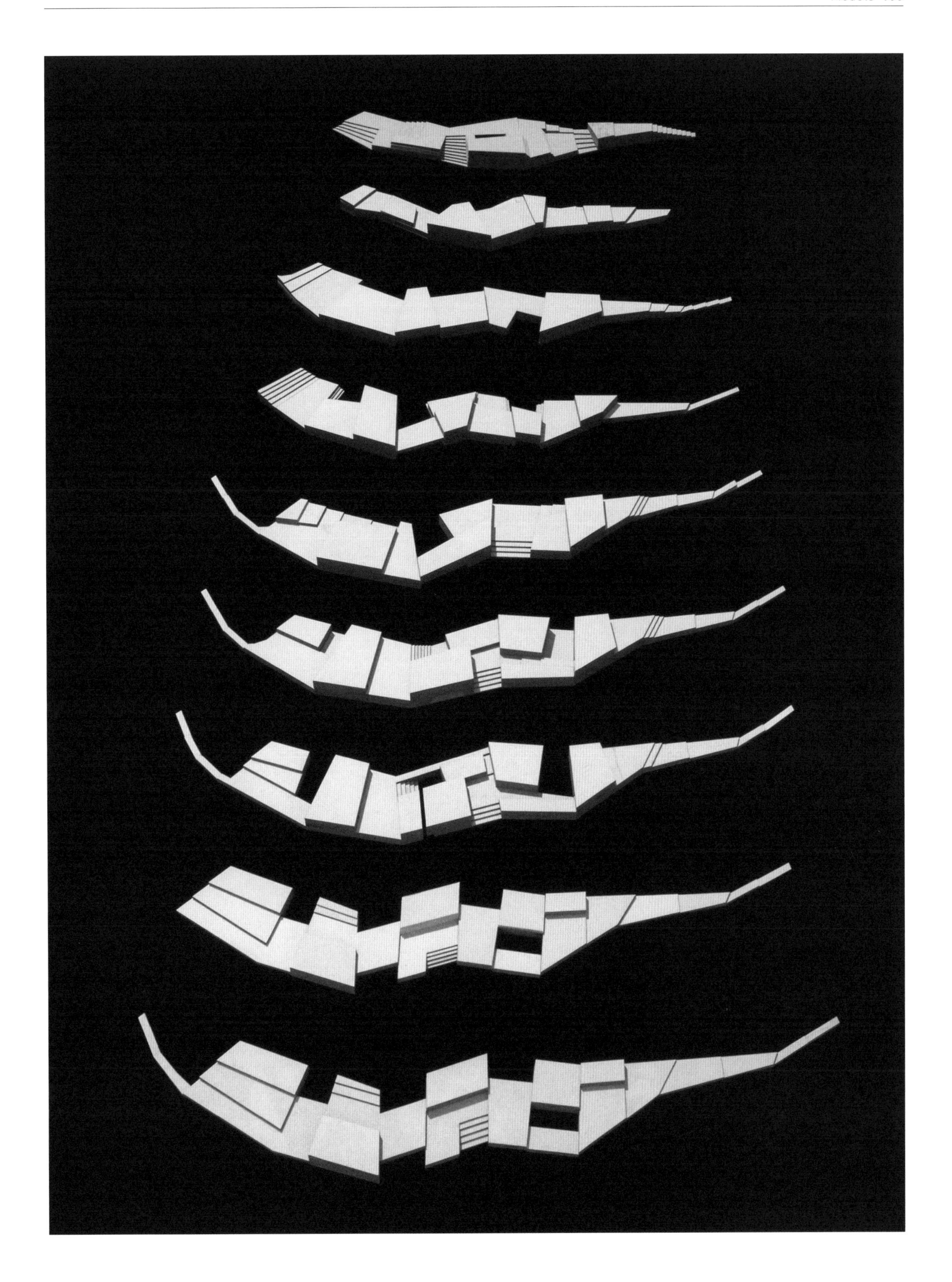

Below
Urban massing can be abstracted to its fundamental elements to provide a core analysis of an urban environment.

Below right
A model for a research project focusing on Groningen, the Netherlands, illustrates the parametric transformation of inner-city, ground-level courtyard blocks into a tower.

Abstract models

Abstract models can be useful to explain the concept for a city or masterplan. These models may convey notions of form, space, mass or material. As with an abstract drawing, the intention is to suggest an idea rather than to determine it. Elements of the model can be exaggerated to communicate the strength or essence of the idea.

The model may be ambiguous and exist almost as a painting, with three-dimensional elements. There may be use of collage to suggest ideas of layering, or the model itself may be pulled apart to reveal a certain aspect of the proposal. An abstract or conceptual model of a complex urban idea is very helpful at the early stages of design to concentrate the idea into a simple form. It can be an important tool as the scheme develops to ensure that the original design intention is not lost.

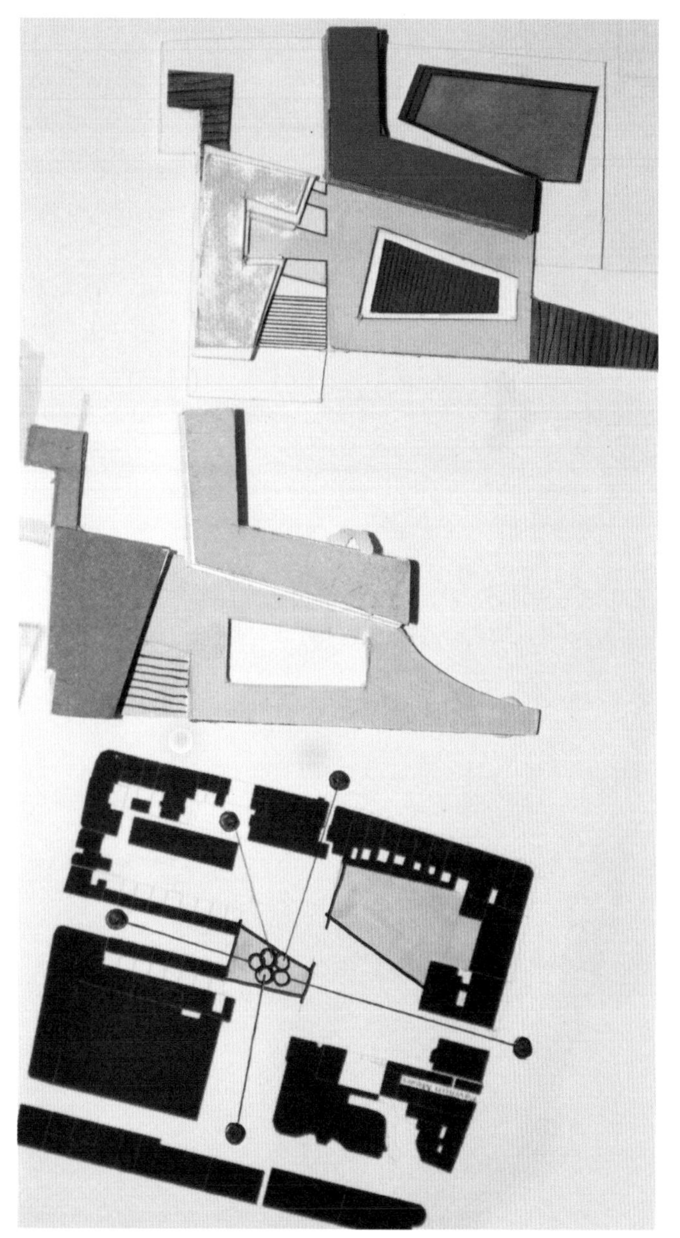

This page
This model series uses abstracts of particular elements from the environment for analysis.

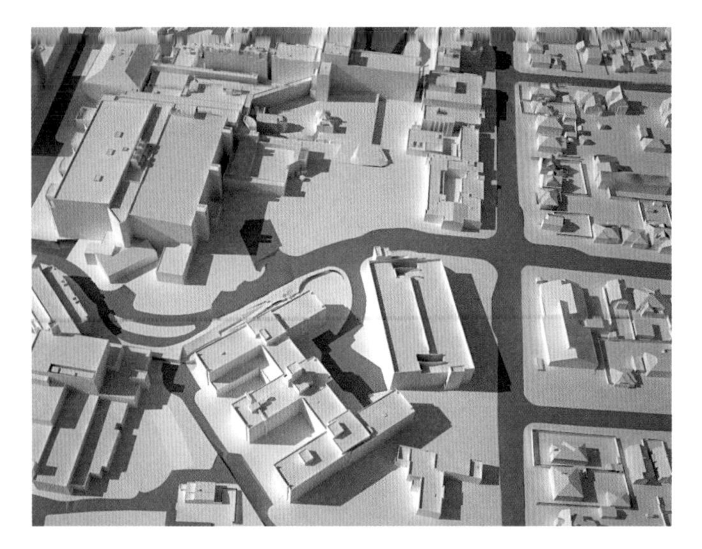

This CAD model of Vancouver, produced by City Vision Network, is sufficiently detailed to allow the viewer to read the roof profiles of the buildings. The model also allows for a realistic visualization of the shadows thrown by the buildings at any given time of day or year, an invaluable tool for studying the impact of a new development.

CAD modelling

Contemporary CAD software enables models to be made by transferring digital files to modelmaking machines at a variety of scales. There is also software that enables visualization, so existing and proposed urban landscapes can be better understood. Virtual-reality environments can simulate real spaces to allow exploration of the city.

The CAD model gives a different impression from the physical model. It can cover an enormous physical area and it can be viewed at a range of scales, from street level to a bird's-eye view of the whole cityscape. It needs to be used at every stage of the design process. Initially a digital map or a Google Earth view can be employed to create a massing model. This can then be used to test a range of different ideas. The best use of CAD models is in parallel with physical models and other drawings: they have enormous possibilities, but also limitations.

A physical model can have CAD images superimposed and vice versa. There are advantages to use every possible sort of visual representation to explore ideas. As the scheme develops, the CAD model can reflect the changing design and forms can be moved quickly from one piece of software to another.

There are specialist rendering pieces of software that can be used effectively to enhance particular views and create impressive visualizations. The CAD model has made it possible to design imaginary spaces that are incredible and fantastical. It has moved from being the tool responding to the idea to allowing designers to think in a much more creative and dynamic way, composing urban landscapes that are sculptural and playful. The city of the future is being presented to us as an exciting new world.

TIP CAD MASSING MODELS

Simple CAD massing models can be developed over time into final presentation drawings. It is important to select the perspective wisely to give the image the most impact.

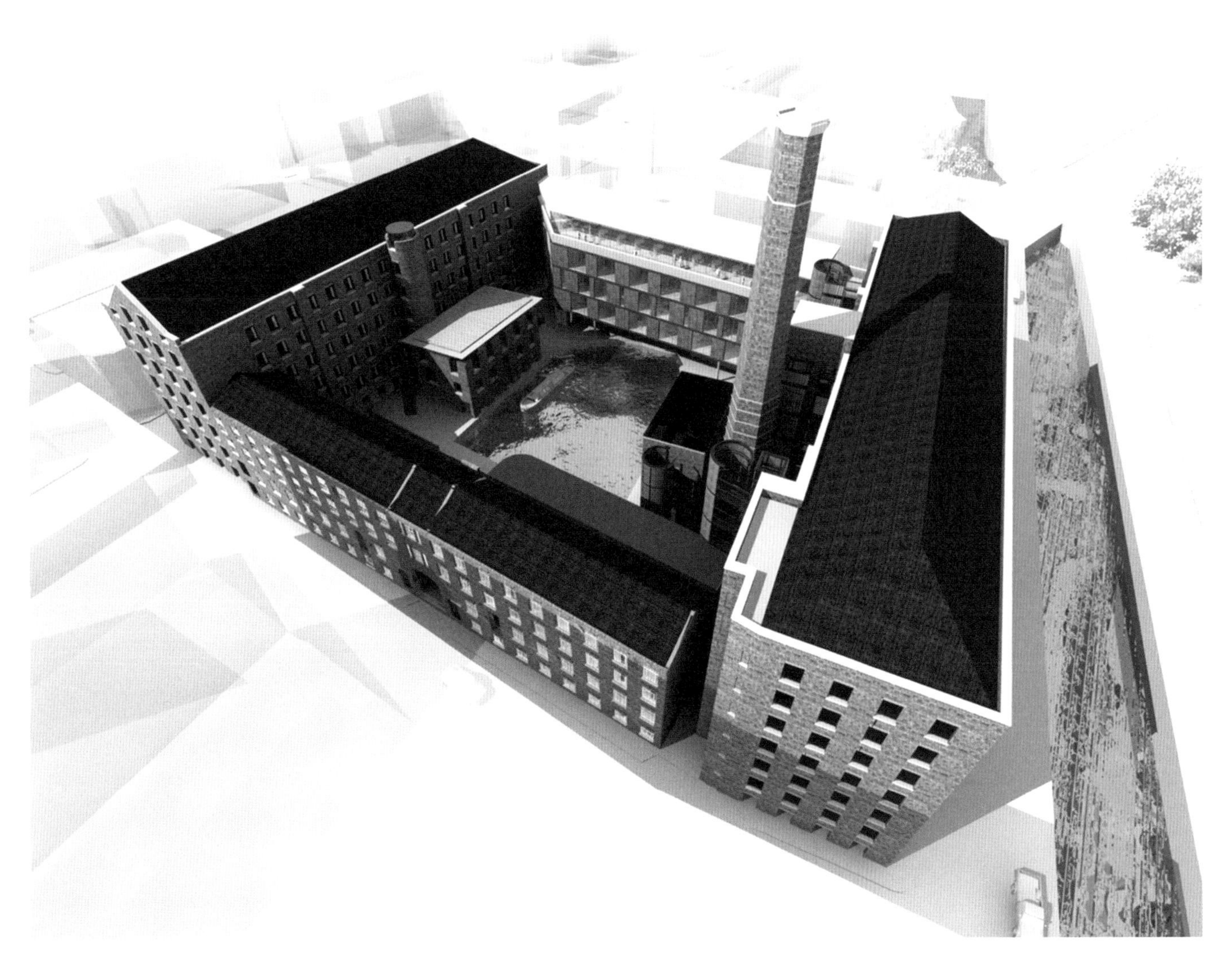

This aerial view of a proposal for Ancoats Village, Manchester, by Richard Murphy Architects demonstrates how, with computer modelling, it is possible to have very tight control over the level of detail applied to a project in contrast to the contextual urban massing.

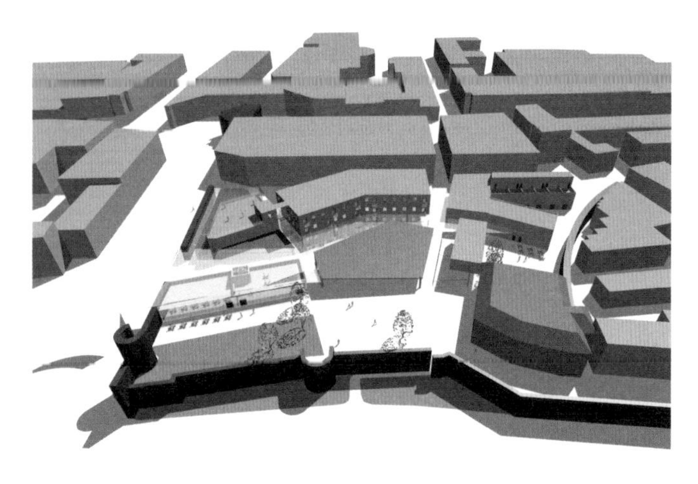

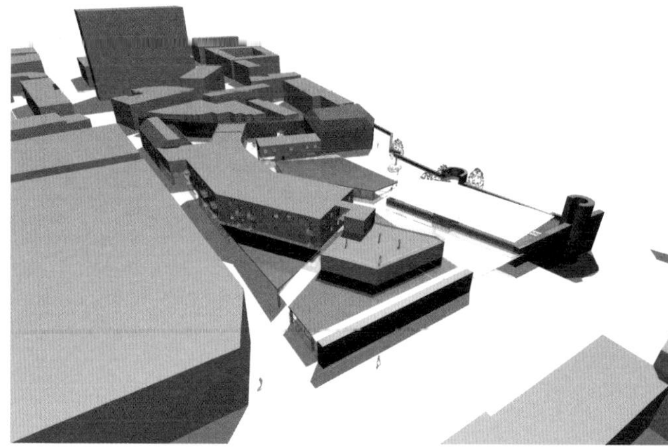

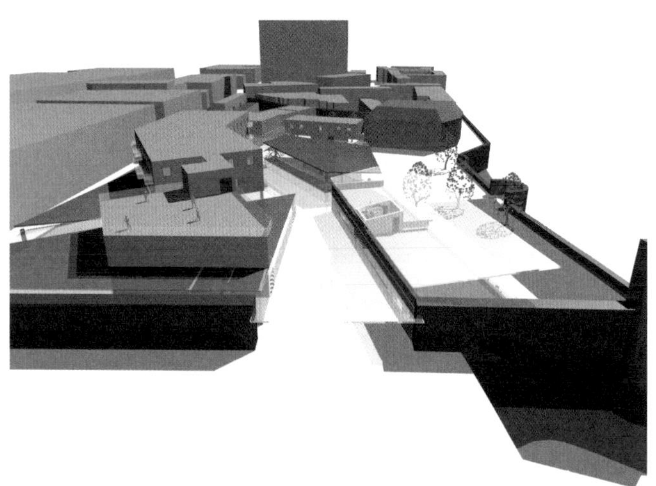

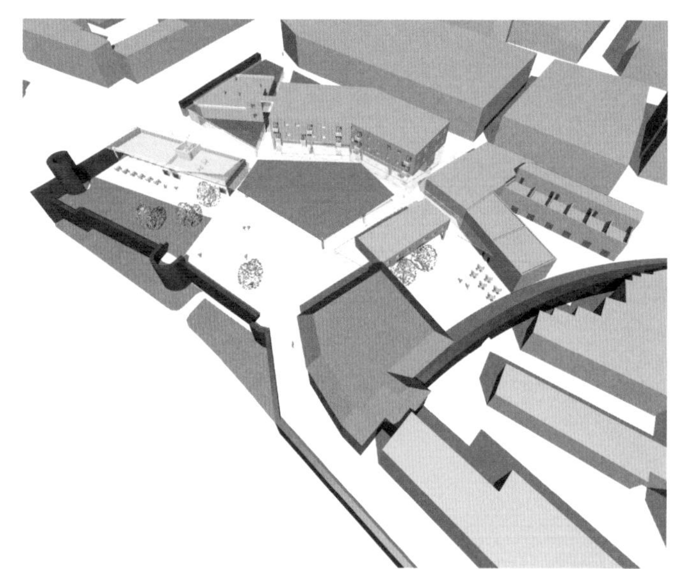

Above
CAD can be used to model the massing of an urban environment. The model can be viewed and recorded from many different angles.

Opposite
In this series of images, CAD software was used to elaborate dynamic visualizations of a proposed scheme for a competition. Rendering software packages are available that can make a proposal look more realistic or more dynamic.

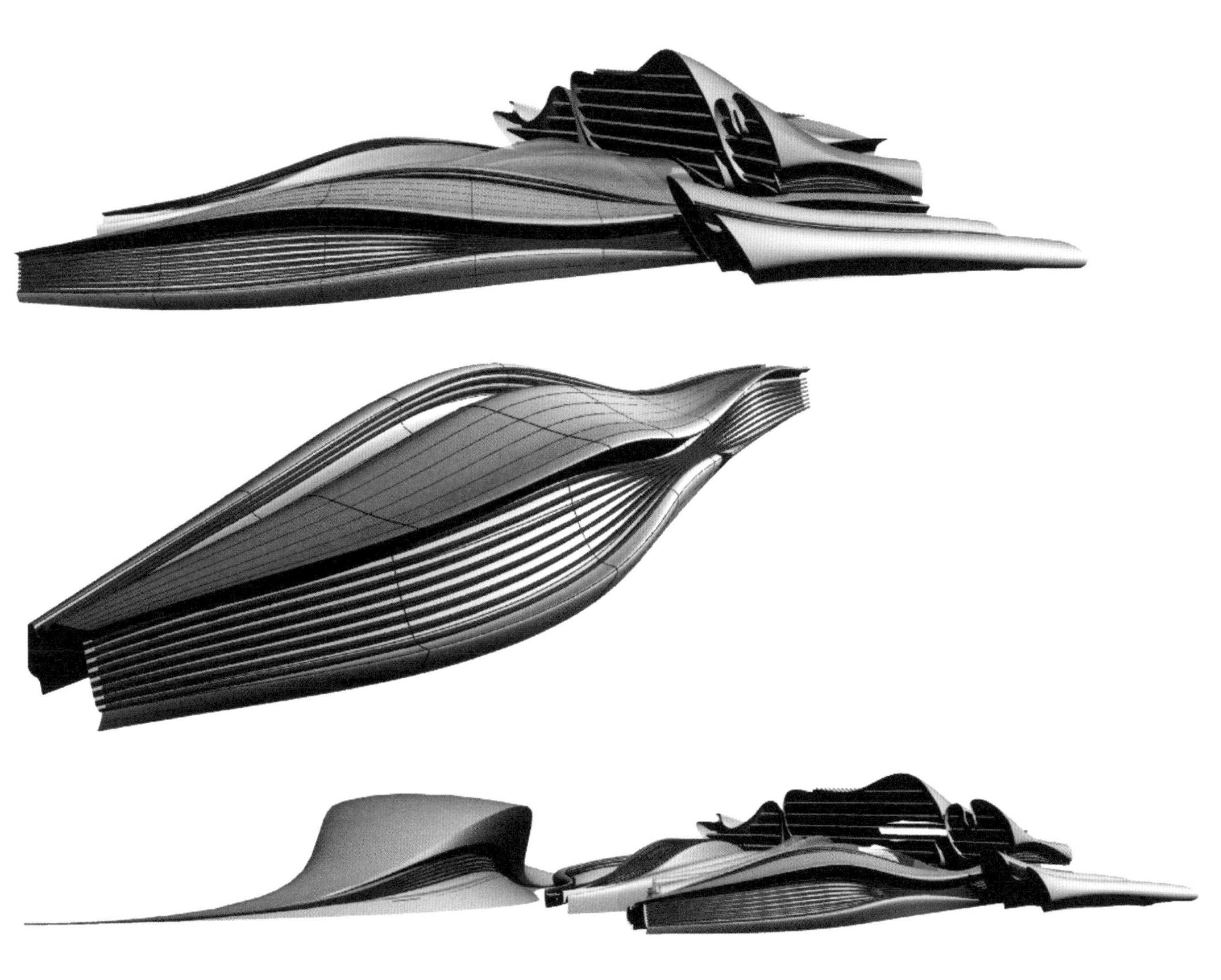

THE CITY IMAGINED

The image of the city

TIP CLARITY

Less is more. Think about how to prioritize the images on the page. Which image do you want to be in focus? Cluttered presentation boards can detract from the power of the design and the quality of the drawings.

Designing cities requires different stages of thinking and a range of communication and representation skills. The city imagined concentrates on the representation tools needed to explain new interpretations of the city. These include design drawings, concept sketches and models, both physical and computer-based.

The new city needs to be imagined as an exciting place of possibilities. The range of images needs to suggest new building forms, inspiring new spaces, and a future that is innovative and stimulating. Drawings and models need to be carefully planned and executed to convince an audience of the possibility of a new world of experience and architecture. New urban environments require a great deal of financial investment: the vision must be articulated so investors are persuaded to engage with the potential of the project.

The presentation needs to be accessible at many levels, with the initial concept connecting to existing contexts, simplifying complex social, physical and ideological ideas. Physical models are important to communicate ideas about cities as they are the most easily understandable three-dimensional medium of communication. The most dramatic developments in CAD modelling make possible an impressive movie-like experience that blurs the boundaries between reality and

The details used in this black-and-white perspective image give it a realistic feel. The view through the trees, the use of figures to give a sense of scale and the reflection of the buildings on the water suggest the proposed scheme is a 'real' place in the city.

This dynamic visualization is animated by the introduction of people and realistic lighting.

fiction. This might include images that appear 'virtually' real, fly-through models that allow a surreal experience of the city.

A vision of the city is the key ingredient in a presentation drawing. There can be an ambiguity between the idea of the drawing as a piece of art in itself and the fact that it is a tool used to promote a project. There are artist–architects who suggest the vision for the city through painting and drawing. These images are extremely important. Unless we can imagine and dream about the possibility of a new city, we will never make it a reality.

Presentation drawing

The presentation portfolio is a prepared set of images that may include one key drawing, but will also have within it a range of complementary drawings that may describe concept, idea, process of thinking, details and materials.

Careful consideration must be given to the intention of the presentation. Urban design schemes may need to communicate complex issues that explain social, economic or cultural conditions.

The main urban idea may involve various contributors. A masterplan may be initiated by one architect or designer and other sections of a scheme may be subject to a competition, or other architects and designers may be involved. This section explores how pieces of the masterplan can then evolve to support the main framework for the city.

The final stage of the process requires presentation drawings. These may include illustrations that can inform the wider public, so the vision is accessible. Images such as set perspective views, bird's-eye views or a series of connected images along an important route can explain a scheme clearly.

Perspective drawings and photomontage may be required: a new urban environment needs to be projected, to be advertised and understood to promote interest and investment. Photomontage images that create a suggested reality are important for this, as are collage images that present perspective views and interpretations of the city environment and streetscape.

A location map or diagram is important. This may be to scale or abstract but it should allow easy orientation. A more detailed map or plan may be part of the description of the site or project.

The organization of images needs careful consideration; there may be drawings at several scales to present a complex idea. Each presentation requires detailed thought. Planning a set of drawings should begin with sketches or scaled-down versions of the final images. Then the layout needs to explain the potential of the idea.

It is important to identify the audience for the presentation, to understand how they will read the project. A scheme may be intended to stimulate public interest and ideas. Or it may be for decision makers, planners and investors and need to be more specific in terms of defined project areas and possibilities.

A scheme can be communicated with a PowerPoint presentation, which is a useful way to order information and to tell the story of a project. However, this should be incorporated with other media, including maps to locate the scheme and contextualize it, physical models to allow a clear three-dimensional representation of the idea, and perspective or other drawings that suggest a more personal interpretation of a view, activity or experience.

Left
In this image of a project in Berlin by gmp architects, line and tone are used to communicate ideas about the scheme's physical structure and the quality of light.

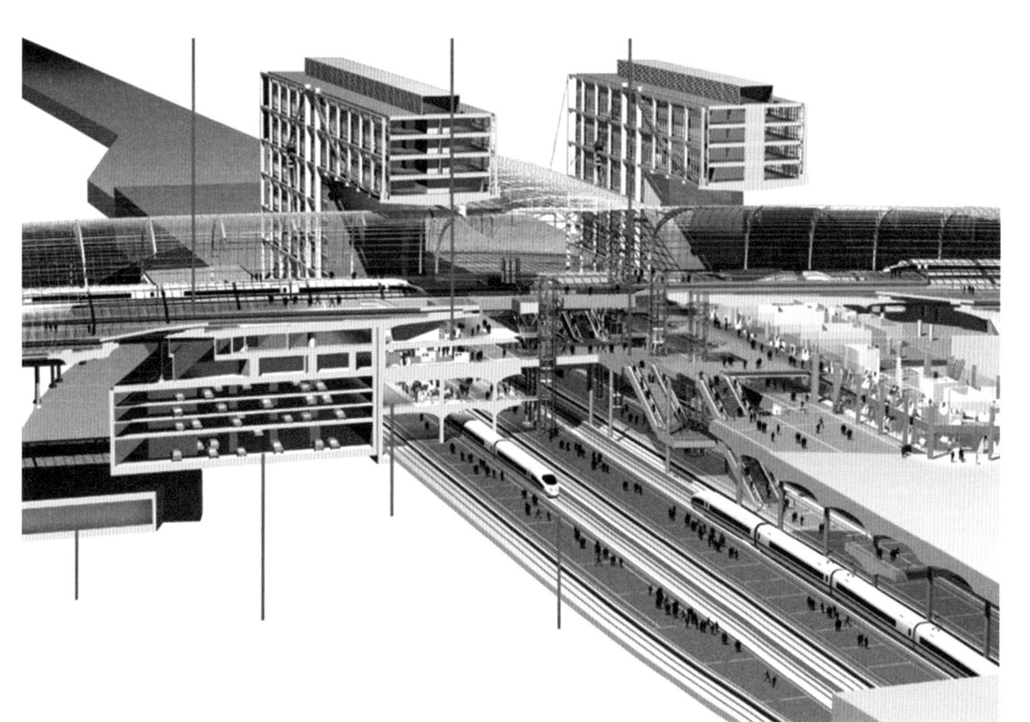

Above
This computer-generated perspective was created by S333 and Balmori Associates as part of the Pennine Lancashire Squared public space competition, and uses digital images of existing elements and CAD visualizations to create a hybrid drawing for the proposed scheme.

Left
This cutaway axonometric of a scheme in Berlin by gmp architects (also shown opposite) efficiently conveys a large amount of information in one drawing.

TIP FONT

It is important to choose a suitable font when laying out your presentation boards. What does a font (classical or modern) say about your design? Look at advertisements and design magazines for inspiration.

Above
This subtle image uses varying opacities to emphasize the main features of the scheme.

Opposite
A sketch section through a proposed residential scheme in Stead Street, London, by Panter Hudspith architects gives a sense of scale and of the intended activity within the scheme, bringing the proposal to life.

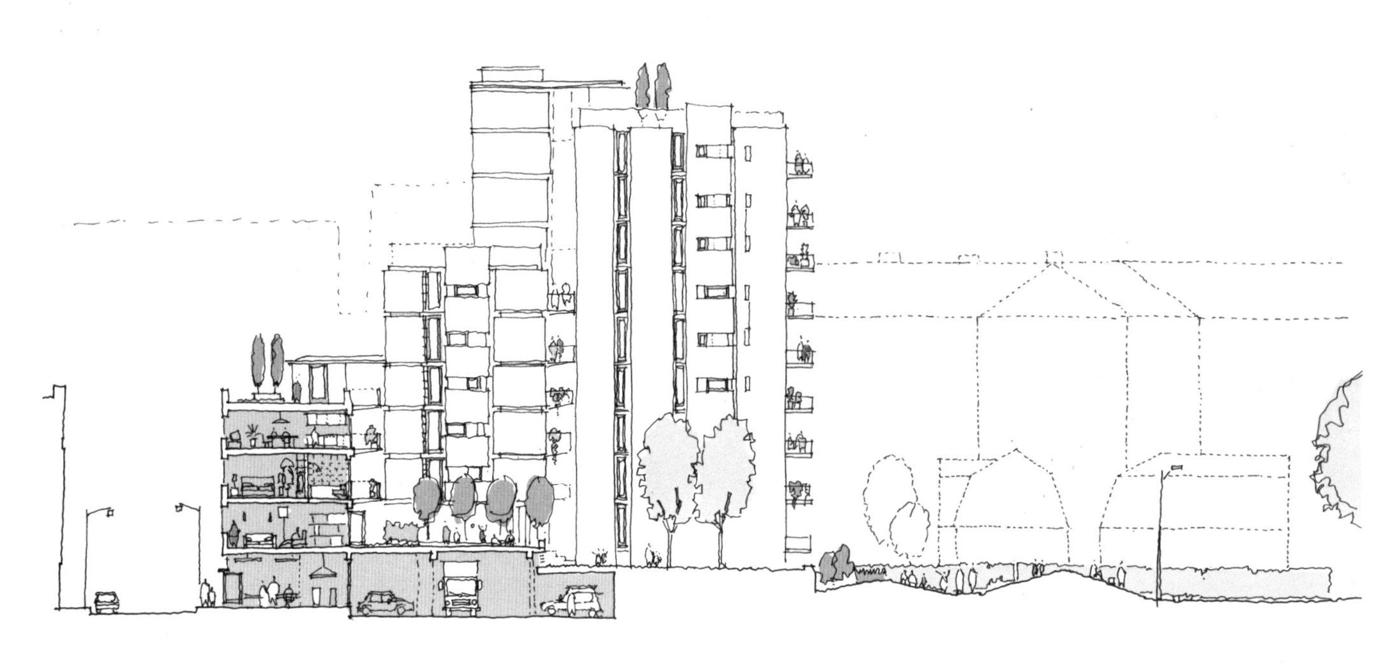

Abstraction

When describing the city, initial ideas may be abstract rather than connected to real impressions or physical dimensions. The city can be interpreted metaphorically: as a tree, as a house with many rooms, as a machine – all of these ideas connect the city to theoretical schemes developed by architects and urban designers.

Abstract ideas can stimulate a new view of what the city could be. Many painters have described their impression of a city or place in terms of emotion, atmosphere or experience. The abstraction may be a conceptual diagram that engenders an understanding of an initial idea. It may be a painting that is used to suggest an impression of a place. Or it could be a physical model that communicates an idea associated with the concept or interpretation of the place.

A city is an environment that is experienced, and sensory description can provide a new set of ways to understand and interpret it. This could be an evocation of movement through a city; it could be an impression of sound, or the use of colour, or scenes from a film or theatrical interpretation of a situation or experience within a place. Each method of communication is valid. An abstraction of an experience can be an exciting way to explain a place creatively.

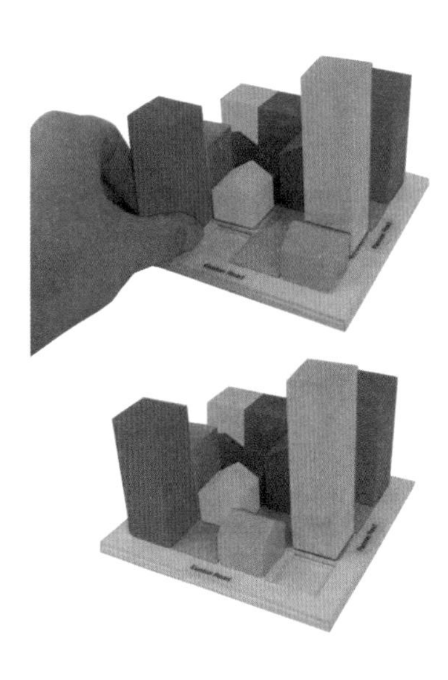

Left and far left
Home Town, one of a series of postcard proposals for urban regeneration by Metropolitan Workshop.

Right
Allies and Morrison's proposal for the Silver Hill urban regeneration scheme in Winchester uses an abstract massing model to pinpoint the proposed development site (bottom centre of the image) within the surrounding context.

Below
Bloomtown, another of the postcard proposals for urban regeneration by Metropolitan Workshop.

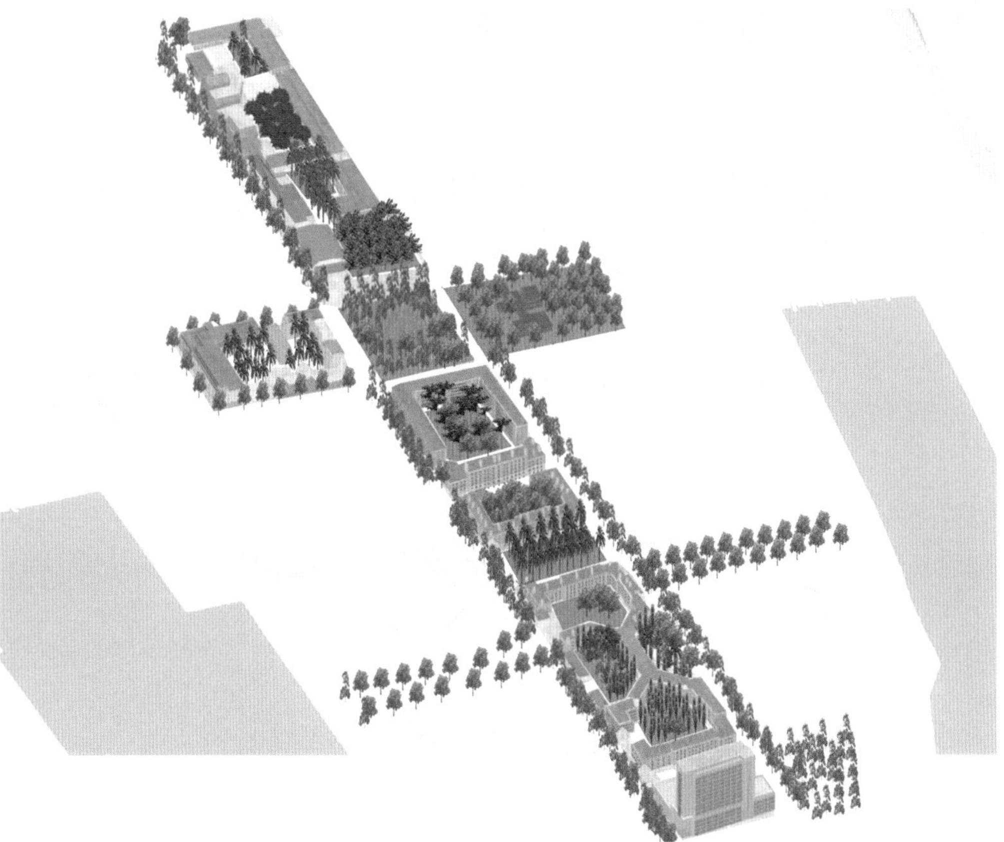

Collage and photomontage

Collage techniques are a useful way to represent a city. Layering a drawing to explore a final concept or to suggest a street scene or activity can be highly effective.

Collage began as a technique that involved literally cutting out images and layering them on top of one another. It derives from the French term *coller,* to glue or stick. Artists who used collage initially cut images from newspapers and other media and created new interpretations of everyday scenes. It is now possible to do this using various pieces of software, meaning that a site can be photographed and an image that has been created in another piece of software can be overlaid on it, or a digital image of a model of a scheme or proposal can be inserted to give a photorealistic impression of an idea.

Photomontage can be used to combine a photograph of a site with a proposed scheme using a digital image or a photograph of a physical model integrated into the final image. This technique can make a street-scene or perspective image of a proposal look more life-like.

This type of image is essential to allow an understanding of how the spaces in the street will be occupied. It conveys the context of a scheme and how the design relates to that context in terms of mass, scale, material and form.

Collage is an essential way to describe a proposal for a city and can create a convincing impression of an idea.

A series of images was used to illustrate this perspective view of a waterside project. The final image was created in Photoshop, and incorporates photographs of the existing area, a three-dimensional CAD model of the proposed idea and figures to indicate scale.

Left
Various textures are used in both the foreground and background of this image to bring a sense of realism to the composition.

Below
This visualization by Niall Bird of a proposal for the regeneration of Hilsea Lido has been composed as a series of slices. The image incorporates layered photographs, some computer-generated concepts, and figures and balloons to suggest activity.

CAD images and modelling

Below
This visual by Imaging Atelier of the James Simon Gallery to be built in Berlin by David Chipperfield Architects shows the connection between the gallery and its immediate urban context.

Digital cities can be built using digital mapping techniques which allow a city to be explored three-dimensionally, at street level, or at bird's-eye level or any point between.

Software used by designers, urban designers and architects to represent cities and buildings varies considerably in price. Some software interfaces with digital maps are available online. These maps can be imported into various software packages and then used as a base for a drawing or computer modelling.

Various software packages can be used to create three-dimensional environments that can be experienced as fly-through sequences or films. These allow the city environment to be represented as it exists and for proposals to be introduced into a model to understand the impact of a scheme or idea in terms of scale and form on its surroundings. For completely new urban projects, the CAD model can create a virtual environment that can be interrogated at street level or from above.

Opposite, top
A digitally rendered visual by Imaging Atelier shows a view looking downriver towards the James Simon Gallery by David Chipperfield Architects.

Opposite, bottom
Imaging Atelier's digital image of the scheme for the Turner Contemporary visual arts centre in Margate, England, by David Chipperfield Architects.

The digital mapping of cities has been transformed by Google Earth software. This software creates an interactive map of the earth from aerial photography, geographic information system (GIS) data and satellite imagery. It allows reproduction at various scales and can be used to create perspective views. This tool can be employed with other pieces of software to superimpose possible schemes, either as two-dimensional plans or in three dimensions to create block models over the existing map information.

GIS software is used to handle urban information and can simulate a variety of propositions. It can create data models of the city. These are not physical models, but abstractions of the real world using a set of data objects to support various analyses.

SketchUp software can be used in parallel with Google Earth. It is a three-dimensional modelling tool and can be used to create a massing model of a site or proposal.

CityCAD allows a quick sketch or diagram to be developed into a three-dimensional CAD model, identifying building types, massing and landscape. Streetscape, by the same company, is a street design tool that allows the user to make a section of a street as well as aiding an understanding of the impact of parking spaces, the height/width ratio in the street, and potential areas of shadow. It also interfaces with other software so that drawing files can be moved into the programme and developed specifically to consider the consequences of an idea on the streetscape.

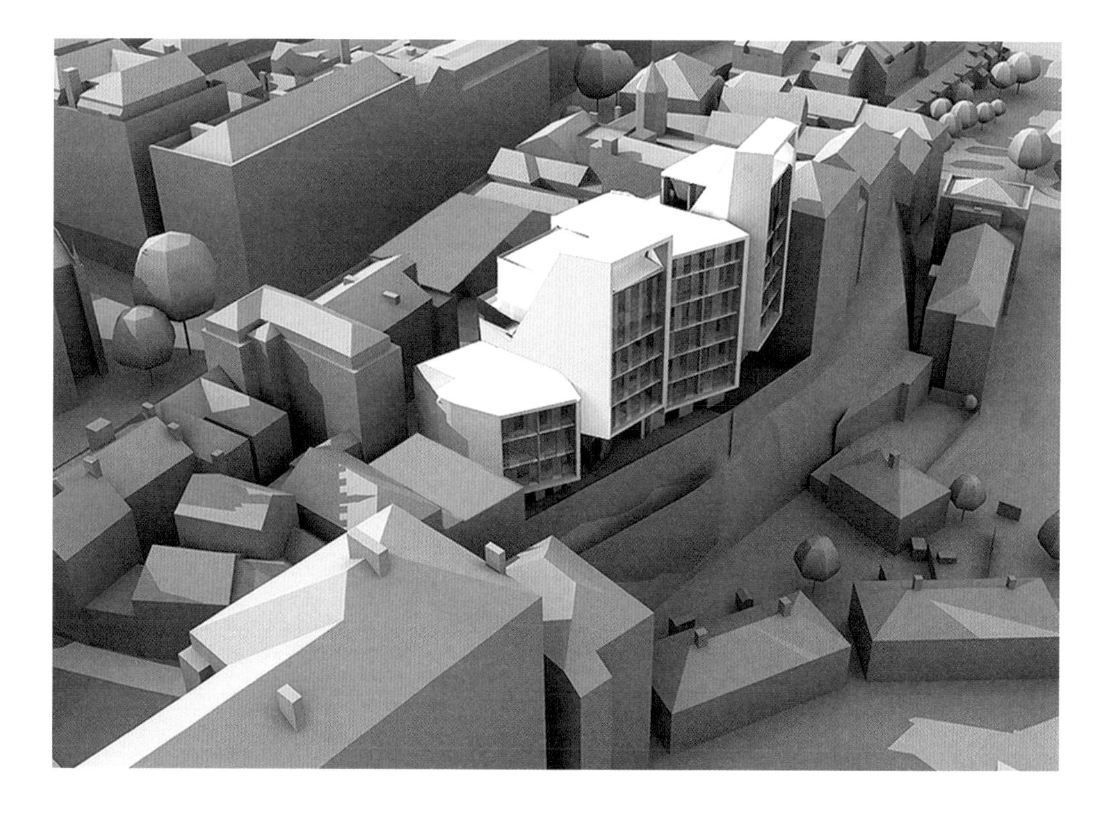

For the Short Hill housing development in the historic Lace Market area of Nottingham, Re-Format architects created this three-dimensional CAD massing model. The proposed housing development is highlighted in white, while the surrounding context is coloured grey.

A digital city model of Southampton created by City Vision Networks Ltd. The image features a scheme by Patel Taylor architects (highlighted in white at the top right of the image).

Software packages such as AutoCAD and ArchiCAD can create two-dimensional drawings and three-dimensional models. They can be used to interface with mapping systems such as Google Earth which can create maps and plans to any scale.

Rendering packages are software programmes used to finish drawings and images, applying colour tone, texture and shadow to make a proposal or idea more realistic.

Rhino, by Autodesk, can create, edit, analyse, document, render and animate images and data. It also provides the tools to model and document designs accurately so that they are ready for rendering, animation, drafting, engineering, analysis, and manufacture or construction.

Maya, also by Autodesk, is a three-dimensional modelling, animation, visual effects and rendering software. It creates extremely photorealistic effects of texture, material and spatial impressions.

Adobe Illustrator manipulates digital images and is used for illustrations and layouts, producing well-organized and graphically impressive presentations using information from a range of media, drawings, photographs and maps.

Adobe makes a suite of integrated software products (Creative Suite) which includes Photoshop. This is a programme specifically designed for graphics editing. It is ideal for professional and amateur photographers and graphic designers, allowing images to be manipulated easily. It can be used for editing images to very high standards and importing them from other software platforms, incorporating special effects such as backgrounds and textures, for television and film, as well as two-dimensional images and presentations.

Space Syntax is a technique developed by Bill Hillier which is used in the analysis of buildings and cities. It is based on demonstrating the role of spatial layout in shaping patterns of human behaviour including pedestrian activity, shopping, residential experience and the working environment (for an illustration, see page 72).

A CAD model of Monaco by City Vision Networks. The model is interactive, allowing proposals to be inserted and viewed in a dynamic context.

STEP BY STEP ENHANCING A THREE-DIMENSIONAL MODEL

A three-dimensional CAD model of a city or building can start as a framework and then be developed graphically to suggest more detail. This can be done by introducing shadow, within the model, followed by texture and detail. The image can also be incorporated into a digital photograph of an existing background using Photoshop.

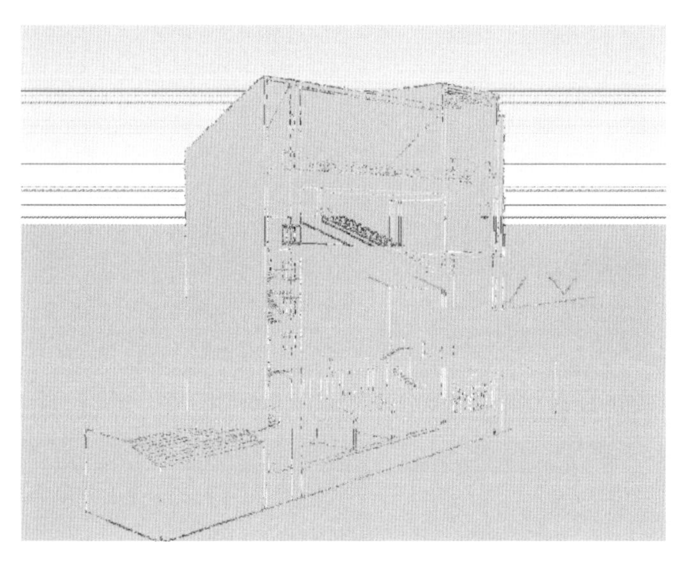

1 Create a model with your three-dimensional modelling software. In this example, SketchUp is used.

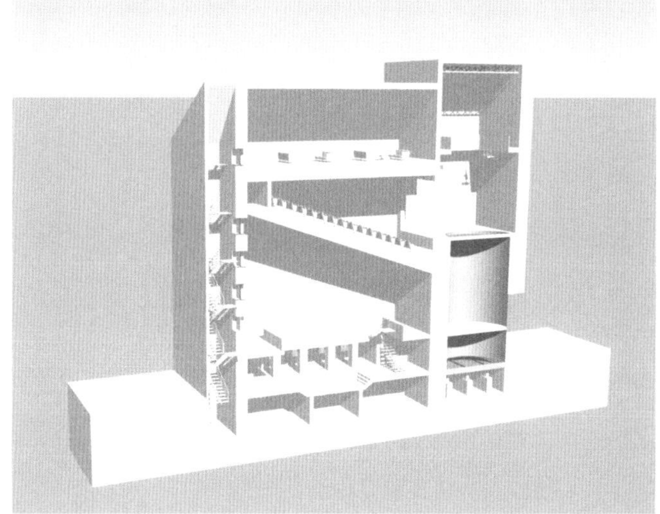

2 Turn off lines and cast shadow within your three-dimensional modelling software. This will give a clearer image to export into Photoshop for enhancing.

3 Export the model into Photoshop as a JPEG file. Add and skew textures in Photoshop. Finally, adjust the opacity of the textures and add gradient shadows to give a sense of depth to your image.

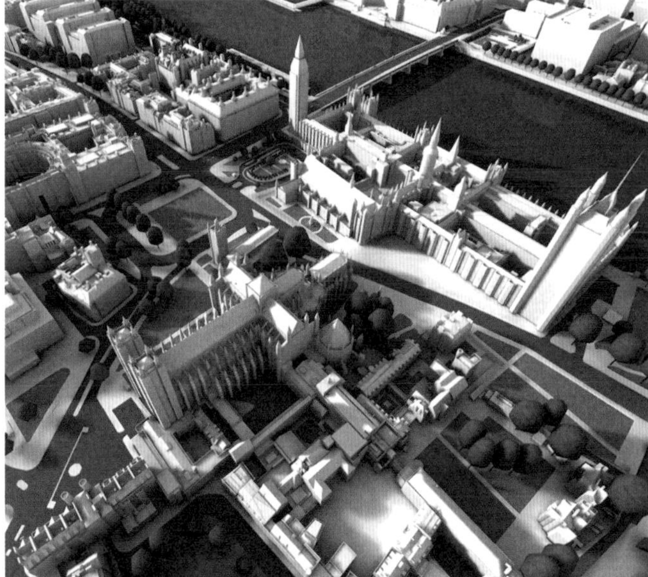

Above and opposite
The images on these pages show parts of a three-dimensional computer model of London, which was generated by Zmapping using specialist software. The model is interactive and proposed schemes can be placed within the model. Views can be generated from any level or height, so that, for example, the model can be seen as if from the air or at street level.

There are companies that create interactive three-dimensional models that can be used with a variety of software programmes to create simulated images of city environments. Zmapping is one such company, which creates computer model cityscapes in three dimensions, ranging from a small area to the whole city environment. The model can show geographical features such as the terrain or ground surface to give a detailed interpretation of a city. The model can then be used as a background against which to model possible design ideas, or to create an animated fly-through or perspective views. It allows the designer to test the impact of proposed buildings on an area, from the effects of massing and form to the way a building affects vistas along streets or an entire skyline.

The basic information is collected from aerial photographs, which are then used in association with ordnance survey maps to produce detailed models. This modelling technique can be used with various software programmes, including Maya, Vectorworks, AutoCAD, MicroStation, ArchiCAD and SketchUp.

There are also three-dimensional versions of the models, which are interactive and designed to allow the viewer to move through and around the modelled environment.

Physical modelling

Presentation models for urban design are important tools in the understanding and development of the city. Many cities have city models as exhibitions to encourage developers and investors to understand their vision of the city and its future development. The city models tend to be at a large scale: 1:1500 or 1:1000. They have interchangeable tiles that allow new ideas to be tested by developers and seen in the broader context of the city.

Models are created as part of the process of design of a city or urban environment. Large masterplanning projects may have models made that are used for exhibition, to display the overall idea of the scheme. This type of physical model may be large and needs to communicate powerfully the impact of the scheme or proposal on its context. These models may be designed to be viewed from a particular point, either from above or at eye level, to allow the viewer to read the urban idea in its entirety.

Models can be produced from digital files connected to physical modelling machines. Computer numerical control (CNC) milling machines will translate information from a CAD model into a physical model.

As part of a European City Studio study at the Portsmouth School of Architecture, this model of Rotterdam was evolved to show a range of proposals on a gridded site layout. The model was photographed in black and white to enhance contrast.

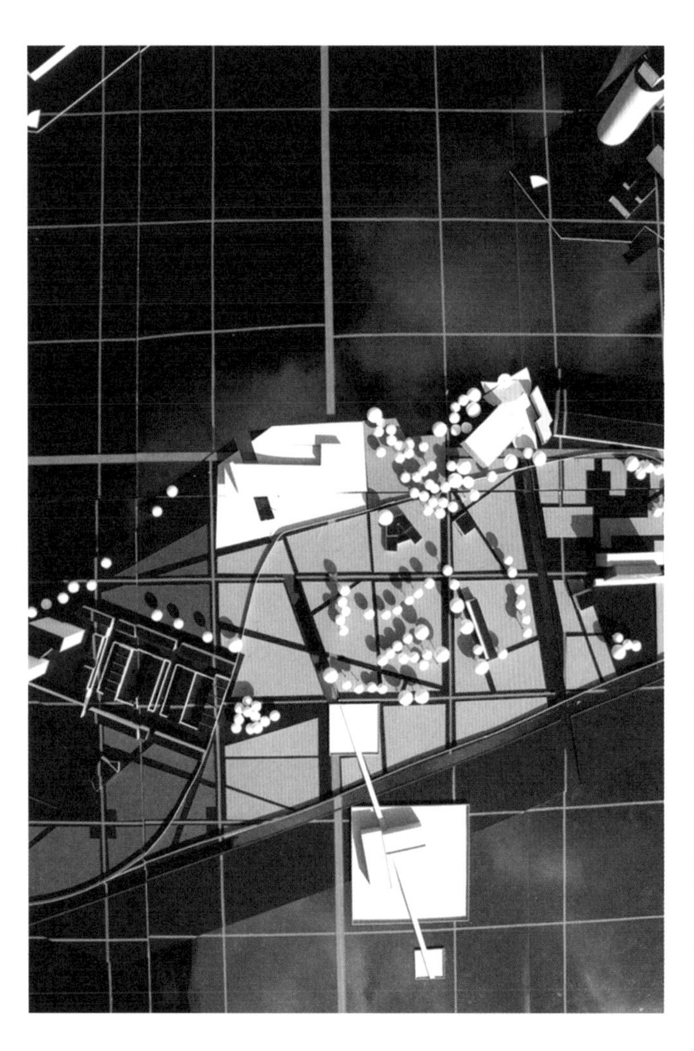

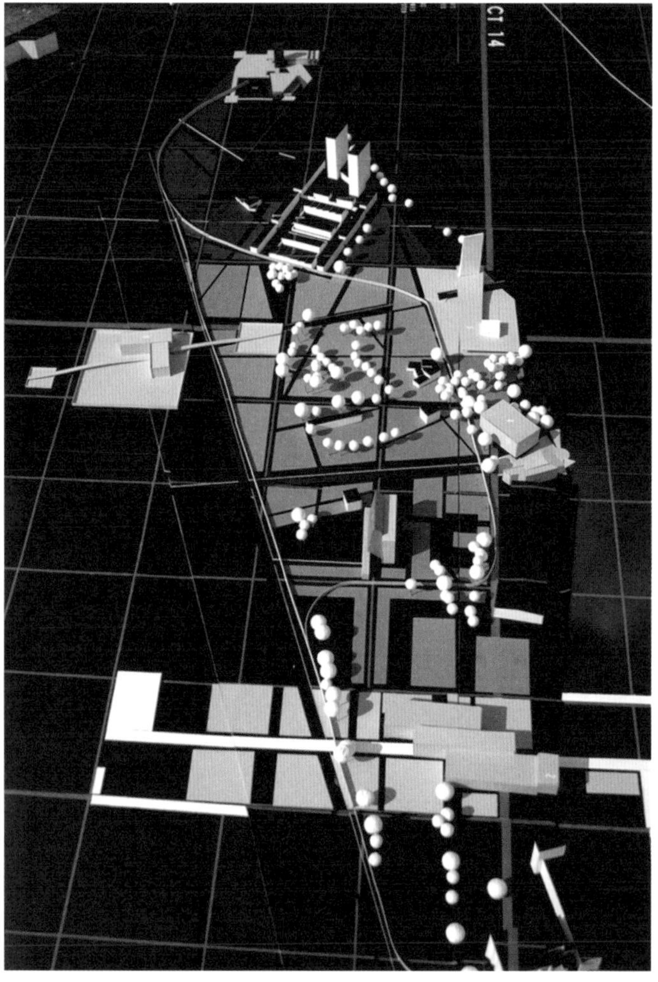

STEP BY STEP MAKING A PHYSICAL MODEL

Physical models can be made to scale or as abstract interpretations of a place. When making a scale model, the modelmaker will start with a map or plan of the site, which should suggest the topography or levels of the surface of the ground. This is a very good base on which to develop the detail of the model, and from this the modelmaker can introduce layers of buildings, spaces and places.

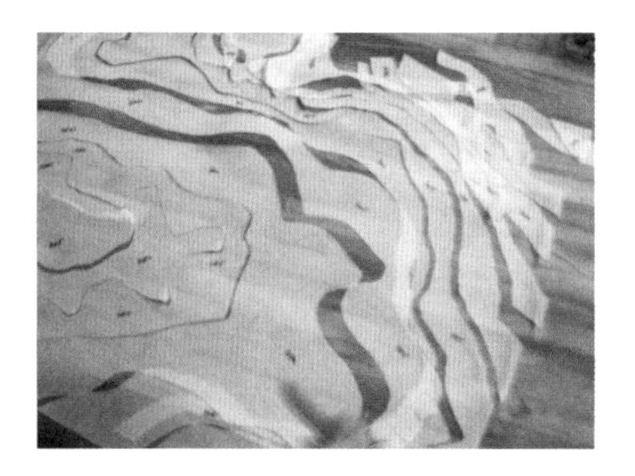

1 Trace the contours of a geographical map onto tracing paper. Cut out the pieces of tracing paper with scissors or a scalpel.

2 Put the trace on some cardboard sheets and cut around it so that you get a series of contours on card.

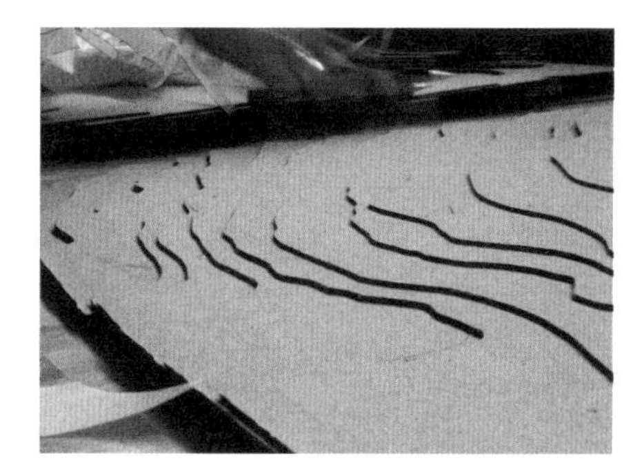

3 Start assembling the pieces of card. Each contour should be raised/lowered according to the original plan. You can create the required thickness underneath each specific piece by using left-over card pieces.

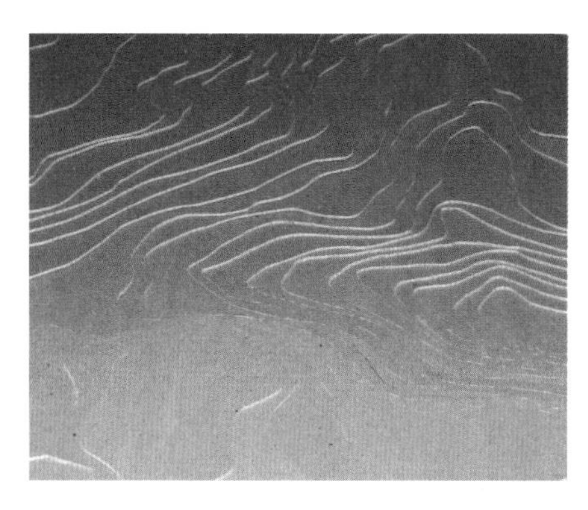

4 Your creation should start to resemble a three-dimensional geographical model, as illustrated here.

5 When the basic model is completed, add finishing touches. You might consider painting the model, or perhaps adding textures, or animating it with buildings or objects made to scale.

6 Finally, add a piece of Perspex (or similar transparent material) on top of your model, supported by bolts to separate it from the model. This will ensure that the model does not get damaged or dirty.

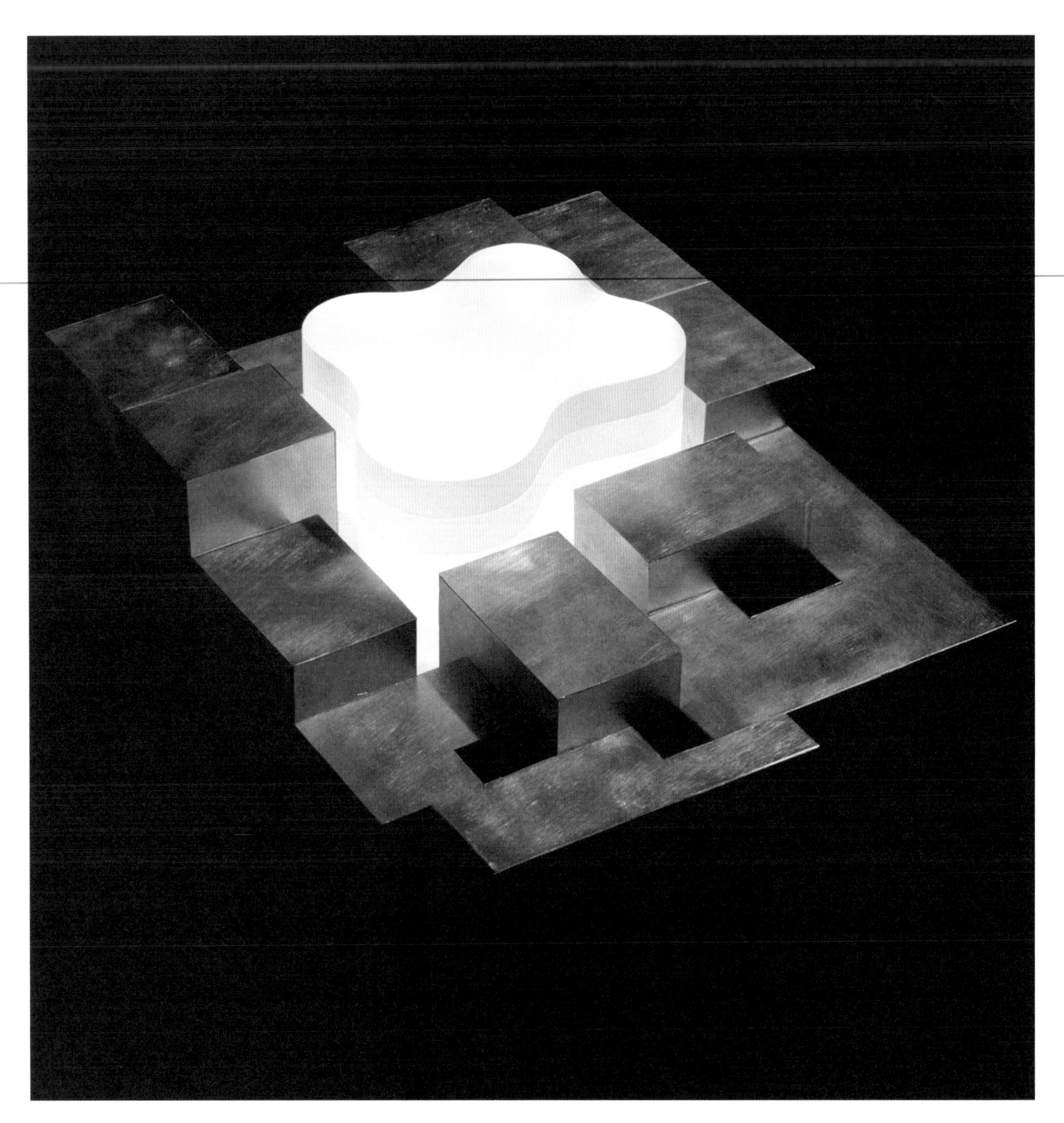

Above
This abstract model for the Ansaldo City of Cultures project in Milan by David Chipperfield Architects explains the concept for a proposal and uses contrasting materials to describe the idea. The central organic form is modelled in a light, translucent material, while the surrounding geometric elements are modelled using metal to exaggerate the contrast of the forms.

Opposite
This model of Rotterdam by the European City Studio could also be viewed as a type of map in relief. It describes a large part of the city and was made from a sheet of cork, which was carefully cut to reveal a black baseboard behind.

Laser-cutting machines can be used to cut large pieces of timber, acrylic or other board material.

One of the key features of these models is that they allow the whole context of the city to be understood: relationships of scale, massing and connection within and across the city can be easily grasped and help to inform the development of a scheme.

Alongside the physical model, many urban development centres have digital models that show design ideas as virtual experiences. Proposed schemes can be interfaced with these digital models to give an impression of a proposal. The physical and CAD models together provide a useful overview of the city.

Final presentation models of urban schemes must incorporate context. Some schemes may need to show the relationship across the whole city, as in the case of a masterplan involving transport infrastructure or topographical features. The city model can become an interpretation of landscape. At a map scale of 1:2500, say, there is very little definition of the built form.

As the model scale increases, so does the detail, affording the possibility to distinguish between features and form. The point and purpose of the model must be clearly defiined before construction begins.

A presentation model may use techniques to feature important aspects of the city. Lighting can be used effectively to highlight a specific site or key sites within an urban development.

MASTERPLANNING PROJECTS

Case study A new quarter for a historic city

David Chipperfield Architects, Art and Technology Quarter, Segovia, Spain

Total project area 120,000 m²

Client Ayuntamiento de Segovia

Design architect David Chipperfield Architects – Georges Batzios, Daniel Blum, David Chipperfield, Trent Davies, Eva Funke, Matthias Heberle, Andrew Phillips, Monica Resines, Peder Skavlan, Niko Wolfromm

Structural engineer Adams Kara Taylor

The masterplan of a new art and technology quarter in Segovia, Spain, comprises a congress centre, an art museum, a technology centre, a hotel, and business-incubator office buildings. It totals more than 120,000 square metres.

The old city of Segovia, surrounded by eighth-century walls, is a UNESCO World Heritage Site spectacularly situated north of Madrid and containing a wealth of monuments. The city has been proposed as the 2016 European Capital of Culture.

One kilometre from the city centre, with links to major road and high-speed train networks, the new quarter is inspired by the old city's walls, plaza, narrow irregular streets and castle, and reinvents a low and dense plan. A sequence of three plazas at the heart of the project establishes a common public identity and spine for the development. New civic buildings are cornerstones of the plan, each including a continuous shaded arcade overlooking the public space. The interiors will be protected from the fierce Castilian sun by shade-giving screen façades. The masterplan endorses continuity in urban approach, learning from the old city, while embracing the inevitable progress and development which will be demonstrated by the architecture of the new buildings.

The Mayor of Segovia commended the scheme in particular for its contribution of new public space to the city. Selected in an international competition, the jury remarked that the project 'shows a singular sensibility being integrated into the environment and the surroundings'.

The scheme originated with a concept sketch which described it as a dense urban block that appeared to have spaces cut into the block form. This was illustrated through various sketch designs. It was also physically modelled as a strong form. The concept built on an understanding of the main urban spaces in Segovia and comprises a series of interlinked spaces that connect the main activities of the project: the congress centre, hotel and technology units.

Located away from the centre of town, close to the new railway station with its fast service linking Segovia to Madrid, the project is intended to act as a catalyst to stimulate urban regeneration. The new masterplan is part of a much bigger strategy for the redevelopment of the adjacent area.

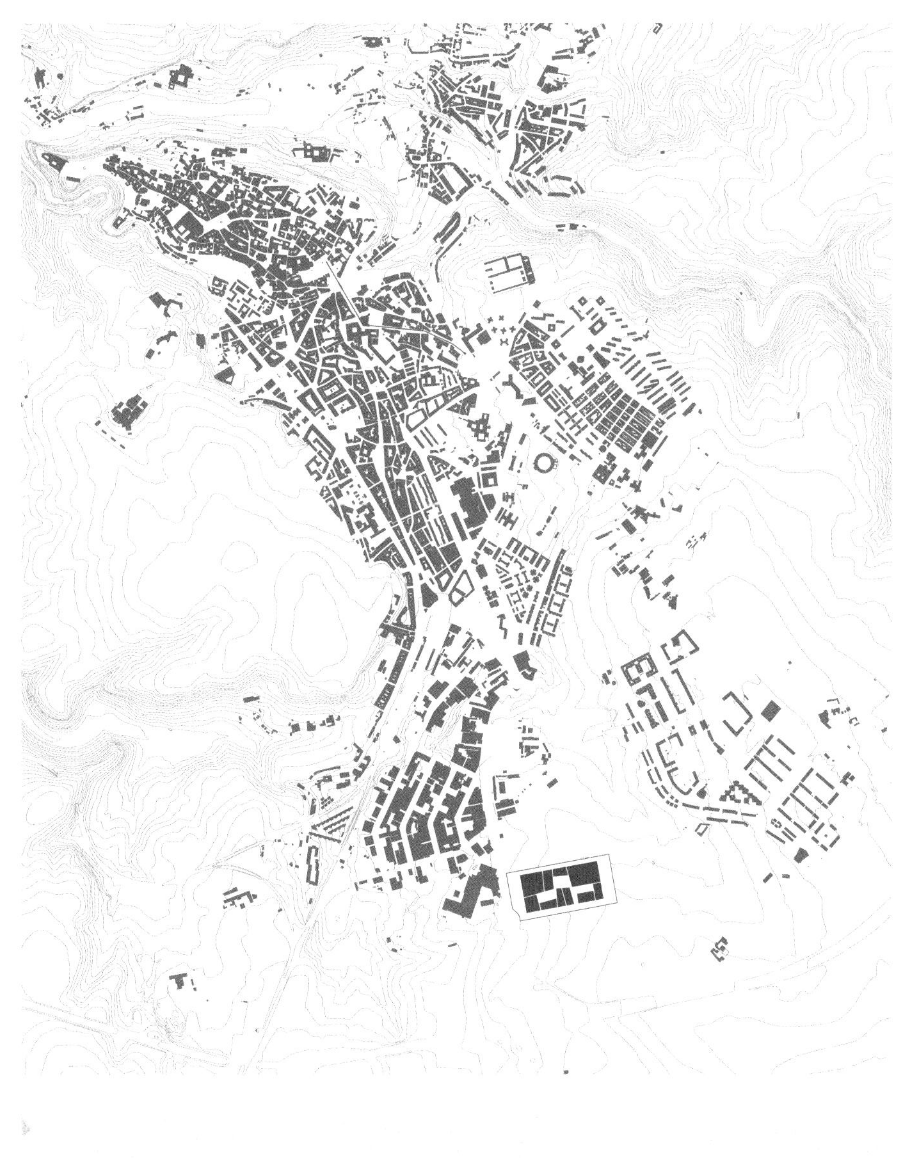

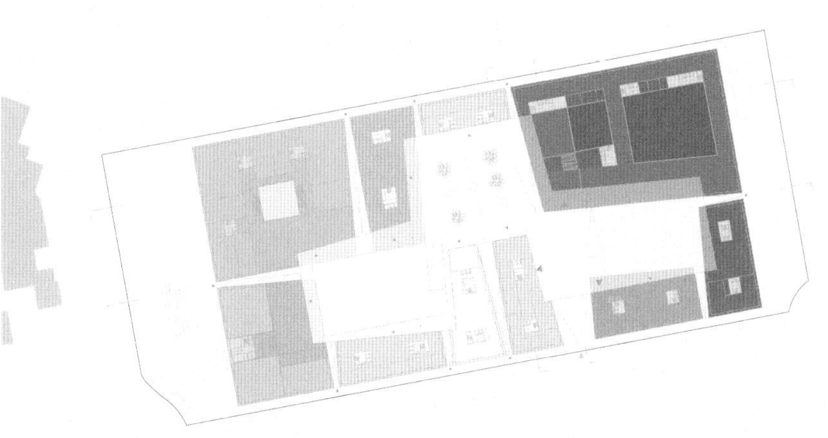

Opposite
A rendered perspective image of one of the three proposed courtyards in the masterplan scheme.

Left
A massing plan of Segovia – the rectangular masterplan of the new quarter can be seen at the bottom.

Centre
Site plan of the scheme. Colours are used to indicate different uses within the proposal, while courtyards are shown as white.

Bottom
Elevation of the masterplan. The mass and position of the buildings respond to the sloping topography of the existing site.

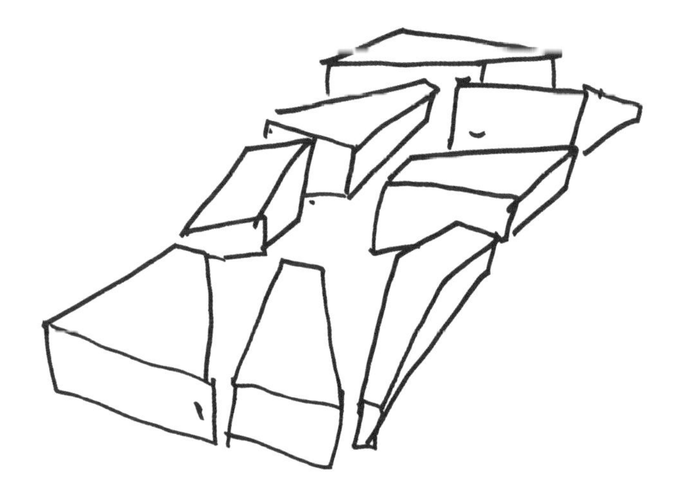

Left
A simple sketch describing the concept behind the masterplan.

Below
An overhead view of a massing model shows the three linked courtyard spaces.

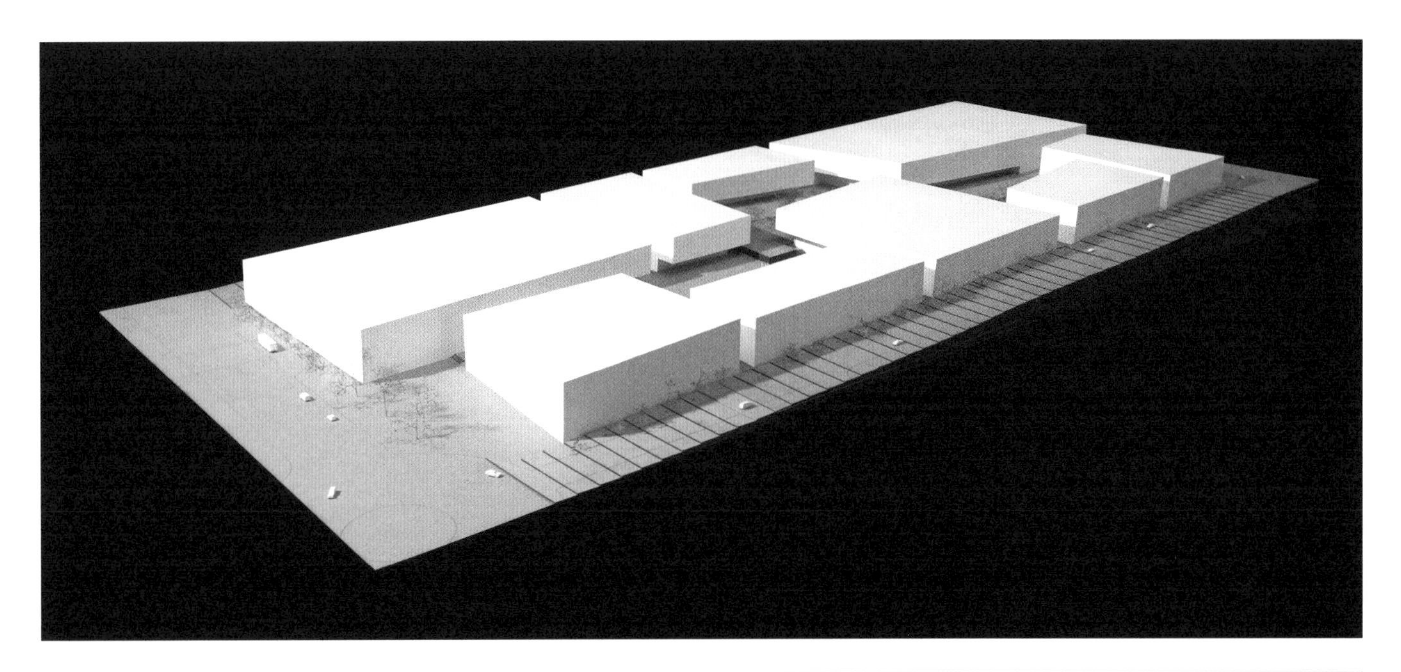

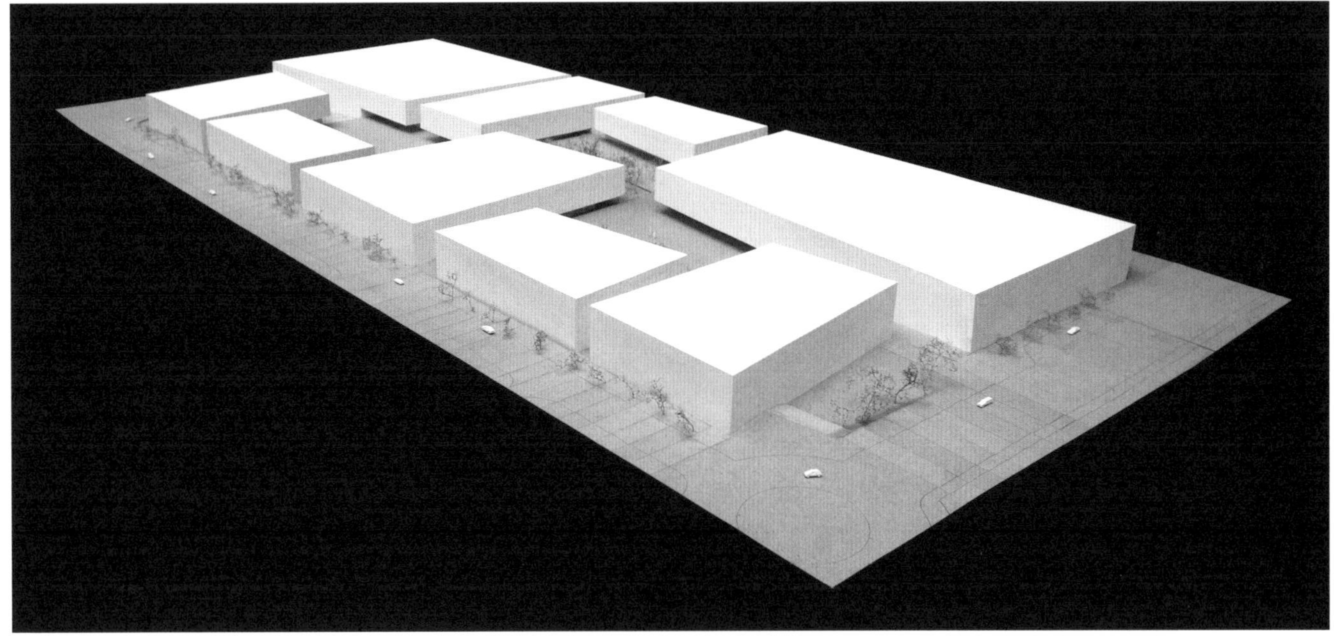

Top
View of the massing model showing the public space to be created at the entrance to the scheme (bottom left of image).

Above
The massing model seen from the opposite angle.

Case study The city of the future

MVRDV, Vision 2030, Almere, The Netherlands

Client City of Almere

Architect MVRDV

The Dutch are experts at reclaiming land from the sea, which brings with it the potential for new cities. One of these, Almere, founded in 1984, is set to become the fifth largest city in The Netherlands. MVRDV are masterplanners for Vision 2030, a project that comprises all of Almere, as well as future development in surrounding areas, and incorporates OlympiaKwartier, a dense urban district masterplanned by Mecanoo architects in 2007. MVRDV's Jacob van Rijs has also been working on part of the OlympiaKwartier – which will incorporate a total of 220,000m² mixed-use development with public facilities – since 2008. Half of the buildings in MVRDV's part of the OlympiaKwartier development will be designed by 24 different architecture practices from Europe, Japan and the United States, with each selected office designing two different buildings ranging from 500m² to 5,000m². The remaining half will be designed by MVRDV. The selection of architects consists of a varied group of offices, from young and conceptual practices to more established classic architects, intended to create true variety. The projects will be realized by experienced construction companies under the direction of MVRDV and Stadgenoot, the joint client to the architects.

By 2030, Almere expects to grow into a city with a stronger identity and a total of 350,000 inhabitants, which necessitates the building of 60,000 new homes – coordinated by the Municipality of Almere – and the creation of 100,000 new jobs for the expected 165,000 new inhabitants.

Vision 2030 marks a collaboration between MVRDV and the city to design a concept structure to accommodate this growth and development. The growth will take place in four main areas: Almere IJland, a new island off the coast in the IJ-lake; Almere Pampus, a neighbourhood focused on the lake and open to experimental housing; Almere Centre, an extended city centre surrounding the Weerwater lake; and Oosterwold, an area devoted to more rural and organic urbanism. Together, the proposals form

the framework that will determine the growth of the city until 2030. The design of IJland has been a collaboration between Adriaan Geuze of West 8 and William McDonough of McDonough + Partners. The concept for Almere is more than an urban masterplan. It has the potential to develop into an ecological, social and economically sustainable city.

Opposite
Masterplan by MVRDV showing Olympiakwartier and the four main areas of the Vision 2030 development.

Below
A computer-rendered aerial perspective showing the IJland geographical context.

Bottom
A computer-rendered aerial perspective showing the OlympiaKwartier district. MVRDV's part of the masterplan is circled in white.

The axis

Today Almere is a city with 185,000 inhabitants, but 30 years ago it was an empty stretch of land reclaimed from the sea. The growth will preserve and further expand Almere's model of a polynuclear city. It will diversify the existing city by adding various densities, programmes and characters.

The vision consists of four major development areas, each with its own character, logic and identity. These new developments are linked by an infrastructural axis which connects the metropolitan area of Amsterdam with Almere. The island known as Almere IJland is a connector between the two cities, literally as well as in economic and cultural terms. The axis then leads to to Almere Pampus, the centre of Almere and Oosterwold in the east, and will in future be extended to Utrecht.

Almere IJland

Together with Adriaan Geuze of West 8 and William McDonough, MVRDV worked on the design for a series of urban and nature reserve islands, with the primary objective of improving water quality in the IJ-lake, an urgent priority. With the new railway connection to Amsterdam, this also offers the potential for 5,000 to 10,000 homes, combined with the nature development. IJland integrates ecological and infrastructural interventions with facilities for living, working and recreation in a natural riparian environment. The island could host special programmes in the future, for example as part of a possible Dutch bid for the 2028 Olympic Games.

Almere Pampus

This area will combine the feeling of a coastal town while accommodating 20,000 homes; all streets within Almere Pampus will lead to the boulevard along the lake. The existing maintenance harbour will be reused for leisure and floating villages, and there will be a new train station with a plaza at the coast.

Above
This computer-rendered aerial view illustrates the landscape proposal within the masterplan.

Opposite
Computer-generated aerial view of Almere Pampus, a neighbourhood that will focus on the lake and be open to experimental housing.

Following pages
An aerial photograph of the existing site has been used to create a computer-generated view of the scheme during the day.

Almere Centre

The current centre will grow until it extends to the south bank of Weerwater, turning the central lake into Weerwater-park and becoming in time the cultural and economic heart of the city. At the junction of the new axis – the motorway and the railway connection – the motorway will be covered, enabling an adjacent development of up to 5,000 homes, offices and public amenities. The central station will be developed into an economic hub and will be surrounded with new projects.

Almere Oosterwold

This large area in the east offers space for up to 18,000 new homes and a variety of functions such as business and retail centres. It will be developed following individual and collective initiatives, both small and large scale, with plots that are always surrounded by green spaces, urban agriculture or local parks. The area will include sites for future development after 2030.

Vision for the future

Vision 2030 is not a blueprint but a flexible development strategy. Adri Duivesteijn, city councillor of Almere, explains: 'It is a framework which can be filled in by the people of the city. By remaining flexible we create possibilities to adjust

the plans to future opportunities.' Almere wants to develop according to this vision to achieve its goal of becoming an ecological, social and economically sustainable city. Large investments in infrastructure are needed to connect the city and its anticipated total of 350,000 inhabitants to its surroundings and to Amsterdam.

Winy Maas of MVRDV will remain involved in the further development of the concept in a supervisory role. The practice has a long history of engagement with Almere. Earlier projects included two studies of innovative organic urban development for Almere Hout and Almere Homeruskwartier, a study for the A6 Boulevard, and the study for Pampus harbour, a neighbourhood of 500 floating dwellings.

MVRDV will be masterplanner for 60,000m^2 of work space, 120,000m^2 of housing (1,000 homes), 15,000m^2 of education space, 2,000m^2 of commercial space, 2,640 parking spaces and various public spaces. This total has been split into 93 volumes of which MVRDV will design 45.

The plan demands individual development of the buildings: a dense mix of living and working spaces leading to a complex urban construct. Retail space, a public square and communal gardens are also part of the comprehensive plan which introduces inner-city life to the mostly suburban typology of Almere. Flexibility is a key objective: all ground floors and parts of the office and apartment buildings are designed to facilitate future change of use. In this way the client, Stadgenoot, can incrementally adapt the built environment to the needs of the growing new town and its inhabitants.

This ambitious project has the potential of becoming a milestone in urban planning. Many urban proposals can be innovative in terms of form or solving individual housing problems. This one has a clear cohesive masterplan: it aims to create a sustainable city of the future.

Adobe Photoshop and 3ds Max software was used to produce the images shown here. Other software used to achieve the design included AutoCAD, Rhino, form·Z and the Adobe Creative Suite package.

Opposite
An aerial view of the masterplan at night, showing the centrally illuminated areas of the scheme.

Below
Computer-rendered perpective of a street scene in the proposal.

Case study The eco city

MVRDV, Eco City, Logroño Montecorvo, Spain

Total project area 61 hectares

Client consortium of LMB, Grupo Progea, Rioja government

Architect MVRDV with GRAS

Environmental engineer Arup

The government of the Spanish province and community of Rioja held a competition (won by architects MVRDV) for the extension to Logroño.

The Eco City designed by MVRDV in collaboration with GRAS envisages the construction of 3,000 social homes and a complementary development programme. The new neighbourhood will achieve a carbon-neutral footprint by producing renewable energy on site.

The 61 hectare site, just north of Logroño on the two small hills of Montecorvo and la Fonsalada, offers views over the city and vast south-facing slopes. The built area of the masterplan is designed in a compact way, occupying only 10 per cent of the site: the linear urban development meanders through the landscape, providing every apartment with views of the city. Sports facilities, retail, restaurants, infrastructure, and public and private gardens are also part of the plan.

The remaining landscape becomes an eco-park: a mix of park and energy-production facility. As the slopes are south-facing, solar energy is easily generated. A tapestry of photovoltaic cells clads the mountain, covering the hills in golden reflection. On top of the two hills, windmills generate part of the energy needed for the new housing and at the same time work as landmarks for the development. All of the energy needed is generated on site by a combination of solar and wind energy. A greywater circuit and on-site natural water purification are parts of the plan, which combines dense urban living with real ecological improvements. All these measures will enable the new development to reach the highest Spanish energy-efficiency rating.

By building as compactly as possible (following the height line of the hill), the building costs are minimized. A further part of the plan is the construction of a funicular railway (a vertical railway system) accessing a museum and viewing point hidden on the top of Montecorvo, which will also house a research and promotion centre for renewable and energy-efficient technology. The on-site production of clean energies and the quality of construction will allow the city to save in excess of 6,000 tons of CO_2 emissions annually.

Of the €388 million total of investment in the project, €40 million will be invested in renewable energy technology. Completion is scheduled for 2015.

Opposite
A computer-generated perspective showing activities along the park strip.

Right
The masterplan map shows the linear development within the larger green site.

Below
A computer rendering illustrating the use of the landscaped recreational space adjacent to the building.

Above and opposite
A major part of the proposal involves using the surrounding landscape for the creation of renewable energy to support the scheme.

Above
Perspective rendering of the Eco City. The land that will be made available by building compactly will become an eco-park, where energy production will be integrated into the landscape.

Opposite
A computer-generated illustration of the massing and topography of the scheme. An array of solar panels can be seen in the foreground.

Case study Rebuilding a community

HOK, Arverne East, Rockaway Peninsula, New York, USA

Total project area 19 hectares

Client Arverne East Development LLC

Architect HOK

Arverne is a neighbourhood in the New York City borough of Queens, on the Rockaway Peninsula. It was initially developed by Remington Vernam, whose signature 'R Vernam' inspired the name of the area. Arverne extends from Beach 56th Street to Beach 79th Street, along its main thoroughfare, Channel Drive. It has been vacant for many years and is being revitalized as part of the Arverne Urban Renewal project. It is a mid-rise development to address the context of mid- to low-rise buildings on the adjacent sites and along the waterfront.

The proposed development at Arverne East will be a vibrant mixed-use neighbourhood with 46, 452 square metres (500,000 square feet) of commercial space, offering integrated retail, entertainment, cafés and restaurants, community services, hospitality, education, and sports and fitness facilities. It will have a broad variety of community parks and open spaces for active recreation, greenways and cycle paths, playgrounds and small pocket parks, and preservation zones. A wide mix of housing types and sub-neighbourhoods will be available to provide for the broadest range of living options, from studio apartments to housing for the elderly. Importantly, more than 50 per cent of the 1,600 planned housing units will qualify as affordable homes. The masterplan takes its cues from the soft forms of the oceanfront environment, amplified by the use of local building and landscape materials throughout. The project

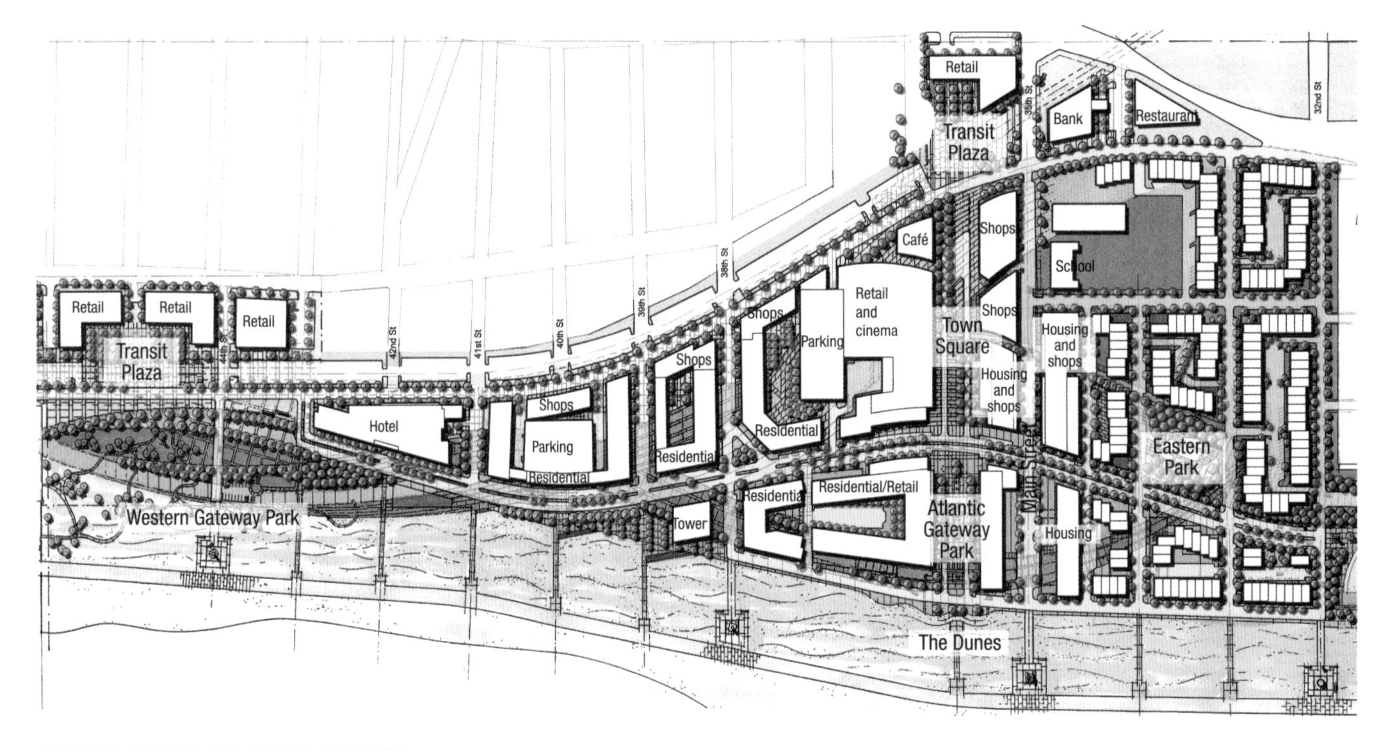

Illustrative masterplan of the development showing the proposed landscaping, residential, leisure and commercial spaces.

Above
Perspective sketch views of Eastern Neighborhood Park.

Top
An aerial perspective axonometric sketch shows the masterplan in its oceanfront context.

Above
Perspective of the beach preserve area with apartment buildings beyond.

Right
A computer-generated street scene in the town square.

will be based on the technology of sustainability and planned on the principles of transit-oriented design, allowing the community to live and work together harmoniously and travel easily to other areas of New York.

The new development is envisioned as a gateway to the ocean and a link to the surrounding community. The design creates strong physical and visual connections with the waterfront and uses the street network as a framework upon which to build a viable and sustainable community. Arverne East includes a town square around its subway station with retail and the Altheus Health and Sport Center.

Altheus will provide sporting venues and activities designed for the waterfront. Existing routes through the city will be enhanced with a series of open spaces that create a beachfront public realm where energy efficiency will be made a high priority.

Artist renderings have been used to give an impression of the activities that will be part of the proposal and to suggest the street scene. These images resemble watercolour sketch drawings. This approach to presentation makes the scheme easier to read. The drawings suggest a softness in the architecture and public spaces, and the relationship of buildings to landscape and public spaces is well described. The images were prepared by urban design and architecture firm Curtis + Ginsburg Architects and the architects HOK.

Case study The new Asian city

von Gerkan Marg and Partners, Lingang New City, China

Total project area 74 km^2

Client Shanghai Harbour City Development (Group) Co Ltd/ Bao Tieming

Architect gmp (von Gerkan, Marg and Partners)

Design Meinhard von Gerkan

Accepting and overcoming the planning and building challenges posed by modern China, while working at a fast pace and at exceptional scales – as well as contributing both economically and culturally, the German practice von Gerkan, Marg and Partners (gmp) has worked on more than 200 design projects in the past few years.

The current transformation of Chinese society, including the immense pressures caused by rural migration into the big cities and the increasing industrialization of rural areas, make it necessary to plan entire cities for the future. Near Shanghai, gmp's Lingang New City, is an entirely new port city for 800,000 inhabitants. The central point of this 'ideal city' is a circular lake, around which the different urban quarters are arranged in concentric rings, like waves rippling outwards from a stone dropped into the water.

Lingang will be the largest laboratory for von Gerkan's ideas. In response to the observation that central business districts are often clusters of unimaginative buildings because only the most conservative institutions such as banking and insurance corporations can afford high-priced central real estate, Lingang has been arranged around a large, immovable space: an artificial lake.

The radial geometry includes a bathing beach and 12 public squares in the innermost ring, a circular light-rail system about 500m from the border, and narrow interior roads admitting only pedestrians and cyclists. The layout ensures that open space, fresh air and human-powered

Above
Computer-generated perspective of the lakeside promenade.

Opposite
The colouring of the masterplan indicates the large amount of landscaped space that will be provided for the city's occupants.

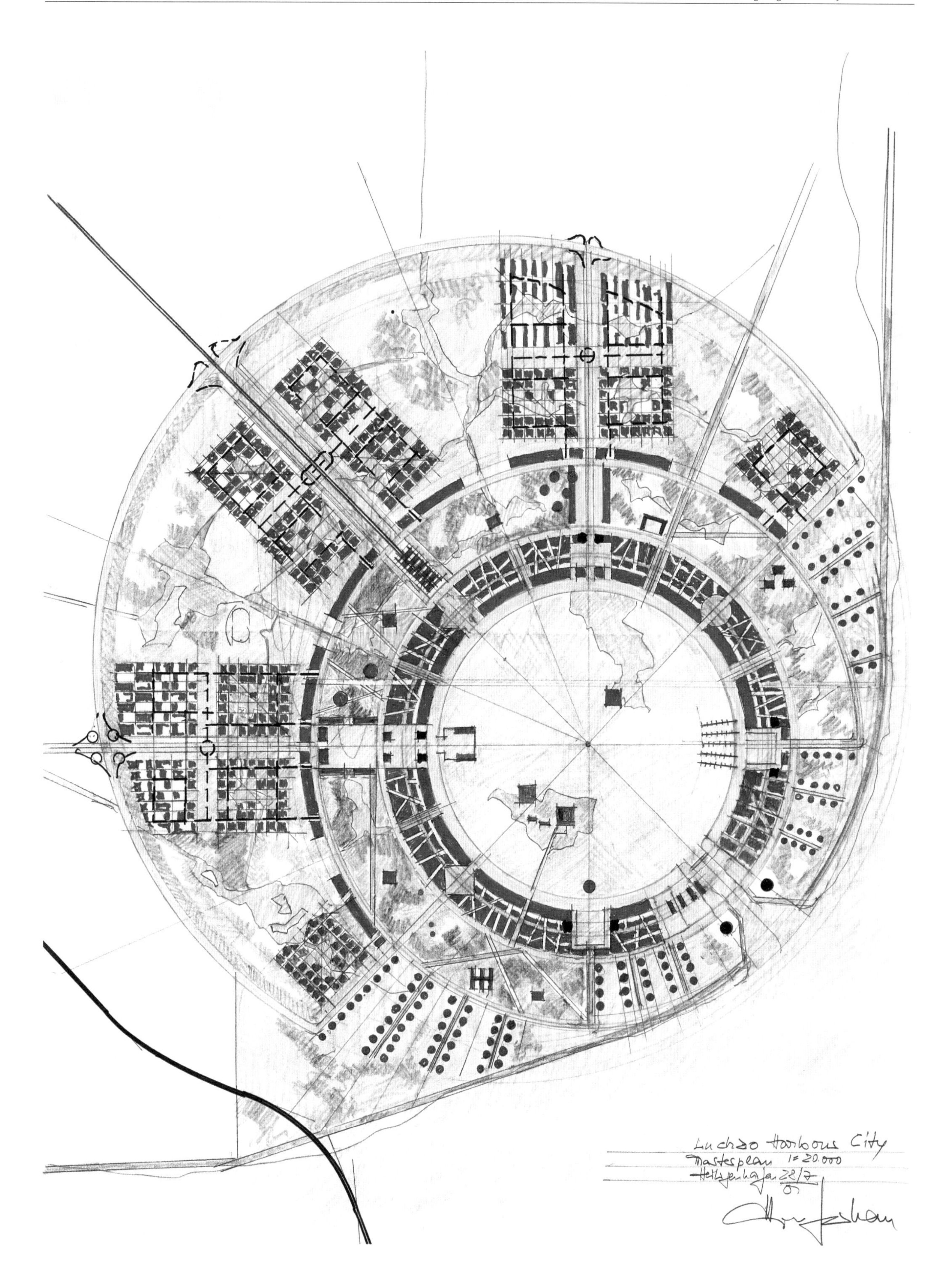
Luchao Harbour City
Masterplan 1=20.000
28/7
05

Preceding pages
Aerial view of a model of the proposed city

Right
Detail map of part of the proposed central concentric ring, showing the network of public spaces, parks and pedestrian and cycle routes.

Below
Computer-rendered photomontage showing proposed activities at the lakeside.

activities dominate the centre, rather than the customary commerce and vehicle congestion.

Like Washington, Brasilia, Chandigarh and Canberra, Lingang starts as a tabula rasa and is organized by the application of elementary geometries. Unlike planned cities that subordinate the quotidian to the theoretical, however, Lingang's abstractions aim to balance what von Gerkan calls the three elements of an ideal city: working, living and leisure. Whether it succeeds over time will depend substantially on how tightly its officials seek to control the disorder that is inseparable from urbanity.

'My thinking,' von Gerkan explains, 'is that the more rational the concept is, the more you can hold your main idea. The more freedom you give, the more chaos you will produce. And if you look around all over China, there is no city anywhere that has a logical system, which is oriented to create a human environment.' In offering Lingang as the first such city, he freely acknowledges its experimental qualities.

Typically gmp develops a master metaphor in the background of each project. In the case of Lingang, this is 'a drop falling from heaven', as exemplified by the organization of the city in concentric ripples; sails for that city's Maritime Museum; a ship for the Grand Theatre in Chongqing. Von Gerkan has found that designs literalizing these metaphors elicit strong approval. 'We never would do that in Europe,' he allows, 'but in China the whole language is based on images. They are very open-minded to metaphors' and to communication in visual or narrative forms.

When complete in 2020, Lingang New City will house 800,000 people, offer Shanghai a solution to accommodating part of its burgeoning population, and serve as a test bed for von Gerkan's highly rational concepts of urban design and transportation.

Opposite, top
Computer-generated perspective illustrating the block massing of the built development.

Opposite, bottom
Computer-generated perspective render showing a street scene illustrating the scale of the buildings in relation to the occupants.

院

Computer-generated view of Lingang's waterfront at night.

Case study Sustainability in an extreme environment

Metropolitan Workshop, Dead Sea Development, Jordan

Total project area 375 km²

Client Urban Workshop, Amman

Project team Metropolitan Workshop, WSP, Gross.Max, Urban Exchange

Metropolitan Workshop has a good track record for delivering large-scale complex urban projects in locations with sensitive contexts. The practice has a reputation for listening and being able to intervene across a wide range of building types. The pervading influence on all their design work emerges from a close analysis of context. The work gains its identity from the particular social, economic and historical associations of the site and from the end-users. The aesthetic and character of each building are unique and derived from these rigorous analyses.

This project is located on the Dead Sea in Jordan. The country is experiencing huge pressures to satisfy the demands for growth within its regions and to promote a diverse and robust economy. In response, planning studies have generated innovative strategies for the nationwide programme of regeneration and urban expansion. The Dead Sea area of the Jordan River Valley is emerging as a new economic engine, playing a potentially significant role within the context of a national plan. A key aim of this study is to identify the latent potential of the region and ways to harness it in a creative and sustainable manner for the benefit of future generations, with the intention that the region should become the Dead Sea Reserve.

The proximity of the Dead Sea to Amman and its inherent qualities combine to create an attractive location that is a natural satellite serving the needs of the city as well as linking to the international market. The Dead Sea area's current growth is based on tourism and its appeal is threefold – the natural therapies of sun, salts and spas; the religious sites spanning the three Abrahamic faiths; and the stunning otherworldly scenery. These attractions are year-round, with high season in the cooler winter months, when the Dead Sea is particularly popular with visitors

Above
A satellite map of the Dead Sea showing the salt pans (right) and the Lissan Peninsula to their left.

Opposite, top
Computer-generated render of the proposed settlement at Contour Zero on the road from Amman.

Opposite, bottom
Computer-generated aerial view illustrating the proposed town of Suweimeh at the north end of the Dead Sea.

from the Gulf. Investors and operators have already been successfully encouraged to exploit new opportunities here.

These developments mark the start of a major expansion of tourist facilities in response to the predicted demand rise from 3,000 hotel beds to 25,000 over the next 20 years. Growth is dependent on a reliable and sustained level of key resources and a resilient model for growth requires the management of resources over the long term.

The region is divided into three zones: the northern area of Suweimeh, the central nature reserve of Al Mujib, and the southern area around Al-Haditha and Al-Mazra. Within these zones current settlements and infrastructure provide the framework for expansion. A coordinated policy of resource management and investment in renewable energy sources will ensure that the existing environmental qualities contributing to the area's attractions are preserved, and will serve as a model for sustainable development throughout the region. Natural and sustainable patterns of growth will be promoted. The harsh climate and the vernacular architecture should inspire built forms that provide shade and use local materials.

The landscape analyses by Gross.Max, along with the requirements of future users, and the availability of flat land for development informs the decisions about where development might be possible. These layers of analysis, when overlaid, give a comprehensive map of elemental land uses and so offer clear guidance on where to build in the future. The combined layers of conservation, protection, existing settlements and current agriculture and mineral activities provide a comprehensive plan illustrating the region's diverse assets, sensible constraints and huge potential. The existing infrastructure investment is the spine linking potential development areas and will be selectively enhanced to create a high-quality experience for visitors coming to the region for commerce or leisure.

A comprehensive and integrated transport system is needed to support sustainable development of the region. The very qualities that make the Dead Sea attractive could be undermined by heavy traffic noise, pollution and congestion. A proposed transport system map illustrates a possible configuration that assists in the process of developing and sustaining the Dead Sea region. Modes of transport to and within the Dead Sea Reserve would be an integral

Below
This coloured map illustrates the proposed transport infrastructure.

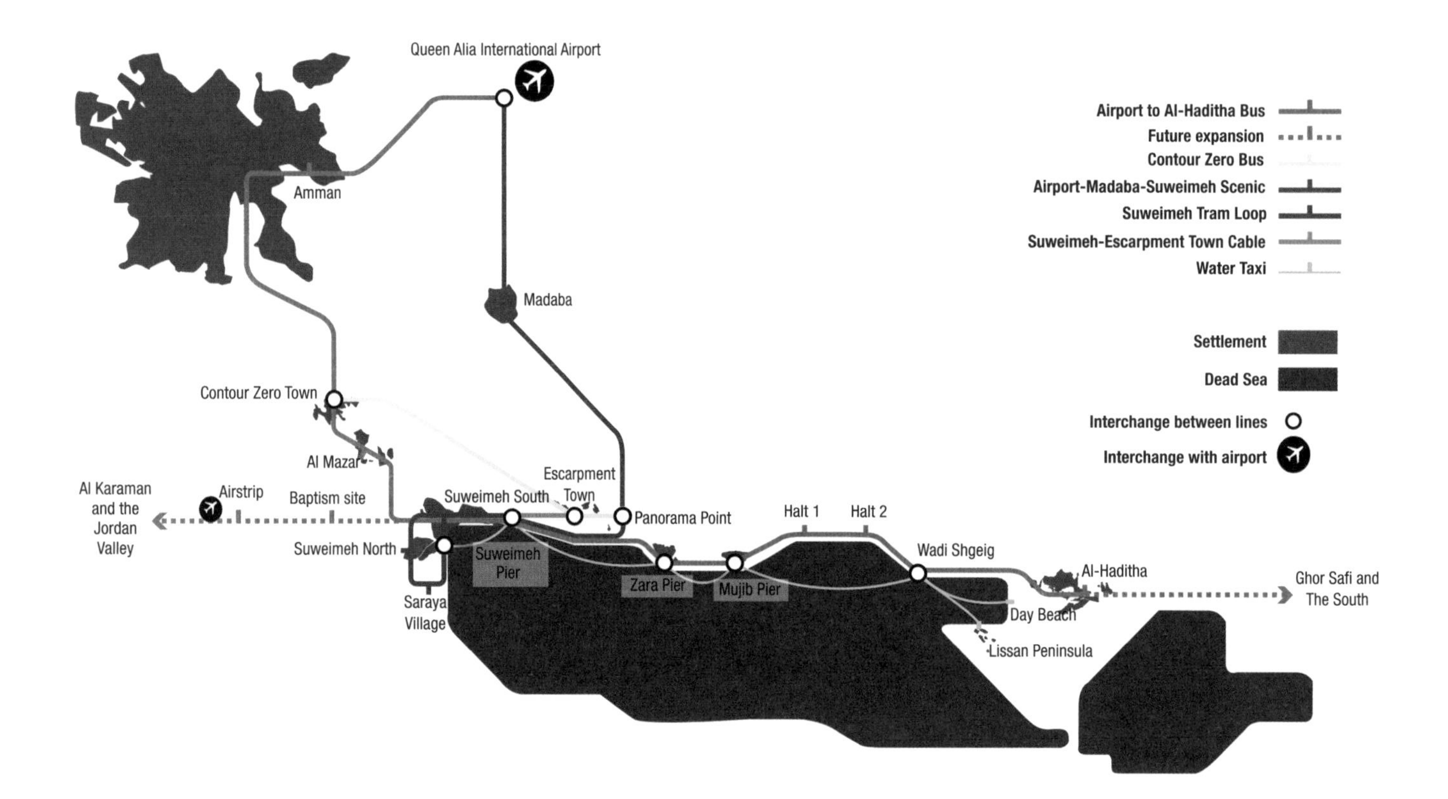

part of its attraction. Overtly green sustainable transport services could be a powerful advertisement. Special biofuel- or hydrogen-powered buses would serve the commuter shuttle route to Amman and the airport transfer route. Water taxis, the tour boats and the tourist tram loop could be electric- and solar-powered. Such smart vehicles would add to the cachet of living, working and visiting the reserve.

The concept is to offer a way of daily life in the region that contrasts with to the typical urban existence or the isolated condition of rural settlements. The modes of transport themselves will be part of the Dead Sea 'experience', offering the opportunity to navigate around the region in comfort on a planned circuit without using conventional motor vehicles.

Suweimeh – currently just a cluster of isolated hotels – is one of the anchor projects and over the next five to ten years is set to become a well-planned tourist town and act as the northern node of the region. A balance of uses is proposed, starting with medical, retail and administrative facilities, closely followed, when the population increases, by civic and recreational uses. The diagonal route between the place of arrival and the public beach will accommodate hotels, retail and entertainment buildings, creating a beach trail for day visitors and tourists. Alongside the tourist attractions will be a considerable amount of residential accommodation, arranged in a variety of apartment buildings. It is envisaged that some apartments will be holiday and weekend retreats for residents of Amman. As the population rises and the need for services increases, more homes will be required for support staff. This will generate demand for education, health, retail and employment facilities. The state will need to deliver the roads and infrastructure and could recover the costs by land levies. The legacy is in the boost to long-term employment and training in the hospitality and well-being industries.

The Lissan Peninsula is a unique landscape even in the context of the Dead Sea. Its bareness provides a platform for land art and programmed events and festivals. In the long term there is potential for hotels and a conference centre here. There have been proposals by Cornell University for a Library of Life as part of their Bridging the Rift Foundation (an organization set up to contribute to peace to the Middle East).

Hotels could be recessed into the landscape, for thermal protection and so

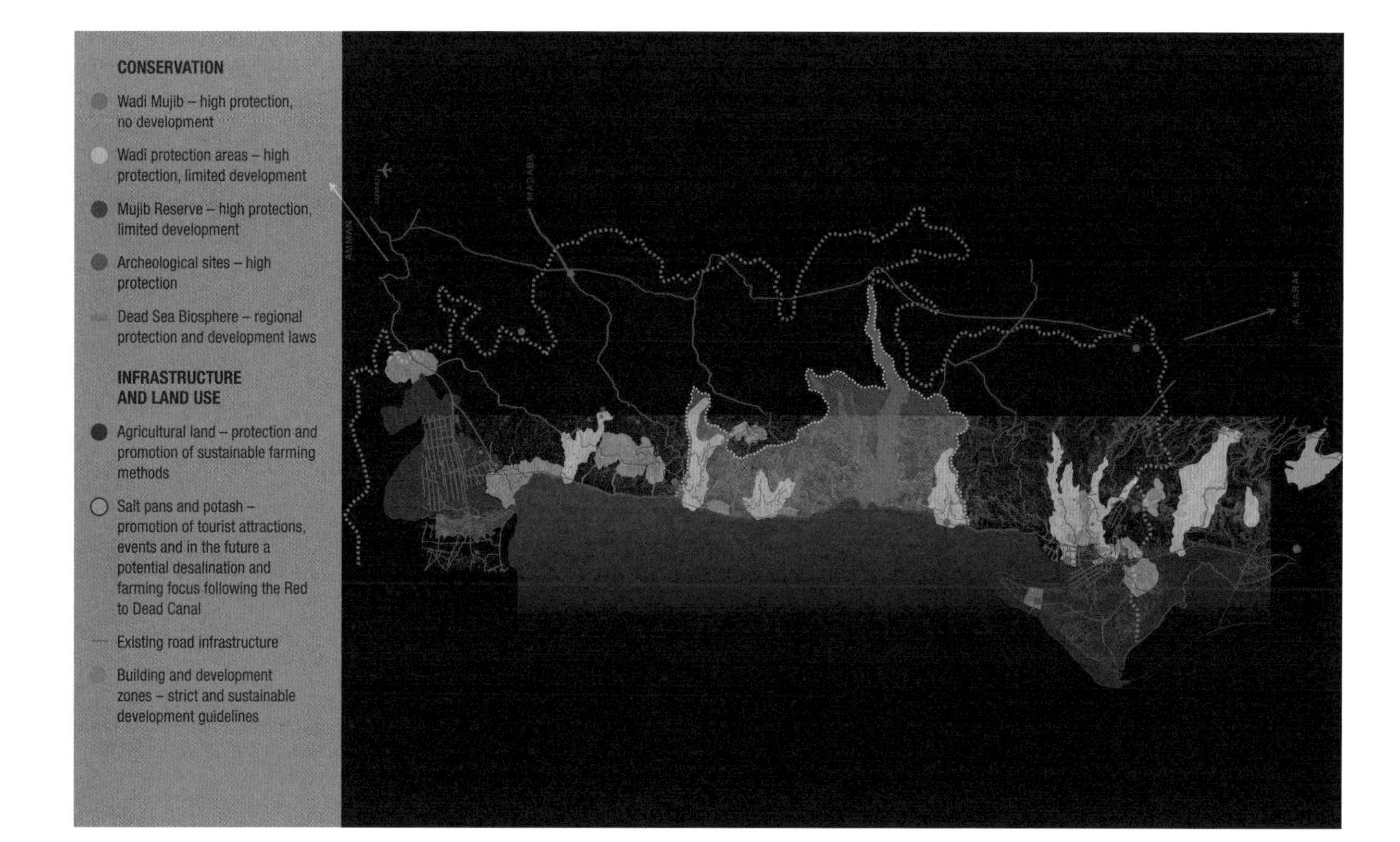

Below
Gross.Max carried out biotic and abiotic analyses which identified the most practical and least environmentally instrusive locations for new settlements.

Above
The importance of on-site energy generation is exemplified by the presence of these solar arrays at the junction of the Amman Road and the Dead Sea Highway.

Left
The Escarpment Town settlement exploits a natural plateau overlooking the Dead Sea and has the potential to be linked by cable car to the town of Suweimeh 400 metres below.

Opposite
A visualization of the Lissan Peninsula hotel development, showing earth-sheltered structures and solar collectors.

reducing mechanical cooling loads. Courtyards would be oases, irrigated by greywater from the hotels. The hotels could be circular in form, as could the solar collectors, irrigation circles and event spaces, a theme that comes from the the sink holes found in the geology of the peninsula. The dramatic plateau of the peninsula will be accentuated by the giant mirrored discs of solar collector arrays. These installations will supply the power requirements to the local homes and industries. This is the most ambitious project and its isolation probably means it awaits the Red to Dead project to bring better road links to Al-Karak in the east and one day to the west. Meanwhile, the blank surface of the promontory serves as a canvas for events and high-profile art installations.

The development has the potential to be a catalyst to develop the ideas, technologies and policies of the future, bringing with it lasting benefits for the people of Jordan in terms of employment, energy and education. The resulting conceptual design demonstrates the extent to which zero carbon can be achieved using existing technologies. To achieve a zero-carbon emission level for the Dead Sea development, a rethinking of standard building design and subsequent resource management is required. Compared with current use, energy and fossil-fuel consumption must be reduced by 30 per cent, water demand by 60 per cent and waste-to-landfill by 90 per cent. Achieving these targets for energy and resource reduction does not necessarily demand a reduced quality of life. Proven and affordable environmental and energy technologies can substantially minimize carbon emissions.

With appropriate masterplanning and energy, water and waste reduction targets, the development could achieve up to 30 per cent reduction in carbon emissions. Maximizing on-site energy generation via renewables could further reduce the carbon emissions to zero. The approach includes solar control for indoor and outdoor spaces, control of site microclimate, controlled daylight supply to reduce artificial lighting, use of thermal mass to buffer temperature swings, passive evaporative cooling and increase of the set thermostat point for air-conditioning from to 22°C to 26°C; buffer spaces and adjusted set point depends on use, reduced water consumption and greywater recycling.

The masterplan report makes the case for the Reserve to have a charter to protect the assets and for there to be a special delivery agency to coordinate and control the execution of these ambitious developments over the coming decades.

Case study The virtual CAD image

Zaha Hadid Architects, Kartal–Pendik Masterplan, Istanbul, Turkey

Total project area 555 hectares (construction area 6 million m²)

Client Greater Istanbul Municipality

Architect Zaha Hadid Architects

Design Zaha Hadid with Patrik Schumacher

The Kartal–Pendik Masterplan is a winning competition proposal for a new city centre on the east side of Istanbul. It is the redevelopment of an abandoned industrial site into a new city quarter of Istanbul, complete with a central business district, high-end residential development, cultural facilities such as concert halls, museums and theatres, and leisure programmes including a marina and tourist hotels. The site lies at the confluence of several important infrastructural links, including the major highway connecting Istanbul to Europe and Asia, the coastal highway, sea bus terminals, and heavy and light rail links to the greater metropolitan area.

Computer-generated aerial view showing the masterplan in its immediate context. The organic form of the quarry is on the left, with the marina on the right.

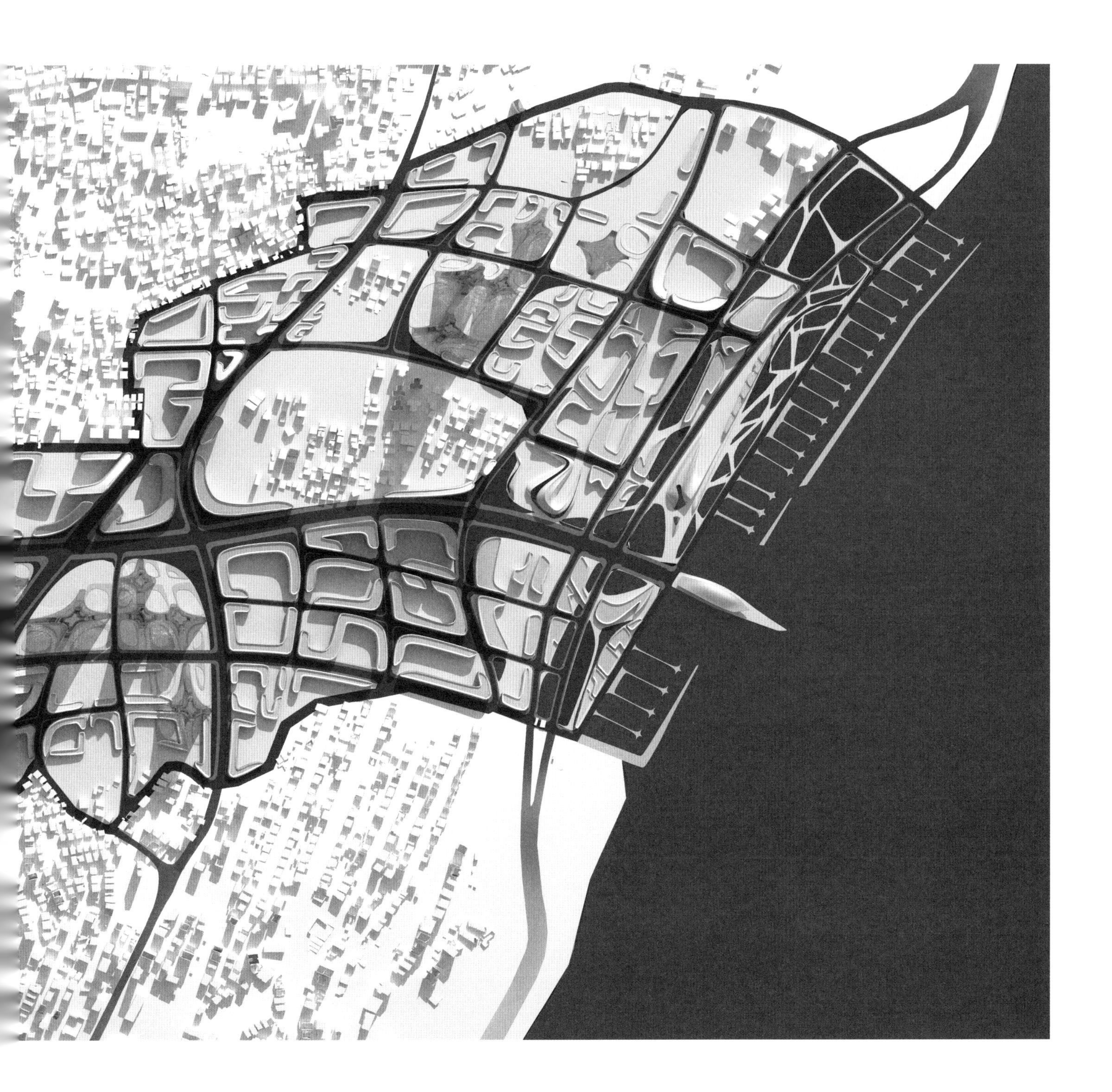

The project begins by linking the basic infrastructural and urban context of the surrounding site. Lateral lines stitch together the major road connections emerging from Kartal in the west and Pendik in the east.

The integration of these lateral connections with the main longitudinal axis creates a soft grid (or net) that forms the underlying framework for the project. Locally, this net can be bundled to form areas of higher programmatic intensity as well as a vertical build-up of the city fabric. In certain areas the net rises up to form a network of towers in an open landscape, while in other areas it is inverted to become a denser fabric cut through by streets, and at other times may completely fade away to generate parks and open spaces. Some areas extend out into the water, creating a matrix of floating marinas, shops and restaurants.

The fabric is further articulated by an urban script that generates different typologies of buildings that respond to the varying demands of each district. This calligraphic script creates open conditions that can transform from detached buildings to perimeter blocks, and ultimately into hybrid systems that can create a porous, interconnected network of open spaces that meanders throughout the city. Through subtle transformations and gradations from one part of the site to the other, the scripted fabric can create a smooth transition from the surrounding context to the new higher-density development.

The soft grid also incorporates possibilities of growth, as in the case where a network of high-rise towers might emerge from an area that was previously allocated to low-rise buildings or faded into open park space. The masterplan is thus a dynamic system that generates an adaptable framework for urban form, balancing the need for a recognizable image and a new environment with a sensitive integration of the new city with the existing surrounds.

An aerial perspective showing the redevelopment of the existing quarry (centre of the image) as a lake.

Opposite
Site plan showing how connections flow across the site.

Above
Computer-rendered building façade studies.

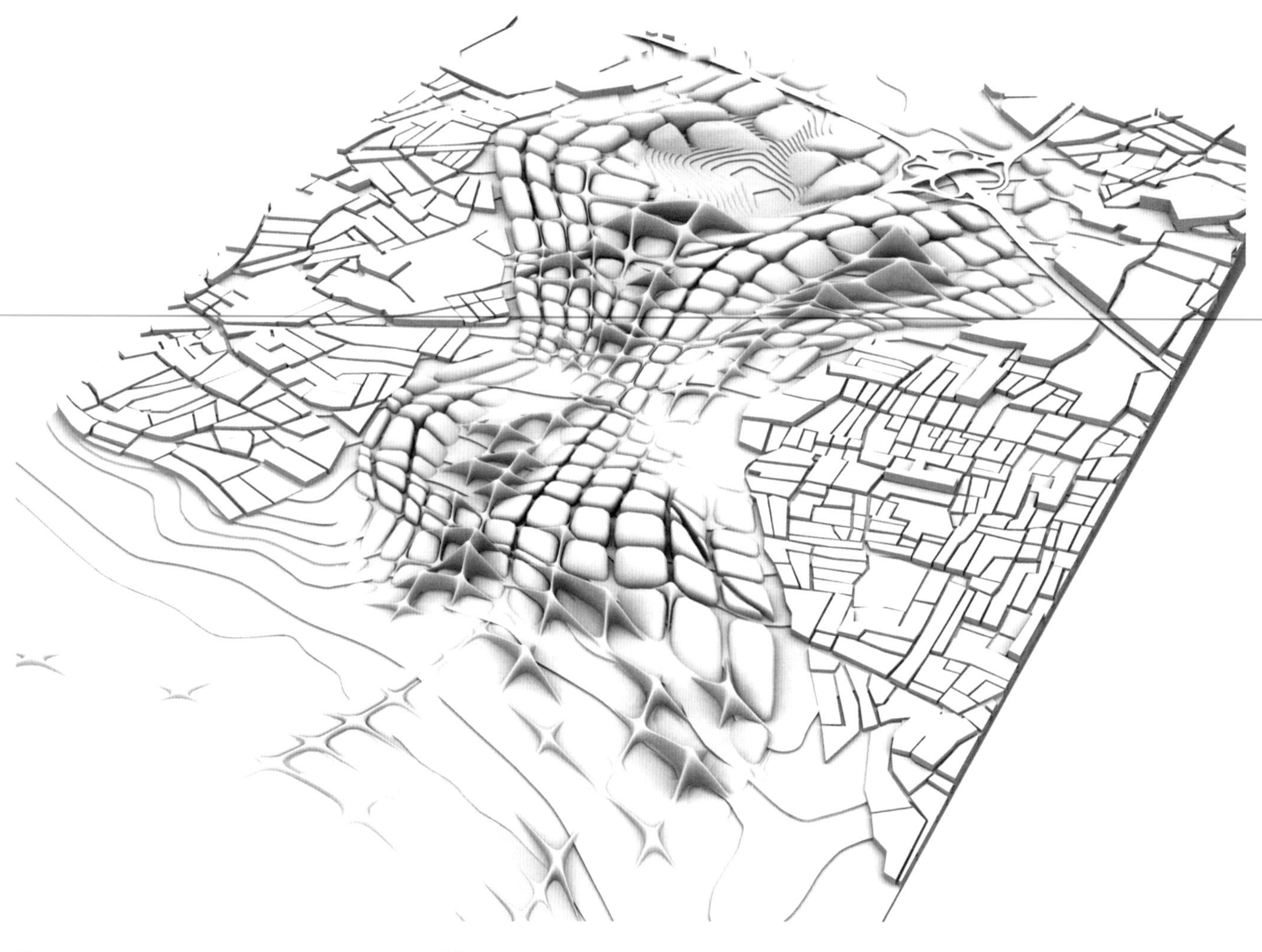

Above
Computer software was used to create this three-dimensional site plan.

Below
Computer-rendered building façade studies.

Below and opposite
Volumetric studies showing the clustering of the urban blocks.

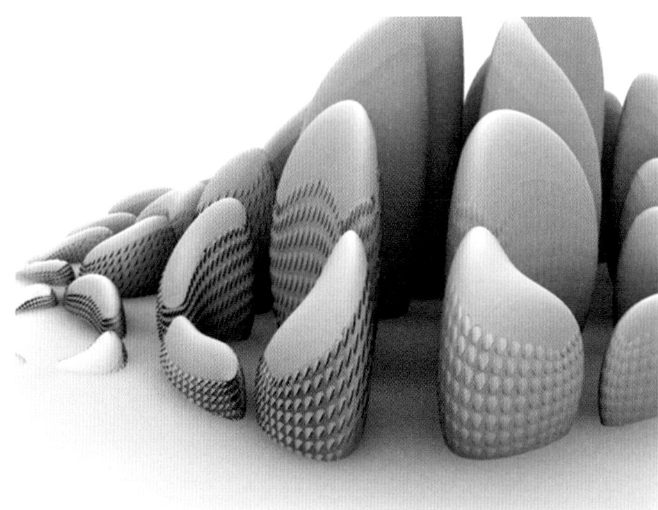

Various programmes were used to create the images of the masterplan shown here. For this project, Rhino, Photoshop, Autodesk, AutoCAD, Maya and Illustrator software packages were used.

For the initial stages of a masterplan for a large city scale such as this, CAD software allows an overall idea to be developed, manipulated and communicated effectively. In this case, the images give a flowing feel to the concept, suggesting that the set of buildings within the masterplan is like a fabric, undulating across different forms and scales to produce an extraordinarily varied landscape. The subtleties of the rendering programmes can further enhance the images, so the overall effect is sculptural and dynamic.

Conclusion

A book about drawing and urban design has to cover a broad range of methods of expression, and the case studies in the preceding pages have been included to exemplify the many ways in which the city can be described. While the key skill of hand-drawing, which requires sensitivity and an enquiring mind, is still essential in the new world of expression and representation, the future for drawing our cities will also involve the use of sophisticated software to create two-dimensional visuals, three-dimensional animations, and even virtual experiences of city environments.

The introduction of digital fabrication techniques, which can allow physical models to be created from CAD images, is an important development in modelmaking that will influence the design of our cities. These new methods of expression are stimulating new ways of thinking and designing. To move from a sketch to a CAD image, a three-dimensional CAD model and then a physical model allows great flexibility in developing an idea of a city, which can be investigated in so many ways before it is realized.

The idea of the masterplan as a remote diagram has also moved on. The city can be described so that it is understood as a series of spaces, square and streets. It can be investigated and evolve through the tools of respresentation that are available. The designer needs to know about these tools and use them at the various stages of a concept development. In the journey from concept

to realization, it is important to have the right tools and methods of representation and use them in an intelligent and skilful way. The exploration of ideas through experimentation with a mixture of media will make our future urban environments even more stimulating in reality than they are in the drawings that describe them.

As Gordon Cullen warns in his book *The Concise Townscape*: 'If at the end of it all the city appears dull, uninteresting and soulless, then it is not fulfilling itself. It has failed. The fire has been laid but nobody has put a match to it.'

Once the designer has communicated his or her thinking through drawing and representing, the work of the imagination has been done. It is then up to others to inhabit the city and live up to the expectations of its designers.

This proposal for a skyscraper competition in Damascus by Rocky Marchant and Ergin Birinci was illustrated using Rhino 4 and Maya for the modelling, and Photoshop, Illustrator and InDesign for the presentation. The cities of the future can be visualized as dramatic sculptures and landscapes, and they are no longer limited by what can be achieved by using a pen or pencil.

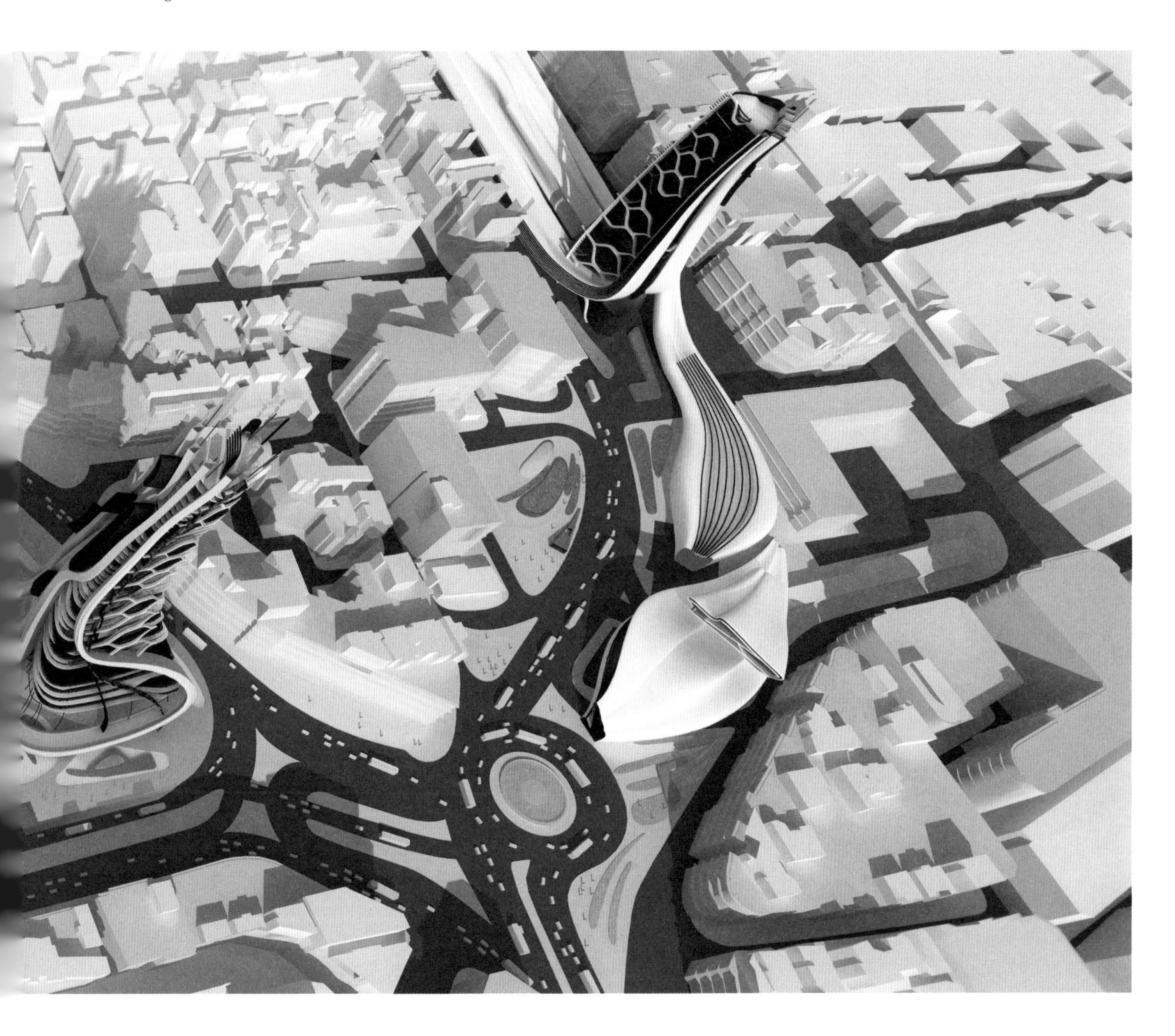

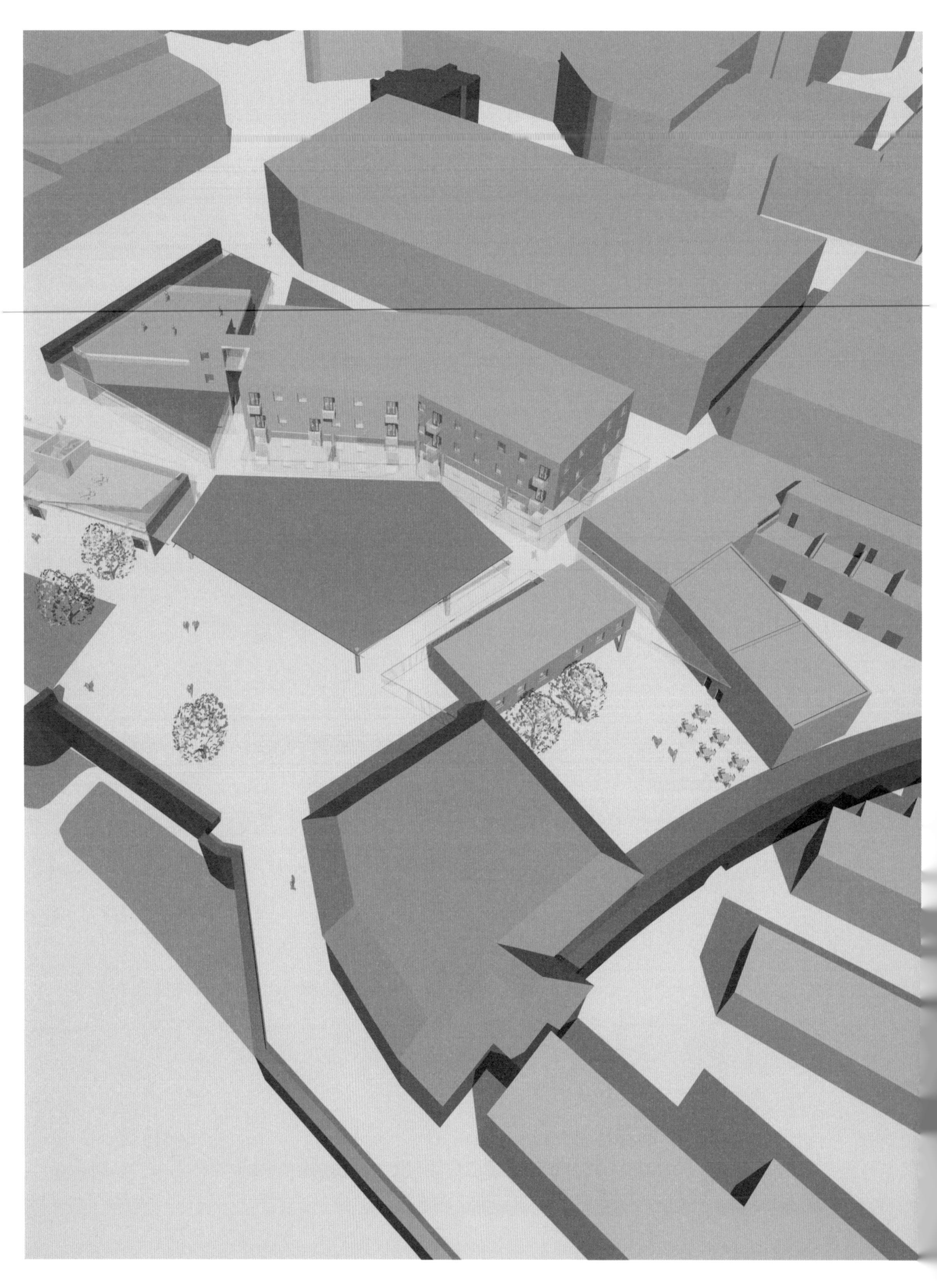

Glossary

access Point of entering or exiting a building or space.

axis A line that is a reference for organization. It can divide a plan, map or building.

axonometric A plan or map that has been projected to a three-dimensional drawing.

bricollage The creation of a drawing or other creative work from a range of different experiences and processes.

CAD (computer-aided design) The use of various types of software to create images of buildings, spaces and places. Techniques can involve two-dimensional images or three-dimensional visualizations.

central city The central city, or core city, is the municipality in an urban or metropolitan area that emerged historically as the most prominent in that urban area.

cityscape Term that is associated with the idea of landscape in an urban sense; the relationship between built forms and the spaces between.

cognitive mapping Methods used to describe problems through certain visual diagramming techniques; also known as mental maps.

collage Derived from the French for 'to stick', this is a technique in which an image is created by using a range of materials that are then reorganized to create a new image. These materials may be paper, photographs, other images or three-dimensional elements or objects.

context A term for the parameters that define either a city, site or building, both physically and culturally. The place where something is located.

density The number of people that occupy a given area, normally expressed per hectare. These statistics can be used to define specific aspects of function, such as residential density or workforce density.

enclosure A space or place that is defined by walls, edges or boundaries.

exurb A municipality (or community) or urban area that is part of a greater metropolitan area but which is beyond the suburbs and separated by a rural zone from the principal urban area.

exurban Refers to non-rural development that is within a metropolitan area, but outside the urban and suburban area.

figure ground A representational technique used to differentiate between objects and the space around them. The object is drawn as a black shape while space around is left as white. This technique, when applied to maps or building plans, allows the building to be seen as distinct from the space around it.

infrastructure The support system that defines a city or urban environment. It can be physical – such as transport and drainage infrastructures – or it can refer to the social support services provided by public bodies and organizations.

massing The volume of a building or group of buildings as described in physical and CAD models.

mapping The description of places, spaces and processes through visual representation. This can involve the use of measured scales or it can take the form of an abstract description.

metropolitan Term for an area that may include more than one urban zone. The surrounding area from which the urban core draws its workforce.

montage Derived from the French, this term refers to the putting together of images or information. For example, a photomontage pulls together different types of image, such as digital, sketch or CAD.

orientation The understanding of the position of a building and how it is affected by the sun.

place A location that has a strong identity or character that enables it to be differentiated from other locations. The idea of a 'sense of place' suggests a physical identity, but a place may also be defined by a strong cultural identity. It may be described in literature, music or painting.

serial vision A phrase coined by Gordon Cullen referring to the visual description of a sequence of spaces in a city as one moves through them.

scale The relationship of one object to another expressed as a proportion: 1:2 scale is half the size of full scale, which is 1:1. Urban scales tend to be quite large; maps at 1:1000 and 1:2500 are necessary to describe large parts of a city.

storyboard A series of grids or frames that suggest image sequence and layout. A graphic technique used primarily by film-makers, it is also used by other artists and designers as an organizational tool.

site analysis A study carried out using diagrams and drawings to describe the factors influencing a site, including access, route, shadow and movement of people.

streetscape Term for everything that can be viewed as part of the street environment, including, for example, pavement, seating, landscape and building forms.

suburban The continuous urbanization that extends beyond the core city.

superimposition The placement of images onto one another to create a new image. This may incorporate hand-drawn, CAD, digital or other media.

topography The description of the surface of the earth, whether a natural or built environment. Within a city the description would include the change of levels from a building to a pavement to a street.

townscape Similar to a cityscape.

urban design The organization and shaping of the urban environment, including the relationship between buildings and public space.

urbanism The study of cities and factors that influence the urban environment.

vista A view from a specific point, for example in the street, between buildings, or through a public square.

Further reading

Crowe, N. and Laseau, P., *Visual Notes for Architects and Designers*, John Wiley & Sons, London, 1984

Edwards, B., *Understanding Architecture through Drawing*, second edition, Taylor & Francis, Oxford, 2008

Choay, F., *L'urbanisme, utopies et réalités: Une anthologie*, Seuil, Paris, 1965

Schorske, C. E., *Fin-de-siècle Vienna: Politics and Culture*, Weidenfeld & Nicolson, London, 1980

Heuer, C., *The City Rehearsed*, Routledge, New York, 2009

Collins, G. R., Collins, C. C., and Sitte, C., *Camillo Sitte: The Birth of Modern City Planning, with a Translation of the 1889 Austrian Edition of his City Planning According to Artistic Principles*, Rizzoli, New York, 1986

Howard, E., *Garden Cities of To-morrow*, Faber, London, 1965

Cherry, G. E., *Pioneers in British Planning*, Architectural Press, London, 1981

Morris, E. S., *British Town Planning and Urban Design: Principles and Policies*, Longman, Harlow, 1997

Unwin, R., *Town Planning in Practice: An Introduction to the Art of Designing Cities and Suburbs*, originally published London, 1909; reprinted 1994 by Princeton Architectural Press, New York

Giedion, S., 'City Planning in the Nineteenth Century' in *Space, Time and Architecture*, Harvard University Press, Cambridge, MA, 1942

Hall, P., *Cities of Tomorrow: An Intellectual History of Urban Planning and Design in the Twentieth Century*, Basil Blackwell, Oxford, 1988

Le Corbusier, *The Radiant City: Elements of a Doctrine of Urbanism to be Used as the Basis of our Machine-age Civilization*, Faber, London, 1967

Garnier, T., *Une cité industrielle: Etude pour la construction des villes*, Princeton Architectural Press, New York, 1989

Mumford, E., *The CIAM Discourse on Urbanism, 1928–1960*, The MIT Press, Cambridge, MA, 2000, pp. 59–130

Jacobs, J., *The Death and Life of Great American Cities*, Penguin, Harmondsworth, 1965, pp. 29–54 and 144–238

Lynch, K., *The Image of the City*, MIT Press, Cambridge, MA, and London, 1960

Cullen, G., *The Concise Townscape*, new edition, Architectural Press, London, 1971

Alexander, C., 'The City is Not a Tree' in *Architectural Forum*, 22 (1–2), 1965, pp. 58–62

Congress of the New Urbanism, Charter of the New Urbanism, 2001, available as a PDF at http://www.cnu.org/sites/files/charter_english.pdf

Krier, L., *Drawings, 1967–1980*, Archives d'Architecture Moderne, Brussels, 1980

Rossi, A., *The Architecture of the City*, US edition, The MIT Press, Cambridge, MA; published for the Graham Foundation for Advanced Studies in the Fine Arts and the Institute for Architecture and Urban Studies,1982

Moughtin, C., *Urban Design: Green Dimensions*, Butterworth-Heinemann, Oxford, 1996

Ritchie, A., and Thomas, R., *Sustainable Urban Design: An Environmental Approach*, second edition, Taylor & Francis, London, 2009

Shane, D. G., *Recombinant Urbanism: Conceptual Modeling in Architecture, Urban Design and City Theory*, John Wiley & Sons, Chichester, 2005

Alexander, C., et al, *A New Theory of Urban Design*, Oxford University Press, Oxford and New York, 1987

Bacon, E., *Design of Cities*, Penguin Books, New York, 1974

Boyer, M. C., *Dreaming the Rational City: The Myth of American City Planning*, The MIT Press, Cambridge, MA, 1990

Castells, M., *The Rise of the Network Society*, Blackwell, Oxford, 1996

Chase, J., Crawford, M., and Kaliski, J., eds, *Everyday Urbanism*, Monacelli Press, New York, 1991

Cronon, W., ed., *Uncommon Ground: Rethinking the Human Place in Nature*, W. W. Norton & Co, New York, 1996

Fainstein, S., and Campbell, S., eds, *Readings in Urban Theory*, Blackwell Publishing, Oxford, 2002

Hall, P., *Cities of Tomorrow*, Oxford, Blackwell Publishing, 2002

Harvey, D., *Spaces of Hope*, University of California Press, Berkeley, 2000

Hillier, B. and Hanson, J., *The Social Logic of Space*, Cambridge University Press, Cambridge, 1984

Kasinitz, P., ed., *Metropolis: Center and Symbol of Our Times*, NYU Press, New York, 1995

Koolhaas, R., *S,M,L,XL*, Monacelli Press, New York, 1998

Krier, L., *Architecture: Choice or Fate*, Papadakis, London, 1998

Krier, R., *Urban Space*, Rizzoli, New York, 1979

Le Corbusier, *The City of To-morrow and its Planning*, The MIT Press, Cambridge, MA, [1929] 1971

Nesbitt, K., ed., *Theorizing a New Agenda for Architecture: An Anthology of Architectural Theory 1965–1995*, Princeton Architectural Press, New York, 1996

Rowe, P. G., *Civic Realism*, The MIT Press, Cambridge, MA, 1997

Rowe, C. and Koetter, F., *Collage City*, The MIT Press, Cambridge, 1984

Scott, A. J. and Soja, E. W., eds, *The City: Los Angeles and Urban Theory at the End of the Twentieth Century*, University of California Press, Berkeley, 1998

Sitte, C., *The Art of Building Cities: City Building According to its Artistic Fundamentals*, Hyperion Press, New York, 1979

Venturi, R., Scott Brown D., and Izenour, S., *Learning from Las Vegas*, The MIT Press, Cambridge, MA, and London, 1972

Useful websites

The websites below provide information on urban design and planning.

Urban Planning, 1794–1918: An International Anthology of Articles, Conference Papers, and Reports
http://www.library.cornell.edu/Reps/DOCS/

The Internet Archive
http://www.archive.org/index.php

Rudi: Resource for Urban Design Information
http://www.rudi.net/

Sustainable Places
http://www.cabe.org.uk/sustainable-places

CABE (Commission for Architecture and the Built Environment)
http://www.cabe.org.uk

Eurocities
http://www.eurocities.eu/main.php

Urban Design Alliance
http://www.udal.org.uk/

Urban Design Group
http://www.udg.org.uk

Create-a-Space
http://www.createascape.org.uk/

Web Urban Design
www.weburbandesign.com

Current City
http://senseable.mit.edu/currentcity/

Index

Page numbers in *italics* refer to picture captions

Picture credits

Front cover **Zaha Hadid Architects**
Back cover **University of Portsmouth**
1 **Zaha Hadid Architects**
3 **S333 Architecture + Urbanism with Balmori Associates**
5 **Joshua Ray/University of Portsmouth**
6 left **European City Studio/University of Portsmouth**
6 right **Eric Parry Architects**
7 **Rocky Marchant and Ergin Kemal Birinci**
8 left **European City Studio/University of Portsmouth**
8 right **Lee Whiteman/University of Portsmouth**
9 top **Design Engine**
9 bottom **European City Studio/University of Portsmouth**
10 **Lorraine Farrelly**
11 top **Niall Bird/University of Portsmouth**
11 bottom **Brad Richards/University of Portsmouth**
14 **CAMERAPHOTO Arte, Venice**
16 **Quattrone, Florence**
18 **Photo: Scala, Florence/© DACS 2010**
19 left & right **Google Earth**
21 top **Property of the Musei Civici di Como**
22 top & bottom **RIBA Library Photographs Collection**
23 **© FLC/ADAGP, Paris and DACS, London 2010**
24 top **Lynch, Kevin, *The Image of the City*, drawings from page 98, upper and centre, page 99, bottom, © 1960 Massachusetts Institute of Technology, by permission of The MIT Press**
24 bottom **Image published on the cover of *The Concise Townscape*, Gordon Cullen, 1971, courtesy Elsevier Limited**
25 **Drawing by Lorraine Farrelly, based on an example from *The Design of Cities* by Edmund Bacon**
26 **RIBA Library Photographs Collection**
27 **© Eredi Aldo Rossi. Courtesy Fondazione Aldo Rossi**
29 **Bernard Tschumi Architects**
30 **University of Portsmouth**
32–33 **Natalie Sansome/University of Portsmouth**
33 top **Allies and Morrison**
34–35 **Khalid Saleh/University of Portsmouth**
35 top **Luke Sutton/University of Portsmouth**
36 top **Niall Bird/University of Portsmouth**
36 bottom **University of Portsmouth**
37 top **Rory Gaylor/University of Portsmouth**
37 bottom **Dean Pike**
38 **Matthew Smith/University of Portsmouth**
39 **Lorraine Farrelly**
40 left and right **Niall Bird/University of Portsmouth**
41 top and bottom **Eleanor Wells/University of Portsmouth**
42–43 **Lorraine Farrelly**
44 **Niall Bird/University of Portsmouth**
45 **Eleanor Wells/University of Portsmouth**
46–47 **Lee Whiteman/University of Portsmouth**
48–49 **Edward Steed/University of Portsmouth**
50 top and bottom **studioKAP**
51 **Rocky Marchant and Ergin Kemal Birinci**
52 **Rocky Marchant and Ergin Kemal Birinci**
53 top and bottom **Owen French/University of Portsmouth**
54–55 **Rachael Brown/University of Portsmouth**
56 left and right **Panter Hudspith Architects**
57 top and bottom **University of Portsmouth**
58 **Eleanor Wells/University of Portsmouth**
59 **Ryan Bond/University of Portsmouth**
60–61 **Joshua Ray/University of Portsmouth**
62 top **Eleanor Wells/University of Portsmouth**
62 bottom **Richard Murphy Architects**
63 **Andrea Verenini/University of Portsmouth**
64 **Richard Davies**
66 **Google Earth**
67 **Rocky Marchant and Ergin Kemal Birinci**
68 **University of Portsmouth**
69 **Christian Tallent/University of Portsmouth**
70–71 **Natalie Sansome/University of Portsmouth**
72 left **Space Syntax**
72 right **Benedict Horsman/University of Portsmouth**
73 top **University of Portsmouth**
73 bottom **Eleanor Wells/University of Portsmouth**
74 **University of Portsmouth**
75 left **Nathaniel King Smith/University of Portsmouth**
75 right **Derek Williams/University of Portsmouth**
76–77 **Brad Richards/University of Portsmouth**
78 **Matthew Smith, Ryan Bond, Andrew Catton/University of Portsmouth**
79 top and bottom **Rocky Marchant and Ergin Kemal Birinci**
80 **Space Syntax**
81 **AA Housing and Urbanism students with Dominic Papa and Lawrence Barth**
82 **Jonny Sage/University of Portsmouth**
83 **Steve Pirk/University of Portsmouth**
84 **Matthew Ingham/University of Portsmouth**
85 **S333 Architecture + Urbanism with Studio Engleback**
86 top **S333 Architecture + Urbanism**
86 bottom **Khalid Saleh/University of Portsmouth**
87 **Andrea Verenini/University of Portsmouth**
88 top **Re-Format**
88 **Design Engine**
89 top and bottom **Re-Format**
90 **Rocky Marchant and Ergin Kemal Birinci**
91 top **Ryan Bond/University of Portsmouth**
91 bottom **Rocky Marchant and Ergin Kemal Birinci**
92 top and bottom **studioKAP**
93 **Andrea Verenini/University of Portsmouth**
94 **Melissa Royale/University of Portsmouth**
95 top and bottom **Zmapping Ltd**
96 **Katherine Burden/University of Portsmouth**
97 top **S333 Architecture + Urbanism with model by AModels**
97 bottom **studio1am/University of Portsmouth**
98 left **Steve Duffy/University of Portsmouth**
98 right **University of Portsmouth**
99 **BA3 Architecture student models/University of Portsmouth**
100 **Christina Marshall and group work/University of Portsmouth**
101 top **European City Studio/University of Portsmouth**
101 bottom **University of Portsmouth**
102 **Katherine Burden/University of Portsmouth**
103 **Richard Davies**
104 left **University of Portsmouth**

104 right **S333 Architecture + Urbanism**
105 **Jonathan Taylor/University of Portsmouth**
106 top **City Vision Networks**
106 bottom **University of Portsmouth**
107 **Richard Murphy Architects**
108 **Katherine Burden/University of Portsmouth**
109 **Rocky Marchant and Ergin Kemal Birinci**
110 **gmp**
112–113 **gmp**
114 **gmp**
115 top **S333 Architecture + Urbanism with Balmori Associates**
115 bottom **gmp**
116–117 **Ryan Bond/University of Portsmouth**
117 bottom **Panter Hudspith Architects**
118 **Metropolitan Workshop**
119 top **Allies and Morrison**
119 bottom **Metropolitan Workshop**
120 **Eleanor Wells/University of Portsmouth**
121 top **Eleanor Wells/University of Portsmouth**
121 bottom **Niall Bird/University of Portsmouth**
122–123 **David Chipperfield Architects/Imaging Atelier**
124 **Re-Format**
125 **Re-Format image with 3D model by City Vision Networks, with scheme by Patel Taylor in background**
126 **Re-Format/City Vision Networks**
127 **Ryan Bond/University of Portsmouth**
128–129 **Zmapping Ltd**
130 **European City Studio/University of Portsmouth**
131 **Urban Studio 2010/University of Portsmouth**
132 **Richard Davies**
133 **European City Studio/University of Portsmouth**
134 **gmp**
136–139 **David Chipperfield Architects**
140–147 **MVRDV**
148–153 **MVRDV**
154–157 **HOK**
158–165 **gmp**
166 **Google Maps**
167–168 **Metropolitan Workshop**
169 **Metropolitan Workshop/Gross.Max**
170–171 **Metropolitan Workshop**
172–179 **Zaha Hadid Architects**
180–181 **Rocky Marchant and Ergin Kemal Birinci**
182 **University of Portsmouth**

Author's acknowledgements

I would like to thank the many contributors who supported the creation, development and production of this book. A book about drawing requires a lot of varied visual material. Many practices and students have generously allowed their work to be used in this book.

Throughout the development of this book the staff and students at Portsmouth School of Architecture have provided examples of many types of drawing at many stages of the design process and their flexibility and interest has been invaluable. In particular, the third-year architecture students and members of my postgraduate design studio 'The European City' have provided examples and experiments of drawings and visual material enthusiastically.

Thank you particularly to Claire Perera, who has managed and organized material for the book throughout its development – she has been an essential part of the production of the book.

Finally, thanks to Philip Cooper at Laurence King who supported the idea of the book and to Liz Faber for her editorial support, encouragement and attention to detail that has been appreciated at all stages of the process. Thanks also to designer John Round and production controller Srijana Gurung.